HUMAN CHARACTERISTICS AND SCHOOL LEARNING

HUMAN CHARACTERISTICS AND SCHOOL LEARNING

BENJAMIN S. BLOOM

DISTINGUISHED SERVICE PROFESSOR OF EDUCATION
THE UNIVERSITY OF CHICAGO

McGRAW-HILL BOOK COMPANY

New York   St. Louis   San Francisco   Düsseldorf   London
Mexico   Sydney   Toronto

LIBRARY OF CONGRESS CATALOGING IN PUBLICATION DATA

Bloom, Benjamin Samuel, 1913– Human characteristics and school
learning. Bibliography: p.   Includes index. 1. Learning,
Psychology of. I. Title. LB1051.B4545   370.15′2   76-4094
ISBN 0-07-006117-3

  4567890 KPKP 754321098

The editors for this book were Thomas Quinn and Cheryl Hanks, the
designer was Christine Aulicino, and the production supervisor was
Milton Heiberg. It was set in Caledonia with display lines in Futura
by University Graphics.

Printed and bound by Kingsport Press.

TO MY STUDENTS

They continue to teach me
even after they have graduated

CONTENTS

Preface   ix

Acknowledgments   xi

1 INDIVIDUAL DIFFERENCES IN LEARNERS AND
   LEARNING   1

2 A LEARNING UNIT   18

3 COGNITIVE ENTRY BEHAVIORS   30

4 AFFECTIVE ENTRY CHARACTERISTICS   73

5 QUALITY OF INSTRUCTION   108

6 AFFECTIVE OUTCOMES OF SCHOOL LEARNING   139

7 SUMMARY OF THE PARTS OF THE THEORY AND
   THEIR INTERRELATIONS IN SELECTED STUDIES   161

8 CONCLUSIONS AND IMPLICATIONS   202

References   219

Appendixes   225

Name Index   275

Subject Index   281

PREFACE

When I first entered the field of educational research and measurement, the prevailing construct was:

1. *There are good learners and there are poor learners*

This was considered to be a relatively permanent attribute of the individual. It was also the prevailing view that individuals possessed it in different amounts and that a quantitative index of it could be made by the use of an appropriate intelligence, aptitude, or achievement test. Furthermore, it was believed that good learners could learn the more complex and abstract ideas, while poor learners could learn only the simplest and most concrete ideas. School systems throughout the world have been organized on the basis of this construct and selection systems, grading systems, and even the curriculum has been built on the basis of it.

During the early 1960s, some of us became interested in the Carroll Model of School Learning, which was built on the construct:

2. *There are faster learners and there are slower learners*

While we were not entirely clear whether or not rate of learning was a permanent trait of individuals, we dedicated ourselves to finding ways by which the slower learners could be given the extra *time and help* they needed to attain some criterion of achievement. In this research, in both educational laboratories as well as classrooms in different nations, it has become evident that a large proportion of slower learners may learn as well as faster learners. When the slower learners do succeed in attaining the same criterion of achievement as the faster learners, they appear to be able to learn equally complex and abstract ideas, they can apply these ideas to new problems, and they can retain the ideas equally well—in spite of the fact that they learned with more time and help than was given to others. Furthermore, their interests and attitudes toward the school subjects in which they attain the achievement criterion are as positive as those of the faster learners.

During the past decade, my students and I have done research which has led us to the view that:

3. *Most students become very similar with regard to learning ability, rate of learning, and motivation for further learning—when provided with favorable learning conditions*

This research questions the first two constructs, especially about the permanence of good-poor learning ability or fast-slow learning characteristics. However, the research does demonstrate that when students are provided with unfavorable learning conditions, they become even more dissimilar with regard to learning ability, rate of learning, and motivation for further learning. It is this research which underlies the theory of school learning developed in this book. It is this research which we believe has profound consequences for the prevailing views about human nature, human characteristics, and school learning.

However, the basic ideas in this book are not matters of abstract theory or faith. They depend on easily observed evidence readily obtainable in most of the classrooms of the world or in educational research laboratories. It is our hope that teachers will test these ideas with the students in their own classrooms and that educational researchers will test the validity and the limits of these ideas in their own research.

Evidence in support of this third construct has far-reaching implications for teacher training, instruction in the classrooms, the organizations of systems of education at the local and national level, selection methods, grading procedures, and the development of new curricula and instructional systems.

But, even more important are the effects of adequate or inadequate learning on the student's view of himself, his interest in learning, and his use of his learning ability as a means of adapting to change throughout his life.

ACKNOWLEDGMENTS

During the period of a decade while I was preparing this book, I also participated in the International Studies of Educational Achievement (IEA). The IEA studies involved surveys of the learning taking place in many school subjects in approximately thirty countries of the world. While we were in the midst of gathering data on large numbers of schools, teachers, and students in these many countries, I was attempting to observe and think about the learning of individual students. The IEA research viewed the entire world as a natural educational laboratory. In contrast, my own research was concerned with the smallest educational situation—one student learning something. Some of the IEA findings have, of course, crept into this work, even though the dimensions are so different. I am grateful to my many colleagues throughout the world who have taught me much about the place of education in their countries.

During the last six years I have been privileged to work closely with three of our graduate students at the University of Chicago. James H. Block worked with me in setting out the general themes of the book and helped to find the research literature which spoke to these themes. Much of our interaction began with assumptions stated as, "What if _____?" followed by long hours of discussions about what would follow if such absurd ideas were possible. From these discussions, we proceeded to collect the literature and do observations and small studies to determine whether there was the slightest shred of evidence to support these ideas.

Having set the major themes and focus of the work, Lorin W. Anderson worked with me for two years in tracking down the literature and in conducting much of the reanalysis of selected studies to test the ideas. Lorin spent long hours discussing these ideas with me and even longer time periods reading and rereading my attempts to put these ideas into prose, graphic, and mathematical form. His encouragement and his good-natured patience with the first fumbling attempts at capturing these ideas made it possible for me to write and rewrite particular sections of the book more times than I would care to admit.

During the past two years, Lawrence Dolan served to find the fugitive material needed for particular points and to rework further data from selected studies until they could be used to test some of the ideas in the theory. Larry also helped me to decide when further rewriting was no longer necessary. In many ways, he has helped to set me free from the bondage in which this author has been held by the book.

Other graduate assistants devoted themselves to specific chapters or parts of the theory. Aurora Benasso, Lawrence Hecht, Edward Kifer, Tamar Levin, Rona Ruben, and Jeffrey Smith did much to summarize the literature, and each became something of an authority on a particular part of the book.

During these years, the many versions of each chapter were patiently and painstakingly typed by Evelyn Murphy, Judith LeFevre, Barbara Koelb, and Jean Babiak. Each secretary not only typed and prepared the tables and charts but also pointed out the many sentences which were found to be incomprehensible.

The financial support for this work—largely the support of graduate assistants—came from a small royalty fund on an earlier book and a small grant from the Benton Educational Research Fund. I am indebted to these sources for providing the necessary assistance for this work. Support for this type of research and writing in education is rarely provided by the project support available from the large foundations or agencies of the federal government.

The first year of full-time work on this book was done while I was a visiting professor at Stanford University. I am grateful to H. Thomas James, then Dean of the School of Education at Stanford, who made it possible for me to devote the entire year to this work, with many opportunities to discuss specific aspects of the book with faculty colleagues and graduate students at that university. The remaining time for this work was made available, in connection with other duties, by the Department of Education of the University of Chicago. I am especially indebted to J. Alan Thomas and Philip W. Jackson, who were chairmen of the Department during this period.

It is to the University of Chicago that I must declare my greatest debt. For three decades it has enabled me to pursue my many studies in a stimulating environment where each scholar is encouraged to find his unique path. Throughout this period I have found much intellectual and emotional support from the community of scholars (students as well as faculty) in this remarkable haven for ideas. May this book prove to be worthy of the support I have been given.

HUMAN CHARACTERISTICS AND SCHOOL LEARNING

1
INDIVIDUAL DIFFERENCES IN LEARNERS AND LEARNING

He allowed very great influence to education. "I do not deny,
Sir, but there is some original difference in minds; but it is
nothing in comparison of what is formed by education."
— BOSWELL's *Life of Johnson* (FRIDAY, MARCH 15, 1776)

INTRODUCTION

This is a book about a theory of school learning which attempts to explain individual differences in school learning as well as to determine the ways in which such differences may be altered in the interest of the student, the school, and, ultimately, the society. It attempts to test the view that most students can learn what the schools have to teach—if the problem is approached sensitively and systematically.

It is fortunate that schools, teachers, and parents do not postpone their attempts to teach the young until an acceptable theory of learning is proclaimed and tested. Learning takes place throughout the world in the *absence* of an acceptable theory. We suspect that Stephens (1967) is correct in assuming that *both* teaching and learning are such natural phenomena that all members of the human species engage in them without being entirely conscious of the processes they are using. There is evidence that some major developments of learning in the homes, in the schools, and in curriculum and instruction demonstrate very high levels of effectiveness in spite of the absence of a guiding theory. Perhaps the best that we can expect is that a theory such as this one may be of help when the process is not going well or "naturally."

The home, especially in the age period of about two to ten, develops language, the ability to learn from adults, and some of the qualities of need achievement, work habits, and attention to tasks which are basic to the work of the schools. While homes vary greatly in their

1

development of these characteristics, there are some homes which do a superb job of developing these and related characteristics. The evidence on the effect of these characteristics—largely developed in the home—has been demonstrated in some of the large-scale national and international studies of school learning such as Coleman (1966a), Plowden (1967), Husén (1967), Thorndike (1973), Comber and Keeves (1973), and Purves (1973). All these studies reveal that a large portion of the variation in school achievement, and especially in verbal ability, is accounted for by the differences in the home environments of children in each of the highly developed nations included in these reports.

Something of the processes used in the home is summarized in the longitudinal studies by Bloom (1964), and in the more detailed studies by Dave (1963), Hanson (1972), and Wolf (1966). These studies indicate that what adults *do* in their interactions with children in the home is the major determinant of these characteristics rather than the economic level of the parents, their level of education, or other status characteristics. Much of this research, which has been replicated in a number of countries, has been summarized by Marjoribanks (1974) and Williams (1974). The point of all this is that the home is a powerful environment (for good as well as harm) for the development of some of the basic characteristics of the child that are fundamental to further learning in the schools. Some homes do it well, while other homes do it rather poorly. It is possible that many homes which do it poorly could do much better if the parents were made more aware of the effects of their interactions with their children.

School systems, especially in many of the highly developed nations, have increased the number of years of school made available to the young. In many countries the official school leaving age is sixteen or higher, and there has been an increase in the proportion of youth completing secondary education. Thus, in the United States in 1975 approximately 80 percent of the age group completed secondary education as contrasted with about 8 percent in 1900. In several of the states the proportion of the youth completing secondary education is now over 90 percent. In Japan, the proportion of the age group completing secondary education in 1964 was 57 percent, while in 1975 it is claimed to be over 90 percent. Although these are about the highest figures reported, it is clear that many nations have moved from the view of schools as performing primarily a selection and classification function to the view that the major function of the schools is to help students develop educationally. The schools are increasingly concerned about the ways in which they can provide for the fullest development of students during the many years they will spend in the schools (White & Duker, 1973). Some schools do a superb job of this, while others have much to learn about ways in which the educational functions of the school can be improved. It is hoped that the theory presented in this book can be of value for those schools concerned about improving this process.

During the past decade-and-a-half there has been much concern about ways in which curriculum and instruction could be improved. In this work at all levels of education from the pre-school to the professional school and graduate levels of education there is evidence that some approaches have been very effective, while others have been no more effective than the ones they replaced. It has become apparent that the amount of money and talent expended on efforts to improve curriculum and instruction is no guarantee of the effectiveness of the new approaches. A summary of some of the more effective approaches in the United States at the pre-school to the grade 12 level has been made by Crawford and others (1972). In general, their findings present evidence that some curricula and instructional strategies result in superior learning for students as contrasted with more conventional approaches. Here again, the theory presented in this book should be of value in explaining why particular approaches are effective and why other approaches are less effective.

Closely related to the work on the development of new approaches to curriculum and instruction is the recent work on mastery learning. This approach makes use of existing curricula but seeks teaching procedures and a set of feedback and corrective techniques to ensure a high level of learning for the majority of students. Using these strategies, many teachers and schools have produced very favorable conditions for learning—long in advance of a theory to explain why the approaches are effective.

MASTERY LEARNING

The basic idea that most students can learn what the schools have to teach—if the problem is approached sensitively and systematically— is a very old one. It has been central in the tutoring of students for several thousand years. It has been well understood by parents (in many historical periods) who find ways of helping their children when they have difficulty with particular aspects of schoolwork. This idea in various forms was emphasized by the Jesuit schools before the 17th century, by Comenius in the 17th century, Pestalozzi in the 18th century, and Herbart in the 19th century. Many other proponents could be cited. In the 20th century, Washburne (1922) and his Winnetka Plan and Morrison (1926) at the University of Chicago Laboratory School provided school situations where mastery of particular learning tasks rather than time spent was the central theme.

A modern approach to the notion that most students can learn what the schools have to teach has been developed under the rubric of mastery learning. There are many versions of mastery learning in existence at present. All begin with the notion that most students can attain a high level of learning capability if instruction is approached sensitively and systematically, if students are helped when and where they have learning difficulties, if they are given sufficient time to achieve mastery, and if there is some clear criterion of what constitutes mastery.

My own thinking in this matter was much influenced by John Carroll's Model of School Learning (1963). As I interpreted the Carroll model, it made clear that if students are normally distributed with respect to *aptitude* for some subject and all students are given exactly the *same instruction* (the same in terms of amount and quality of instruction and learning time allowed), then achievement measured at the completion of the subject will be normally distributed. Under such conditions the relationship (correlation) between aptitude measured at the beginning of the instruction and achievement measured at the end of the instruction will be relatively high (typically about +.70). Conversely, if students are normally distributed with respect to aptitude, but the kind and quality of instruction and learning time allowed are made appropriate to the characteristics and needs of *each* learner, the majority of students will achieve mastery of the subject. And, the correlation between aptitude measured at the beginning of instruction and achievement measured at the end of instruction should approach zero.

My students and I worked out various procedures and strategies for achieving mastery in selected school subjects. Basic to this work was the problem of defining what was meant by mastery on an achievement test. One approach to this problem was to use identical or parallel achievement tests in non-mastery and mastery classes and to set the level required for a grade of A in a non-mastery class as the definition of *mastery* for the mastery classes. Also important in this work was the idea that mastery and non-mastery classes should have much the same original instruction—sometimes even having the same teacher teach in the same way to the mastery and non-mastery classes. This way of viewing the original instruction enabled us to disentangle the effects of mastery learning from the particular characteristics of the teacher and the subject matter. That is, it placed the central focus of the research on the effects of particular strategies of teaching-learning rather than on the characteristics of the teacher or the characteristics of the students.

More central to the mastery learning strategies was the development of feedback and corrective procedures at various stages or parts of the learning process. While a variety of feedback processes are possible—including workbooks, quizzes, homework, etc.—we found that the development of brief diagnostic-progress tests proved to be most useful. Such tests were intended to determine what each student had learned in a particular unit, chapter, or part of the course and what he or she still needed to learn. However, the key to the success of mastery learning strategies largely lies in the extent to which students can be motivated and helped to correct their learning difficulties at the appropriate points in the learning process. Here is where many teachers have been highly creative in both motivating students to do the necessary additional work and in finding the most effective ways of providing correctives. My general appraisal of the work done so far suggests that providing opportunities for small groups of students to help each other has been an effective method of motivating each student to make the correctives and providing the additional time and help he or she needs. Teachers' aides, programmed instruction, audio tapes or cassettes, and other instructional material also appear to work quite well in particular situations. In very few cases has the teacher provided the additional instruction or help needed. In most cases, the corrective work following the diagnostic-progress feedback testing is done *outside* the regular classroom time.

In the many studies reported by Block (1971, 1974) and by Peterson (1972), there is considerable evidence that mastery learning procedures do work well in enabling about four-fifths of students to reach a level of achievement which less than one-fifth attain under non-mastery conditions. The time costs for this are typically of the order of 10 to 20 percent additional time over the classroom scheduled time. The efficiency of the correctives and the additional time needed are direct functions of the quality of the diagnostic-progress feedback testing— the formative tests.

There is little question that mastery learning strategies have been effective in many classroom situations at all levels of learning from the elementary school level through the graduate and professional school levels. It is also clear that there are some situations in which mastery learning approaches do not work well. We have tried to understand something about the situations in which mastery learning works well and the situations in which it works poorly. In large part, this book regards mastery learning as a special case of a more general theory of school learning. Properly used, the theory should be useful in predicting the learning situations and characteristics of students necessary for mastery learning to succeed, as well as the conditions under which mastery learning is likely to produce about the same levels of learning as non-mastery learning situations.

But more important for the present work, we have attempted to do research using mastery learning strategies as research tools to determine the conditions under which most students can learn well and to determine the conditions under which they learn less well. It is this research and our reviews of the literature that have raised serious questions about our present views of individual differences in school learning. After almost a decade of work on mastery learning and research on some of the variables involved in mastery learning, we have come to the conclusion that individual differences in school learning under very favorable conditions of schooling will approach a vanishing point while under the least favorable conditions they will be greatly exaggerated. We must remind the reader that it is education that we are primarily concerned about, rather than individual differences. We are interested in the conditions under which education and the schools are most effective—individual differences in learning and the level of learning are two symptoms of the effectiveness of our educational methods under school conditions.

The research on mastery learning, our research using mastery learning as research tools, and the review of the relevant research literature have been the basis for a series of generalizations about schooling, learning, and human characteristics, which we have attempted to summarize in a theory of school learning. The theory attempts to explain school learning in terms of a small number of variables. It begins with almost no assumptions about human capacity for learning but attempts, on the basis of empirical evidence, to establish the extent to which our present common sense and common observations about students and learning should be questioned.

While this theory owes much to the Carroll Model of School Learning (1963) and to the ideas underlying mastery learning as it has been used in schools and colleges, it attempts to go beyond these. Perhaps the reader should be apprised at this point of the final conclusion of this work. Essentially, it is that what any person in the world can learn, almost all persons can learn *if* provided with appropriate prior and current conditions of learning. While there will be some special exceptions to this, the theory provides an optimistic picture of what education can do for humans. It holds out the possibility that favorable conditions of school learning can be developed which will enable almost all humans to attain the *best* that any humans have already attained. What is defined as *best* will, of course, vary with time, place, culture, and even individuals. However, the theory holds promise that in any time and place, the schools can provide the best of education for virtually all of their students—if the schools choose to do so.

THE PROCESS OF SCHOOLING

While "education" may be provided by many institutions in a society (e.g., home, church, mass media) and by varied experiences of living within a society, systematic education is most frequently provided by schools and colleges. Much of the theory to be provided in this work is directly applicable to the process of schooling and the schools. It is to be hoped, however, that aspects of this theory may be seen as relevant to any form of systematic education—whether it be in the schools or elsewhere in a particular society.

Throughout the world, schools have been created to provide a major part of the education for the young. While the purposes and content of this education varies greatly between nations as well as within nations, the process of schooling is much the same everywhere. Schools are organized in which teachers and instructional materials provide instruction to *groups* of students (usually between twenty and seventy students in each group). Much of the instruction is intended to be systematic in that the learning that takes place in one term or year is regarded as a base or prerequisite for the learning to be provided in subsequent years or terms.

In this process of schooling, students tend to be classified by age or grade level with some assumptions that what is to be learned and the ways in which it is to be learned are appropriate to the age-grade level of the students. There is also an assumption that the teachers at a particular level are sensitive to the special characteristics of the students at that level and to the content and objectives of the instructional materials and processes to be learned at that level.

At each stage or level in the schools, some measure of attainment is used as a determiner of the students' status and as a basis for decisions about the further opportunities for learning to be provided the students in subsequent stages. At each stage in the schools, the measures of achievement typically show greater individual differences in the learning attained than was true in the previous stage. Students who are denied further opportunities for learning, students who are expected to repeat a set of learning experiences, and students who are provided with further opportunities for learning are all regarded as meriting these decisions. Individual differences in learners are invoked to explain and account for individual differences in learning and as a rationalization for the differential opportunities for further learning to be provided by the schools and the communities that support them.

The main thesis of this book is that *individual differences in learning* is an observable phenomenon which can be predicted, explained, and altered in a great variety of ways. In contrast, *individual differences in learners* is a more esoteric notion. It frequently obscures our efforts to deal directly with educational problems in that it searches for explanations in the person of the learner rather than in the *interaction* between individuals and the educational and social environments in which they have been placed.

That large individual differences in school learning exist is clearly testified to by parents, teachers, and by almost every research publication dealing with the measurement of learning outcomes since the turn of the present century. The ease with which these differences can be observed by trained or untrained observers makes the existence of individual differences in learning a commonsense type of phenomenon. This common sense is further supported by the elaborate system of achievement tests created and used in the United States (and other countries) which reveal individual differences in learning in great detail and with considerable reliability and objectivity.

Furthermore, large-scale studies of educational achievement in entire nations (Coleman, 1966a; Plowden, 1967; Comber & Keeves, 1973; Husén, 1967; Purves, 1973; Thorndike, 1973) reveal very great individual, group, and national differences in measures of school achievement.

There is ample evidence that individual differences in school learning do "exist." Indeed, the existence of the phenomenon is unquestioned. Furthermore, there is considerable evidence that differences which appear relatively early (by grade 3) in school achievement tend to remain and even *increase* over the many years of school. Studies using longitudinal research methods make it clear that the differences found between students in measured achievement at one grade level do not disappear at a later grade level (Bloom, 1964). These studies show that there is a substantial relation between the achievement differences among a group of students at one time and their achievement differences several years later (Bracht & Hopkins, 1972; Payne, 1963).

In spite of all the evidence on the existence and stability of differences in school learning, this writer is convinced that much of the variation is attributable to the environmental conditions in both the home and the school. Much of individual differences in school learning may be regarded as man-made and accidental rather than as fixed in the individual at the time of conception.

Part of the differences are produced in the home and the school by the particular practices used in these two institutions. Efforts to teach the child may be effective or ineffective—in either case a judgment is made about the learner and *only rarely* is a judgment made about the teaching or the previous preparation of the learner. These judgments about the learner by parents, teachers, and the schools are effective in convincing the learner that he is different from other learners and that he can learn better or that he can learn less well than others of the same age or school level. Having convinced the student and themselves, both the student and the significant adults in his life act accordingly. Students, parents, and teachers expect differences and they make arrangements and engage in processes which maximize and enlarge the differences. In turn, educational scholars and testers provide major theoretical, experimental, and practical justifications for the entire process.

One of the most important elements in accounting for individual differences in school learning is the centrality of instruction for groups of learners. Instruction provided to a group of twenty to seventy learners is likely to be very effective for some learners and relatively ineffective for other learners. This aspect of the process of schooling is likely to be replete with *errors* which are compounded over time. Unless there are ways of identifying and correcting the flaws in both the teaching and the learning, the system of schooling is likely to produce individual differences in learning which continue and are exaggerated over time.

Quite in contrast with such an "error-full" system might be the conception of an "error-free" system of instruction and learning. An approach to such an error-free system of schooling might be seen in the interaction between a gifted and sensitive tutor and *one* learner. If the communication processes between tutor and learner are ideal, it is likely that there would be a minimum of error in both the teaching and the learning. Whether or not group instruction and learning could ever approach the reduction in error present in an ideal tutor-student rela-tionship, it is likely that a systematic way of *identifying* and *correcting errors* in group instruction and individual learning might be one way of approaching a *minimal-error system* in the process of schooling.

This theory attempts to identify the variables which account for much of the "error" in the schooling process and brings evidence together to determine the amount of error contributed by each variable and the effect of controlling or altering this variable. While it is unlikely that the schooling process could ever be a completely error-free system, it is possible to determine the reduction in error (or the reduction in individual differences in learning) which could theoretically and practi-cally be accomplished in the schools.

A THEORY OF SCHOOL LEARNING

If we could have a system of schooling which is virtually error free or with a significant reduction in error, we assume it would result in most of the learners attaining a high level of learning, a relatively small amount of variation in levels of learning achieved, and a very small amount of variation in the learning time required.

Our theory is an attempt to determine a small number of variables which will account for much of the variation in school learning. We have selected three interdependent variables which if properly attended to should enable schools to approximate an error-free system of education.

The three interdependent variables which are central to this theory of school learning are:

   a. The extent to which the student has already learned the basic prereq-uisites to the learning to be accomplished *b.* The extent to which the student is (or can be) motivated to engage in the learning process

c. The extent to which the instruction to be given is appropriate to the learner

More specifically, the theory deals with student characteristics, instruction, and learning outcomes (see the following chart on major variables in the theory of school learning).

One of the student characteristics which is believed to be central in determining student learning is the student's *Cognitive Entry Behaviors* —the prerequisite learning held to be necessary for the learning task(s) on which instruction is to be provided (see Chapter 3). The second characteristic is the *Affective Entry Characteristics*—the student's motivation to learn the new learning task(s) (see Chapter 4).

The instructional variable of greatest importance is believed to be the *Quality of Instruction*—the extent to which the cues, practice, and reinforcement of the learning are appropriate to the needs of the learner. This is considered in detail in Chapter 5. Since it is necessary to consider these variables in relation to something to be learned, we have attempted to define the nature of a learning task (see Chapter 2).

It is the central thesis of this work that variations in the *Cognitive Entry Behaviors* and *Affective Entry Characteristics* and the *Quality of Instruction* will determine the nature of the learning outcomes. These outcomes are the *level and type of achievement,* the *rate of learning,* and the *affective characteristics of the learner* in relation to the learning task and self. Where the student entry characteristics and the quality of instruction are favorable, then all the learning outcomes will be at a high or positive level and there should be little variation in the measures of the

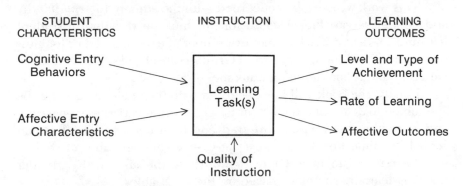

MAJOR VARIABLES IN THE THEORY OF SCHOOL LEARNING

outcomes. Where there is considerable variation among students in their entry characteristics and where the quality of instruction is not optimal for the different students, there should be great variation in the learning outcomes. The degree to which one or more of these variables is less than optimal will determine the level and type of learning achievement, the difficulties encountered in the learning process, the time and effort required to accomplish the learning that does take place, and the student's affect about the learning, the learning process, and the self.

The theory is ideally intended to explain the interaction between an individual learner, the instruction, something to be learned, and the learning finally accomplished. However, it should be equally appropriate for accounting for the interaction between a number of learners, the instruction, the learning task, and the *differences* in the learning finally accomplished.

The intent of this book is to develop a theory of school learning which will enable us to predict, to explain, and to modify individual differences in school learning.

Much of this book will be concerned with the review of relevant research to determine the effectiveness of these three variables in *predicting* levels of school achievement and the differences within groups of students in their school learning. There is a relatively large body of educational studies which bear on this prediction problem. One aspect of the prediction problem is to determine the extent to which each variable separately and in combination accounts for the differences among students in a great variety of school learning situations and school subjects.

This work will also be concerned with the attempt to *explain* why and how these variables account for much of the variation in student learning. Here a somewhat smaller number of experimental or longitudinal studies will be utilized to determine causal links between these variables and school learning outcomes.

Finally, the book will be concerned with the evidence that can be assembled to determine the extent to which these variables (separately and in combination) may be *altered* and their consequent effects on school learning. For this purpose an even smaller number of studies will be referred to in order to demonstrate the effects of particular teaching-learning strategies based on these variables.

One primary purpose of the book is to develop a theory of school learning which may be useful in *predicting* and *explaining* the variation in school learning under a great variety of conditions. For these purposes, the theory is value free and should be judged on its effectiveness in predicting and accounting for individual differences in learning in a great variety of schools, curricula, and countries.

However, the merits of this theory in the long run must rest on its usefulness in *altering* school learning and in producing school and other conditions which provide for more effective learning for the vast majority of students. If the theory is to be useful, it should enable educators to determine the conditions in students and in the schools which need to be altered *if* it is desired to alter *both* the level of school learning and the variation in individual differences in learning. Here the author must register his own value point of view that better learning is to be preferred to poorer learning and that smaller individual differences in learning are to be preferred to larger individual differences in learning. Or, to put it in the terms of the previous section of this chapter, a system of schooling with a minimum of error is to be preferred to one with a maximum of error. The reduction in the amount of error in a system of schooling is, in this author's view, to be determined by the extent to which students attain a high level of learning while, at the same time, variation in student learning approaches a minimum.

TWO BASIC ASSUMPTIONS

One assumption underlying this work is that the *history* of the learner is at the core of school learning. Each learner begins a particular course, class, school grade, or school program with a history which has prepared him differently from other learners with regard to the learning to be accomplished. If each learner entered each class as a "tabula rasa" or with similar relevant histories, it is assumed that much of the differences in school achievement would disappear. Thus this is a theory largely concerned with the varying histories of a collection of learners. What is at issue then is how these histories can be understood or taken into consideration in relation to the learning which is intended to take place. Also, we may wish to understand how these histories and the schools' response to them may increase or reduce individual differences in school learning.

Quite in contrast with this historical assumption for school learning is the attempt in learning theory and in much of laboratory research on learning to account for learning in a group of subjects presumed to be equal or similar in most respects for the learning to be studied. In much of this research or theorizing, elaborate efforts are made to find learners who are equivalent in major respects or to find learning tasks which are minimally affected by the previous history of the individual learners. Such theories and research seek to establish principles or generalizations about learning. It is quite possible that the great difficulty we have had in applying *learning theory* to school learning is largely attributable to the fact that learning theory and research ignore or attempt to minimize or control the effect of the history of the learner, while this is a central and dominant fact in school learning.

Although we have indicated the importance of the individual's history in influencing his or her learning, it is obviously impossible to fully know an individual's history or to take it into consideration in actually teaching a student or in helping each one learn some task. What is necessary is to search for some economical way of knowing a student's history and taking it into consideration. For many purposes we are not interested in the details of how someone developed in a particular way, but in what the individual has already developed in relation to what is yet to be learned.

For each learning task, we regard the student's level of attainment of the prerequisites for the learning to be accomplished (Cognitive Entry Behaviors) as one measure of the student's history relevant to the learning task. The individual's motivation for the learning to be accomplished (Affective Entry Characteristics) is, we believe, a resultant of prior experiences with learning tasks which the student regards as similar or related. Thus, rather than making a detailed study of the history of each individual, we will attempt to demonstrate that these two measures of the individual represent an economical current summary of the individual's history with respect to the learning yet to be accomplished.

A second assumption underlying this theory is that modifications are possible in the entry characteristics of the individual (prerequisite learning and motivation for learning), in the instruction for the learner (Quality of Instruction), or in both. Thus, it is assumed that the characteristics of the learners as well as the characteristics of the instruction can be modified in order to effect a higher level of learning for individuals and groups.

While we will stress the point that adequate preparation of the learners is to be preferred to attempts to modify these characteristics at the point of entry to a learning task, the selection of a learning task, modifications in the learning task, and even remedial measures on the specific prerequisites and motivation can be strategies which will ensure the highest proportion of the learners being adequate to the learning situation.

We will attempt to provide evidence that generalized characteristics of the learner—such as intelligence and aptitudes—are highly resistant to modification, while characteristics such as the specific prerequisites and motivation for a particular learning task are modifiable to a greater degree at most stages in the individual's history.

But even more important are the notions (1) that the student's ability to learn as indicated by the time and effort required to learn a particular set of tasks is highly alterable and (2) that under ideal conditions there will be little variation in students' ability to learn when judged in terms of time and effort required to learn one or more learning tasks for which the students are adequately prepared and motivated and for which the instruction is appropriate to the learners.

THE LIMITS OF THE THEORY

A limiting factor in this theory is that it deals with learners and instruction in relation to something to be learned. A particular learning unit or learning task (see Chapter 2) will be an important limiting condition for this theory. Thus, while the theory deals with relatively abstract qualities in the learner and the instructional process, these must finally be related to one or more specific learning tasks before much can be done to demonstrate the power of the theory in predicting, explaining, or altering the learning.

While the theory purports to deal with any learning task, most of the examples will be drawn from learning tasks which are cognitive in nature. A few examples of psychomotor learning tasks will be included, but the evidence on such learning tasks is not as readily found in the literature as that on the cognitive tasks. We believe the theory has relevance for learning tasks which are primarily *affective* in nature, but we will have little evidence for this. Affective variables will be treated in this work as largely entry variables as well as outcomes of cognitive and psychomotor learning.

Our focus on the *individual* learner (and the history a student brings to a task), something to be learned (a learning task), and a particular set of instructional conditions (quality of instruction) means that there are many other educational conditions and educational problems which will be regarded as peripheral in this work. As a result, this work on school learning will neglect a large number of factors which might claim central attention for many other educational scholars. School organization, administration, finance, control, etc. are believed by many scholars to affect school learning. While we would agree, we place them as peripheral to our concerns in this work. Similarly, curriculum and teacher training will be referred to only indirectly in this work since we are primarily concerned with particular learning tasks (already developed) and teachers (already trained). Hopefully, curriculum makers and teacher trainers may find the theory helpful in their work.

Finally, the theory does not deal with the underlying values of the educational enterprise and the choices among these values in a given educational situation. Nor does it deal with the many specific conditions and personal experiences in the student's history which may have determined the particular characteristics he brings to a particular learning task.

SUMMARY

The central thesis of this book is that variations in learning and the level of learning of students are determined by the students' learning history and the quality of instruction they receive. Appropriate modifications related to the history of the learners and the quality of instruction can sharply reduce the variation of students and greatly increase their level of learning and their effectiveness in learning in terms of time and effort expended. Where conditions for learning in the home and school approach some ideal, we believe that individual differences in learning should approach a vanishing point.

Learning in the home and in the school is a process with a very large magnitude of errors. In contrast, a *minimal-error* educational system should enable almost all learners to learn effectively and with considerable pleasure. The level of learning, individual differences in learning, and variation in student satisfaction with learning and with themselves as learners are useful indicators of the extent to which the process of schooling approaches such a *minimal-error system.*

The remaining chapters of this book go into some detail on the effect of the major variables on individual differences in school learning. These variables, separately as well as in combination, present many research problems for education, many implications for educational and social policy, and specific detailed consequences for school practices, teaching, testing, and curriculum development.

However, the main import of the entire book is that human nature is not the barrier to educational and cultural development that philosophers, politicians, social scientists, and educators have frequently alleged. The characteristics of the students and of the instruction dealt with in this book are claimed to be alterable, and *if this is so,* changes in the school environment can relatively quickly (in a single decade) make great changes in the learning of students. In contrast, attempts to make changes in the home and the larger social environment which are believed to be related to education and learning are likely to take many decades before major effects would be felt in the schools.

Societies in the past have relied largely on prediction and selection of talent as the means for securing a small group of well-educated persons. Modern societies stress the development of a very large number of well-educated persons and attempt to produce this by legal and social pressures which require individuals to attend school for a minimum of 10 to 12 years.

A society which places such great value on education and schooling that it requires the individual to attend school for long periods of time must find the means to make education attractive and meaningful to the individual learner. Modern societies no longer can content themselves with the *selection of talent;* they must find the means for *developing talent.*

2
A LEARNING UNIT

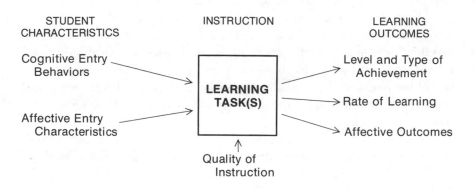

STUDENT CHARACTERISTICS	INSTRUCTION	LEARNING OUTCOMES

Cognitive Entry Behaviors → **LEARNING TASK(S)** → Level and Type of Achievement

LEARNING TASK(S) → Rate of Learning

Affective Entry Characteristics → **LEARNING TASK(S)** → Affective Outcomes

↑
Quality of Instruction

THE HISTORY OF THE LEARNER

We have stated in Chapter 1 that we are attempting to develop a theory of school learning which takes into consideration the history of the learner. While such a theory must recognize the large effects of the home environment and other out-of-school factors which have an influence on the student, the center of attention in this theory is the *learner in the school.* A student spends about 1,200 hours in school each year. Students in the United States as well as other developed countries will attend school for 10 to 16 years. We are concerned here with what takes place in the student's learning over the approximately 12,000 to 20,000 hours he attends school.[1] It is this history with which we will primarily be concerned. We believe that the school can do great good or great harm to the student in the long period of time in which he is expected and required (legally as well as socially) to attend school.

At the end of each year we may try to understand what the student

[1]By school we mean elementary, secondary, as well as higher educational institutions.

has learned, what the year has meant to him, and the great variety of factors in and out of school which have had some effect on him. We can do this repeatedly until we have attempted to understand his learning history over the 10 to 16 years he has been in school. Many studies have attempted to do this by a variety of techniques and procedures. However, we are here concerned with the way in which the history of the learner must be taken into consideration in the very process of the day-to-day interaction that takes place in the school. Furthermore, in order to reduce the many aspects of this history to a more manageable dimension, we will concern ourselves in this theory with only the very small number of variables which we regard as most central in explaining school learning. Fortunately, these happen to be the variables which are most amenable to modification within the school.

SEARCH FOR A UNIT OF ANALYSIS

Just as we find it necessary to reduce the history of the learner to a small number of aspects of this history, so we find it necessary to confine our attention to smaller units of analysis than years and terms of school attendance.

It is true that at the end of some long period of schooling some students have learned a great deal of what the school had to teach while others have learned relatively little. But the dimensions of this are so great that we can do little more than report on these differences and attempt to account for them by the use of intelligence and aptitude variables, personality and motivational variables, school variables, and home variables. Even when we have accounted for a large portion of this variation, we are left with the feeling that while we have done the right bookkeeping, there is little that we can do to change the conditions for the next generation of students. And there is little information we can give to teachers, curriculum makers, or educational leaders which will be helpful to them in improving learning conditions in the school or classroom.

Even when we view school learning as the learning of a school subject over a single semester or year, it is difficult to be very specific about what determines the variations in the achievement (cognitive and affective) of the students. While schooling is usually divided into subjects, terms, and classes, these are such large and complex learning units that it is difficult to examine them or to probe for the reasons why our students vary so much in their learning.

We have searched for a unit of school learning that is more manageable and analyzable. We regard the problem as one of determining a unit that has some relevance for the ways in which school learning is organized, the ways in which most students and teachers confront existing learning situations, and the curriculum and learning material with which they work. Such a unit should have an independent (or semi-independent) existence, and each unit should be large enough to have elements and parts that form a separable whole or *gestalt*.

SOME OF THE POSSIBILITIES AND CONSTRAINTS

School learning throughout the world is largely group learning. A teacher is held responsible for the learning of a group of 30 or so learners. (Countries differ in class size with the largest number of highly developed countries attempting to have classes between 20 and 40 [Husén, 1967; Comber & Keeves, 1973].) While much of the teaching and learning is group based and teacher paced, it should be recognized that a smaller number of classes or schools attempt to individualize the instruction and learning so as to permit variation in what the students are learning at any point in time. The learning unit selected should be applicable to school learning situations which are individualized as well as to those which are group based with most of the learners expected to learn many of the same things at the same time.

At present, most school learning throughout the world is subject centered. That is, the learners are expected to learn a subject like arithmetic, reading, social studies, science, a second language, etc. For the most part, much of this learning is related to a set of learning materials, a set of expectations as to what the students are to learn, and even a set of preferences as to the activities in which teachers and students are to engage. While there may be great variations in these learning materials and expectations and preferences, there are some very powerful constraints which place limits on these variations. The age-grade division of students means that the learning at one age or grade level is constrained by the learning expectations of the subsequent grades or courses. Examinations at various points in the schooling process, whether given by the teachers, the school, or external authorities, also place constraints on what is to be learned at any given school level or in any given subject. Other societal constraints (expectations of parents, employers, teachers, other schools) also place limits on these variations. In any case, while the learning unit selected should be applicable to graded subject-centered school situations, it should also be relevant to more open and less formal learning situations.

A third constraint in schools is that students are expected to learn from a set of materials and a teacher. Although there may be some school situations with a variety of instructional materials, teachers, tutors, or aides made available to the student, schools by and large expect the student to accommodate to the instructional characteristics of the teacher and the learning material selected by or for the student. While it is possible for the student to learn a great deal by himself from a great variety of life experiences outside the school, in the school he must adjust to the instructional properties and characteristics of the material and the teacher. That is, he must learn what is contained in the instructional materials, what the teacher emphasizes in these instructional materials, and what else the teacher emphasizes in the instruction.

What we are searching for then is a unit of learning which can be related to group or individualized learning, to graded subject-centered as well as non-graded less formal learning situations, and which can reflect the style and characteristics of the instructional materials and the instructor.

Were we free from these constraints, we might search for what has been termed *learning experiences* of the individual. As Tyler (1950, p. 41) puts it, "learning experience refers to the interaction between the learner and the external conditions in the environment to which he can react! Learning takes place through the active behavior of the student; it is what *he* does that he learns, not what the teacher does." While this is what we are trying to get at, and this is what the teacher and the instructional material are trying to stimulate, we find this to be a difficult concept as the basis for developing learning units for our research. A learning experience is a highly individualistic experience, while we are attempting to account for variation in the learning of something that two or more learners are expected to learn at the same or different times under relatively similar conditions.

For some purposes, it might be desirable to move to an atomistic level where each interaction of student, teacher, and material can be recorded and related to every other interaction and to other variables such as aptitudes, achievement, etc. (Bellack, 1966; Flanders, 1970; Smith & Meux, 1962). We grant the usefulness and meaningfulness of such an atomistic approach, but have preferred, for reasons which will become explicit throughout this book, to work with a somewhat larger or molar unit.

In the Carroll (1963) Model of School Learning and in the Mastery Learning strategies (Bloom et al., 1971; Block, 1971, 1974) derived from this model, it is necessary to relate the learning and instruction to a smaller unit than an entire course or curriculum. This basic unit may be a learning activity, a learning project, a learning task, or some other way of conceiving of an interaction between a *learner, something to be learned,* and a *teacher* or *tutor.*

The unit that we believe is most relevant for our purposes is a *learning task* comprising what is usually referred to as a learning unit in a course, a chapter in a textbook, or a topic in a course or curriculum. Such a learning task may take somewhere between 1 to 10 hours for the students to learn it. Defined in this way, a learning task may include a variety of subject matter or content elements as well as a variety of behavioral or learning process elements. The point of all this is that this type of unit contains a variety of ideas, procedures, or behaviors to be learned over a relatively short period of time.

It is a useful unit since it fits in well with existing courses and curricula, and it is about the size of the learning unit that teachers, students, and curriculum workers have been using for many years.

Finally, one or more learning tasks may include relatively complex cognitive educational objectives such as *analysis* or *application* as well as less complex objectives such as *knowledge* or *comprehension*. Similarly, in the psychomotor domain a learning task may include complex or difficult educational objectives as well as simpler and less difficult objectives. While the affective domain has not been stressed in the work which has been done with learning tasks, we believe affective objectives are also learned over a series of learning episodes and that elements of affect can be found in particular learning units.

SOME CHARACTERISTICS OF A LEARNING TASK

In the research reported by Airasian (1969, 1970, 1971) and in the work on formative testing by Bloom, Hastings, and Madaus (1971) it has been found that two independent judges who are competent in the subject can, with a minimum of training, identify the elements to be learned in a learning task with more than 90 percent agreement. In this research, the judges concentrated on the learning materials provided for the learning task. Undoubtedly, the agreement would be somewhat lower if they observed the instruction and what went on in the interaction of students and teacher for a period of several hours.

When independent judges were asked to determine the relations among the elements, in terms of what elements had to depend on prior elements and in terms of necessary (but not sufficient) learning relations among the elements, they agreed about 85 percent of the time.

The point to be made then is that a cognitive learning task as indicated by the materials of instruction can be analyzed with considerable objectivity by competent judges. This suggests that a learning task can be defined, its elements analyzed, and the relations among the elements made explicit. Whether affective and psychomotor learning tasks can be defined equally clearly is a matter for further research. However, it is the impression of the writer that given the state of the art with regard to the different kinds of learning, psychomotor learning tasks should be easier to define than cognitive learning tasks, while affective learning tasks may be the most difficult to define and analyze. We are contending that any learning task can be defined and analyzed whether it be largely cognitive, psychomotor, or affective. While much of the work so far has been confined to school learning tasks, it is believed that similar procedures can be applied to learning tasks to be learned through other types of experiences and encounters than those provided by structured school learning situations. Some learning tasks and the relation among the elements within the task are suggested in Chart 2-1.

A further question about learning tasks has to do with the validity of the definition and analysis. In the research reported by Airasian (1969), he hypothesized that the elements which required little more than *knowledge* types of learning would be easier for students to learn than those requiring *comprehension* and that the most difficult types of learning would be those involving *application* and *analysis*. In general, when formative tests containing items at each of these levels were used with several classes of students, the results support these hypotheses. That is, the difficulty level of the questions were, with few exceptions, supportive of the view that different levels of learning were involved from knowledge to application or analysis.

A second type of validation of the arrangement of elements in a learning task was also provided by Airasian (1969). The subject matter experts had agreed that certain elements could not be understood or learned unless the student had mastered other elements in the task.

Chart 2–1. Three Learning Tasks with Different Degrees of Structure and Interrelatedness of Elements

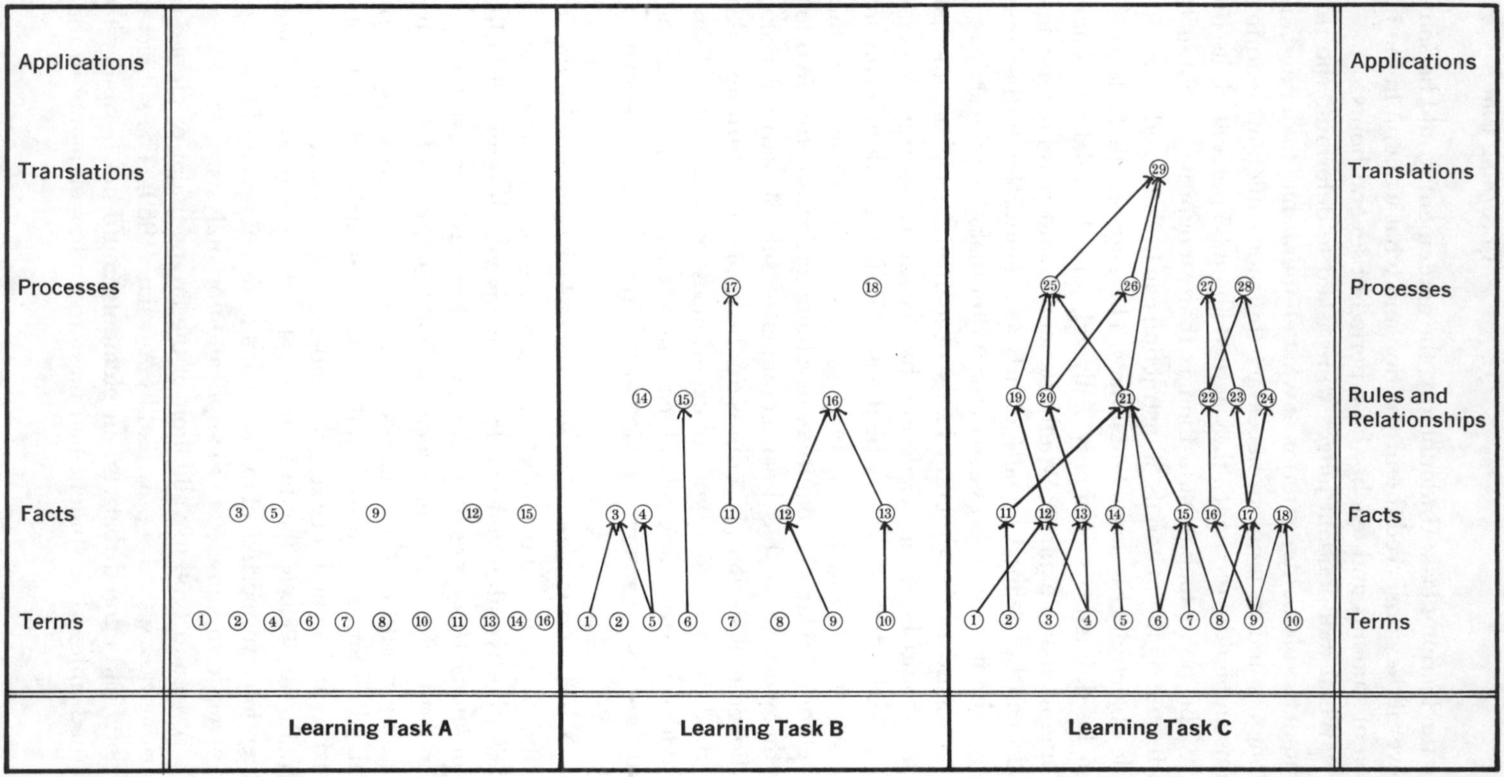

That is, certain elements were necessary for the learning of more complex elements. Again, in several classes, the hypothesized relations among the elements were borne out by pattern analysis of the test responses which involved those elements. Altogether, 75 percent of the responses fitted the hypothesized relations, while 25 percent did not. Further research is necessary to establish the conditions under which the results vary from the constructs established a priori. However, this type of validation further establishes the lawfulness of the relations among the elements in a learning task. This research on the hierarchical relations among the elements in a learning task is largely based on the ideas developed by Gagné, 1968; Gagné and Paradise, 1961; and Resnick, Wang, and Kaplan, 1970.

We should note here that not all learning tasks contain a hierarchical arrangement of elements. There are a great many learning tasks in which there are a large number of elements that are unrelated, other than by the structures and mnemonic devices imposed upon them by individual students. The learning of a large number of terms, specific facts, etc., may be without any clear pattern or structure, that is, the learning of one element has no necessary arrangement with other elements (see Learning Task A in Chart 2-1).

We have noted learning tasks in which the burden of remembering terms and definitions in the tasks was unusually great. In single chapters in widely used textbooks we found as many as 100 to 150 new terms introduced and defined. When we studied the relations among these terms and other materials in that chapter and other chapters in the course, we found that up to 80 percent of the terms were used only on the page in which they were introduced—and never again used in the course. It is unlikely that students will remember such terms very long, and we may question the value of burdening the students with a terminology that even the author of the textbook doesn't find useful. That all students can be brought up to mastery (at least temporarily) of such terms is not questioned. That students should learn such material may be questioned from the viewpoint of its utility, its meaningfulness, and the likelihood of long-term retention.

The point to be made is that a learning task can be analyzed with considerable objectivity. Once it has been analyzed, it may be evaluated from the viewpoint of the subject material to be learned, the structural relations among the elements, and learning theory and research. We would venture the hypothesis that a large number of unrelated elements can be learned relatively easily but not remembered very long, while a more complex set of relations among the elements may provide far greater difficulty in the original learning but are likely to be retained much longer (see Learning Task C in Chart 2-1).

RELATIONS AMONG LEARNING TASKS

A learning task in the schools is rarely completely isolated from other learning tasks. We can imagine some learning tasks which take relatively short periods of time to learn and which may be learned in isolation from other learning tasks—fire drill behavior, behavior expected in the school under particular circumstances, how to use the library. For the most part, however, learning tasks are clustered in groups or sets and taught by the same teacher over a term or year. While the logic of the relations among the learning tasks may not be entirely clear, learning tasks do tend to be grouped by subjects, courses, or fields. We are not arguing that this should be the case; we are only pointing out that this is what we most commonly observe in the schools. We suspect that the provision of a teacher for a group of students makes this kind of organization an economical one and that curriculum makers, textbook writers, teacher training, and school organization make use of these groupings of learning tasks.

When we examine the learning tasks in courses or subjects, we find a variety of organizations among the learning tasks. For some courses, we find that the learning tasks are typically taught (and learned) in a particular order, but that what is learned does not require that order. That is, the different learning tasks do not require each other and they could be learned in many different orders—and could even be learned in random order (see Chart 2-2).

What such an order suggests is that there are no necessary relations among the learning tasks, and that, in terms of cognitive, psychomotor, or affective tasks, the learning of one task is not required for the learning of the other tasks in the series. To restrict it to cognitive tasks, where it is easier to comprehend, the learning of one task does not materially facilitate or impede the learning of the other tasks. The student who has difficulty in learning the first task may perceive the remaining tasks in the series as difficult and may react to them in the same manner. Thus, his affect toward the series of learning tasks may be affected by his experience with the early tasks in the series (see Chapter 4). But his learning (or lack of learning) of the first task does not

Chart 2–2. A Set of Nonsequential Learning Tasks

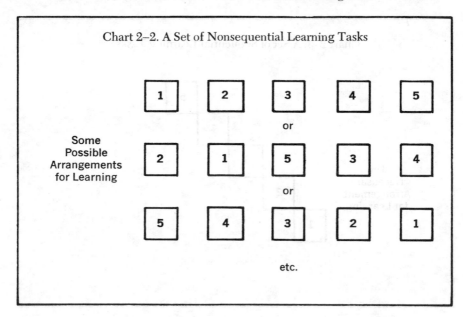

Some Possible Arrangements for Learning

1	2	3	4	5

or

2	1	5	3	4

or

5	4	3	2	1

etc.

facilitate or obstruct his learning of the later tasks, at least from the viewpoint of cognitive entry behavior (which we will discuss in Chapter 3).

We have also found subjects and courses where each learning task was sequentially related to the other learning tasks in the series. In such arrangements, each learning task becomes a prerequisite for the next task in the series and is, in turn, dependent on the achievement of certain prerequisites in the previous task(s). Such an arrangement is suggested in Chart 2-3.

Such learning tasks presumably cannot be learned in other orders and this is fixed by the intrinsic nature of the subject and/or by the logic of the pedagogical relations among the tasks. The level of achievement of each task thus becomes all-important for the learning of the later tasks, and each task has a necessary relation to the later tasks in the series. Here the cognitive structure of the sequence of tasks makes each task in the series necessary (but not sufficient) for the learning of the next task(s) in the series.

If a student fails one task, presumably he cannot learn the next task, unless he remedies his failure before proceeding on to the next task (see Chapter 3). Here also, the student's perception of his ability to learn each task affects his motivation (and effort or perseverance) for the next task in the series (see Chapter 4).

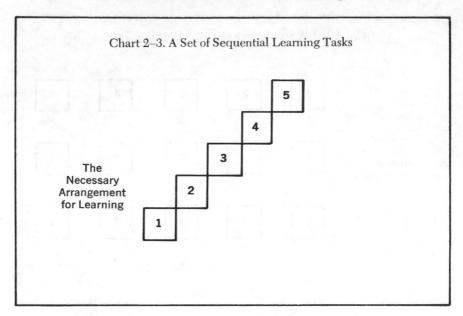

Chart 2–3. A Set of Sequential Learning Tasks

Not all groupings of learning tasks are so neat and clear as suggested by Charts 2-2 and 2-3. Many arrangements of learning tasks are possible, but these are the two extreme possibilities.

If each learning task is learned in an ideal student-tutor relationship, we believe that each student would be able to accomplish successfully each learning task for which he has the necessary prerequisites. We will develop this set of ideas more completely in a later chapter on the quality of instruction (Chapter 5).

However, the one-to-one relation between learner and teacher is rarely available in our mass school systems. The more customary relation is one teacher to thirty learners, with little time for a teacher to give individual attention to the problems of each learner.

No matter how good the teacher is in instructing the group, there must be great variations in the learning of the individuals in the group. Unless the teacher is able to get feedback on the difficulties each student in the group has had with particular aspects of the learning task and unless each student is able to get feedback on the particular difficulties he has had with the learning task, both students and teacher must stumble on from task to task with an inadequate understanding of what learning is or is not taking place.

Furthermore, unless the specific difficulties each student is having are corrected, it is unlikely that he can adequately learn (or master) a particular learning task. We will not go into here the variety of strategies which may provide both feedback and correctives for individual students (see Chapter 5), but it is likely that the strategies and correctives which work for some students may be different from those which are likely to be effective for other students.

All this is to say that group instructional procedures with individual students who vary in many characteristics *must* produce variation in the accomplishment of a learning task—both in the level of achievement of the task and the rate at which it is accomplished. Feedback and corrective strategies are necessary if this variation in achievement or rate of learning is to be reduced to any significant extent.

SUMMARY

We have been primarily interested in defining each learning task and the internal relations of its elements. We may wish to study what each student brings to a particular task, the quality of instruction provided to the students, and the achievement of the students at the end of the task. Much of our theory is an attempt to explain what occurs for a given learning task with respect to these characteristics of the student, the task, the instruction, and the outcomes at the end of the task. This represents the basic unit in our theoretical formulations.

We are also interested in the relations among a series of learning tasks and the ways in which the learning of one task influences the learning of subsequent and related learning tasks. Here again, we will attempt to utilize the theory to explain achievement over a series of learning tasks.

Finally, we are interested in the ways in which learning over each task and the series of tasks influences results on summative achievement measures as well as affective measures at the end of the entire series or at the end of sets of learning tasks within the series.

3
COGNITIVE ENTRY BEHAVIORS

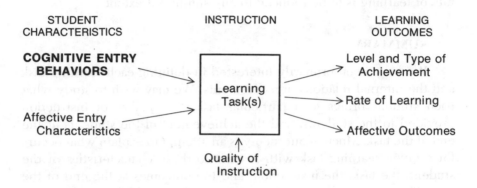

STUDENT CHARACTERISTICS	INSTRUCTION	LEARNING OUTCOMES
COGNITIVE ENTRY BEHAVIORS	Learning Task(s)	Level and Type of Achievement
Affective Entry Characteristics		Rate of Learning
	Quality of Instruction	Affective Outcomes

INTRODUCTION

A student enters each new learning task with a particular history of previous development and learning. The central thesis of this chapter is that some of that previous history will determine the nature of the student's interaction with the learning task and the learning outcomes of that interaction. We have termed the prerequisite learning needed for a particular learning task the *Cognitive Entry Behaviors,* and we plan to define and describe these behaviors and to demonstrate their effects on the students' interactions with a learning task and the learning outcomes.

In Chapter 2, we have defined the concept of a learning task. It is a task in which a number of elements are to be learned. These elements may be separable or unrelated terms, facts, or rules, or they may be so interrelated that the learning of one element is dependent on the learning of other elements. In school learning, a learning task is typically a part of a series of such tasks as provided in a course, textbook, or curriculum. In describing a learning task in this way, we are deliberately seeking to include more than the learning of a single element, such as a term, fact, or relation, and we are including less than an entire course, curriculum, or learning program. The reader may find it helpful to think of a learning task in school as the equivalent of a section or part of a course such as a chapter in a textbook, a unit of a curriculum, or a separable part of the course. We have found it useful to think of a learning task as requiring several hours to learn.

When school learning is thought of in terms of specific learning tasks, it is difficult to conceive of any single learning task which is beyond the capabilities of most human beings who wish to learn it and who have been properly prepared for it. With some exceptions, such as persons who suffer from severe retardation, brain damage, or deep-rooted personality problems, learning tasks provided in the schools are likely to be within the grasp of most humans who have the prerequisites for them. Stated another way, very few learning tasks provided in the schools require neurological or other capabilities which exceed that potentially available to most humans.

Yet it is a common observation that groups of students show considerable variation in their achievement over almost any learning task in the schools. Or, if all the students in a group are taught or helped until they reach a criterion level of mastery on a single learning task, some students will need more time and help to attain this criterion than will others. Furthermore, we do find some learning tasks in the schools that are learned by only a few rare students—at least as they are taught in particular classrooms.

In our attempt to explain or account for variation in level or rate of achievement on a learning task—or why some students can't learn it at all—we place great emphasis on the history of the learner. Our working assumption is that if all the students have the necessary prerequisites for a particular learning task, they would be able to learn it with less variation in level or rate of learning than if the students vary greatly in their attainment of the prerequisites.

While variation in the learning of a particular learning task may be explained in part by the student's motivation for the learning of the task and by the quality of instruction, in this chapter we will attempt to deal primarily with the extent to which the variation may be accounted for by student differences in the possession of the prerequisites for the task. Since the majority of school learning tasks are largely cognitive in nature, we will confine our consideration to what we have termed the

Cognitive Entry Behaviors (Glaser, 1970) or cognitive entry characteristics of the learners. By Cognitive Entry Behaviors we are referring to those prerequisite types of knowledge, skills, and competencies which are essential to the learning of a particular new task or set of tasks.

In terms of measurable variables, we assume that much of the variation in the learning of any particular task may be attributed to variation in the relevant knowledge, skills, and previous achievement that the students had *at the beginning* of the learning task. There are several considerations on which this assumption is based.

a. The whole history of research on prediction of school achievement demonstrates that particular tests of achievement and/or aptitude given prior to a learning task or a set of learning tasks enable one to predict to some extent the level or rate of achievement of students by the end of the task, course, or set of learning tasks. While these predictions are far from perfect, they do make it clear that attributes of the student *prior* to the learning tasks have much to do with how well he or she will learn the tasks or the conditions of time and help needed for the student to learn the tasks to a particular criterion level.

b. Longitudinal studies of learning achievement over a year or more reveal that the achievement variation of students at the *end* of the year or term is highly related to their variation in achievement over related school subjects *prior* to the beginning of the year or term (Hicklin, 1962; Payne, 1963; Bloom, 1964; Bracht & Hopkins, 1972). Even when the longitudinal research is over several years, the achievement measures at the end of one year are positively related to the student's achievement several years later in the same subjects (e.g., reading, arithmetic, a second language). Later in this chapter we will attempt to differentiate that part of the earlier achievement which represents prerequisite learning from other characteristics included in such longitudinal evidence.

c. School learning tasks typically represent some developmental sequences in which later tasks assume some prior learning on the part of the students. This is especially true in sequential sets of learning tasks such as are frequently found in mathematics or science. But, even in less sequential subjects such as language learning, literature, history, or the social studies, the learning tasks at one level of schooling are set on the assumption that the students have had certain prior learning. Related to this is the way in which many teachers begin their teaching at the beginning of the term, viz., by assuming that *all* students enter the course or subject with these prior learnings—an assumption which is unlikely to be equally true for all the learners.

d. Finally, we find it impossible to conceive of any learning task which is not built on some prior learning. Even a simple learning task such as learning to draw a circle or triangle, assumes that the learners have some prior experience with pencils (or chalk), some understanding of the words used in giving directions, and some specific psychomotor skills. That is, almost every learning task we can conceive of, no matter how simple, has a base in some prior learning. We believe this is especially true of the learning tasks found in the schools.

PREREQUISITE LEARNING AND ITS AVAILABILITY

If *all* the learners lack the *necessary* prerequisites for a learning task, it should be theoretically impossible for them to adequately learn (learn to criterion) the learning task. That is, if true prerequisites are established, then no amount of effort, persuasion, reward, or quality of instruction will enable the learners *without* these prerequisites to adequately learn the task under consideration. Thus, the prerequisites, or *cognitive entry behaviors* (for cognitive learning tasks), constitute a necessary link between the learners and the accomplishment of the learning task—they cannot be ignored or omitted if the student is to adequately learn the task. Given this view, only if the student acquires the necessary entry behavior can he or she possibly attain the criterion of achievement specified for the learning task.

If *all* the learners do possess the necessary prerequisites for a new learning task, then it should be possible for all of them to adequately learn the task—*if* they are motivated to do so and *if* the quality of instruction is appropriate to their needs. If these conditions are met, then all the students should be able to learn the new task with little or no variation in level of achievement or time required to reach the criterion of achievement.

Where there is great variation in the possession of prior requisite learning, there is likely to be great variation in the level of achievement of the new task or in the time required to reach the criterion of achievement.

While it is possible that all the students have had an opportunity to acquire the prerequisite learning, and it is even possible that all the students did acquire it, the critical point is the *availability* of the prerequisite learning at the time it is required in the specific new learning task. By *availability*, we mean that the student remembers and can use these prior learnings when and where they are required in a specific new task.

It is our view that each learning task may differ from every other learning task in the prerequisite learnings required. It is even possible that each teacher's approach to a particular task may require specific prior learning different from that of other teachers. One can imagine a never-ending search for the prerequisite learning. However, we believe the problem of determining the necessary cognitive entry behaviors for a particular learning task can be solved at a satisfactory level without engaging in a complex and interminable set of research procedures. We will say more on this on pages 36 and 38, but here we may leave the matter by noting that a careful logical and pedagogical analysis (by teachers of the subject) is a useful way of determining what is *given* in a learning task and what it is assumed the student already *possesses* at the beginning of the learning task.

SEQUENCE AMONG A SET OF LEARNING TASKS

So far we have been considering learning tasks as though they were single and isolated tasks. For our purposes in considering entry characteristics, it is useful to remember that in school it is rare that learning tasks are taught as isolated tasks. Most learning tasks in the schools are grouped in some ways. Perhaps the most common way of grouping them is by courses, subjects, or fields of study; that is, there are a series of learning tasks grouped in relation to arithmetic, literature, reading, science, geography, second language, economics, psychology, etc. These are further subdivided by terms, grades, or other curricular units.

Within each term or subdivision of a subject, the learning tasks are placed in some order. This order may be a preferred or convenient order as viewed by the curriculum makers, the textbook writer, or the teacher. However it is determined, the students are expected to encounter the learning tasks in some arrangement or order.

It may well be that the sequence of learning tasks is purely one of convenience and that the same learning tasks could be learned equally well in any of a great variety of sequences. When this is so, the learning of unit 1 is not a *necessary prerequisite* for unit 2, and the learning of unit 2 is not a necessary prerequisite for unit 3. If this is true, the initial entry behaviors for the entire course are likely to be equally relevant to the different learning tasks within the course, while each learning task does *not* contain the prerequisite or entry behaviors for the later learning tasks.

In contrast, where a set of learning tasks are arranged in a truly sequential order, mastery of the first task is a prerequisite for the learning of the second task, and, in turn, mastery of the second task is a prerequisite for the learning of the third task, and so on. Under these conditions, the cognitive entry behaviors for the first task are the prerequisites for the entire course or set of learning tasks. However, in addition, once the student has begun the sequence of learning tasks, each of the tasks includes the prerequisites or cognitive entry behaviors for the next task.

Under highly sequential arrangements of learning tasks, the most critical tasks are likely to be the early ones in the sequence, since if these are not learned adequately (or to some criterion), the student is likely to have great difficulty with all the later tasks. In Chart 3-1 we have suggested that the distribution of achievement on a sequence of learning tasks is likely to become more and more varied where inadequate learning on one task is not corrected (by the student or the student-teacher). That is, uncorrected difficulties on the first task are likely to be compounded by more uncorrected difficulties on the second task, and by even more difficulties on the third task.

In contrast, if the students learn all or most of the essential parts of the first task (or their inadequate learning is corrected) before they begin the second task, and if their learning over the second task is

Chart 3–1. Theoretical Achievement Distributions
Where Inadequate Learning Is Not Corrected
at the End of Each Learning Task

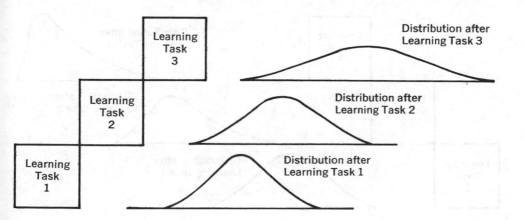

adequate (or corrected), then there should be equal or decreasing variation on achievement over each subsequent learning task. Whether the achievement variation remains equal or decreases is probably dependent on whether the students gain feelings of adequacy or competence with each successive task or whether they enter each task with the same affective qualities as they entered the previous learning tasks.

In any case, inadequate learning of each task should show more and more varied distributions of level or rate of achievement, while adequate learning of each task should show similar or decreasing variation in level or rate of achievement (see Chart 3-2). When we turn to the micro-studies on pages 55–65, we will bring together some of the evidence bearing on these points.

Identification of Specific Learning Prerequisites
In the sequential learning tasks discussed here, it should be relatively easy to identify the cognitive entry behaviors. If the learning tasks are truly sequential, then each learning task contains the entry behaviors for the subsequent learning task or tasks. A criterion-referenced measure or a content-valid achievement test over Learning Task 1 in the sequential series will include the prerequisite elements for Learning Task 2 in the series. Appropriate testing and statistical methods (see Airasian & Bart, 1973; Airasian, 1970, 1971; and Chapter 6 in Bloom, Hastings & Madaus, 1971) can be used to identify the *necessary but not*

Chart 3–2. Theoretical Achievement Distributions
Where Inadequate Learning over the
Previous Learning Tasks Has Been Corrected

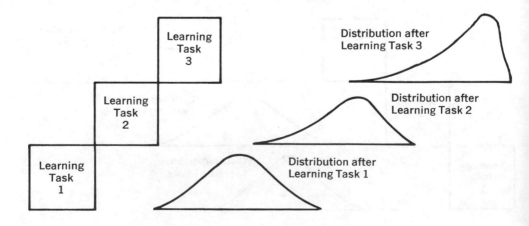

sufficient relationships between the test items over Learning Task 1 as related to the test items and performances over Learning Task 2 (or over subsequent learning tasks).

Where a learning task is viewed by itself (whether it is in a sequential series or not), it is necessary to do a logical and pedagogical analysis of what is given in the learning task and what it is assumed or required that the learners must have learned previously. Here the hierarchical types of analysis proposed by Gagné and others (Gagné, 1968; Gagné & Paradise, 1961; Resnick et al., 1970) may be utilized. Essentially these are techniques for determining the simpler or prior learning required before the learner can be expected to master a subsequent learning step. Again, it is possible to use testing procedures and statistical procedures to determine whether the *logical* and pedagogical analyses of what is *given* and what is presumably required *prior* to the learning task are empirically verified in the learning of students.

The determination of what the learners need at the beginning of an entire course or set of learning tasks (e.g., algebra, geometry, physics, first grade reading, introductory Spanish) is more difficult. Curriculum makers and textbook writers frequently attempt to define the prerequisite learnings required. However, only rarely has there been an empirical verification of this. One would hope that, in the future, curriculum developers would assume more of the burden of specifying the necessary cognitive entry behaviors for the first course in each series of courses (i.e., Arithmetic 1, Reading 1, History X, Science 1, Spanish 1). Such identification should be made on pragmatic as well as pedagogical types of analyses. Cognitive entry behaviors for later courses in a sequential series are somewhat easier to identify since the first course usually contains the prerequisites for the second course in the series— much in the same way as the first learning task includes the prerequisites for the second learning task in a sequential series.

It should be pointed out that it is unlikely that *all* that has been learned in previous school courses constitute the necessary cognitive entry behaviors for subsequent courses or subjects. Thus, for example, ninth-grade algebra does not require all the previous eight years of arithmetic. Undoubtedly, algebra does make some use of previous arithmetic competence—probably the competence developed in the first four or five years of arithmetic—depending on the way in which the arithmetic and algebra have been taught. A great deal of research will be needed to identify some of the *necessary* cognitive entry behaviors for particular school subjects. Once this is done for a particular set of learning tasks, one can begin to determine where such entry behaviors are likely to be learned in the usual school curriculum and the special learning conditions needed to ensure that they are available when they are needed.

MACRO-MICRO STUDIES

While the concept of prerequisite learning is a very old one in the history of education, the operational definition and measurement of cognitive entry behaviors is not found frequently in the educational research literature. In the micro-studies to be reported in a later section of this chapter we will deal more directly with cognitive entry behaviors for particular learning tasks within a set or series of learning tasks.

In reviewing the relevant literature on *something* approaching cognitive entry behaviors we will make use of the literature dealing with aptitude tests and achievement measures for the prediction of subsequent achievement. In these *macro-studies* there is no differentiation of particular learning tasks or measures of achievement over such tasks. Rather, the emphasis is on a course, term, or year of instruction in a subject, the achievement at the end of the course or term of instruction, and certain measures available prior to the beginning of the course.

Insofar as possible, we will make use of relatively large scale studies with samples of 100 or more students with carefully developed instruments for measuring the cognitive characteristics of the students prior to the instruction as well as following it.

In addition to the macro-level studies which only approximate the concept of cognitive entry behaviors and their effects on subsequent achievement, there are a small number of micro-level studies which provide more direct evidence on the relation between cognitive entry behaviors and achievement over subsequent learning tasks. Since most of these studies are experimental studies, we can also determine the effects of changes in cognitive entry behaviors on subsequent achievement variables.

In short, we are interested in (*a*) the predictive relation of cognitive entry behaviors to later achievement and in (*b*) the causal relations between cognitive entry behaviors and later achievement. It is unfortunate that most of the available evidence in the literature is on the predictive value of cognitive entry behaviors for subsequent achievement. Hopefully, the evidence available on *(a)* and *(b)* will stimulate educational researchers to devote more effort to the detailed study of cognitive entry behaviors, and the relations between such behaviors, the learning processes, and the subsequent achievement of students under conditions which permit causal inferences about all three.

MACRO-LEVEL STUDIES OF COGNITIVE ENTRY BEHAVIORS

In this section we are concerned with the relations between cognitive entry behaviors prior to a course or term of instruction and achievement at the end of the instruction. Here we have turned to the research literature on the prediction of achievement over a course (a set of learning tasks) by measures of achievement or aptitude prior to the beginning of the course.

Prior and Later Achievement

We first turn to longitudinal studies of achievement where there is a measure of achievement, followed by a period of learning, followed by another measure of achievement. In some instances the longitudinal study is over a single term or year, while in other instances it is over several terms or years.

In Chart 3-3 we have made use of the longitudinal studies of achievement to determine the predictability of achievement at grade 12 from earlier measures of achievement. In general it will be noted that the estimated correlation between general measures of achievement at grade 2 and grade 12 is +.60, between achievement at grades 6 and 12 it is +.78, while between achievement at grades 10 and 12 it is +.90. Put in another way, after grade 3 the prediction of achievement at grade 12 is +.70 or higher. Chart 3-3 also shows that by grade 3 the correlation between general achievement measures at adjacent years (or grades) is +.90 or higher.

While this chart is based on general measures of school achievement, such as the standard achievement batteries, the chart does demonstrate that measures of school achievement at any one grade are much influenced by the earlier measures of the students' achievement. Especially is this the case with adjacent years of school. It also demonstrates the increasing stability of achievement with increasing age or grade level.

In a more recent study, Bracht and Hopkins (1972) report that for

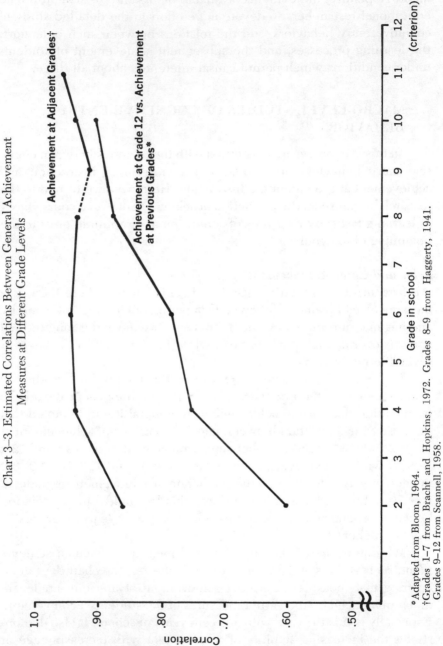

Chart 3–3. Estimated Correlations Between General Achievement Measures at Different Grade Levels

Achievement at Adjacent Grades†

Achievement at Grade 12 vs. Achievement at Previous Grades*

Grade in school

Correlation

*Adapted from Bloom, 1964.
†Grades 1–7 from Bracht and Hopkins, 1972. Grades 8–9 from Haggerty, 1941.
Grades 9–12 from Scannell, 1958.

one sample, the correlation between composite achievement tests given at grade 3 and grade 11 was +.82. Thus about two-thirds of the variance of 11th grade achievement was predictable from 3rd-grade achievement. For this sample, the correlation between 7th grade achievement and 11th grade achievement was +.90—that is, 81 percent of the variance of 11th grade achievement was predictable from a measure of achievement four years earlier.

In another longitudinal study, Payne (1963) demonstrated that arithmetic achievement at grade 6 could be predicted by arithmetic achievement at grade 2 with a correlation of approximately +.70, while reading achievement at grade 5 could be predicted by reading achievement at grade 2 with a correlation of approximately +.75.

What is demonstrated in these two studies and in the longitudinal data summarized in Chart 3-3 is that early achievement in school has a powerful effect on later achievement in the school—as the school subjects are at present taught. In the Payne study the high predictability of achievement in reading and arithmetic over so many years was regarded as an indictment of the schools since it indicates that relatively little was done in the intervening years to change the pattern of achievement for individual children. This, of course, involves the assumption (made in this chapter) that school achievement is an alterable characteristic and that altering the achievement at one school level will have consequences for the achievement at a later school level.

In Table 3-1 we have shown the longitudinal relations between achievement in specific school subjects such as reading (and English) as well as arithmetic and mathematics. In column A it will be noted that for measures of achievement on a subsequent related course (one year later), the median relation is in the neighborhood of +.85. In general, almost three-fourths of the variation in achievement at the end of a course is predictable from the measure of achievement or pretest before the course started. We believe that such prior measures of achievement include the effects of *cognitive entry behaviors* (prerequisite content plus prerequisite general skills), *affective entry characteristics*, as well as the *overlap* between the two measures of achievement.

In the case of the overlap, it is likely that some students at the beginning of the course already had to a considerable degree attained some of the characteristics measured by the final measure. Furthermore, the same or similar achievement tests were administered at both times, so that the later achievement measure includes what the student

TABLE 3-1. RELATIONS BETWEEN PRIOR AND SUBSEQUENT ACHIEVEMENT MEASURES

	COLUMN A* Achievement at grade X vs. achievement at grade X + 1 Grades			COLUMN B† Achievement at grade X vs. achievement at grade X + 2 or more Grades		
	1–5	6–8	9–12	1–5	6–8	9–12
Reading and English	.85 (.89)‡	.84 (.91)	.86 (.94)	.79 (.85)	.81 (.91)	.77 (.87)
Mathematics	.74 (.81)	.73 (.81)		.71 (.76)	.68 (.86)	.68 (.86)
Science						.68

*See Appendix Table 3-A.
†See Appendix Table 3-B.
‡Values in parentheses are corrected for attenuation.

TABLE 3-2. RELATIONS BETWEEN APTITUDE TEST SCORES AND ACHIEVEMENT FOR A FIRST COURSE IN A CURRICULUM SEQUENCE

Composite aptitude scores vs. achievement*		Selected aptitude subtest vs. achievement†	
Aptitude scores vs. first-grade reading	.63 (.70)‡	Word meaning scores vs. first-grade reading	.43 (.56)
Aptitude scores vs. first-grade arithmetic	.64 (.69)	Knowledge of numbers vs. first-grade arithmetic	.63 (.72)
Aptitude scores vs. ninth-grade algebra	.67 (.72)	Fundamental arithmetic operations vs. ninth-grade algebra§	.53 (.73)
Aptitude scores vs. first course in a second language	.60 (.70)	Words in sentences vs. first course in a second language	.52 (.63)

*See Appendix Table 3-C.
†See Appendix Table 3-D.
‡Values in parentheses are corrected for attenuation.
§Based on very limited evidence.

had already attained on the prior measure plus the change that took place during the single academic year. Thus, for our present purposes, these are overestimates of the effects of cognitive entry behaviors on subsequent learning.

In column B of Table 3-1 we have included only longitudinal studies where two or more years intervene between the two achievement measures. Here we believe the effect of overlap is considerably reduced and what remains is largely the effect of cognitive entry plus affective entry characteristics. (In Chapter 7 we will attempt to separate the effects of cognitive entry behaviors and affective entry characteristics.) However, Table 3-1, column B, suggests that the combined effect of cognitive (prerequisite content plus prerequisite general skills) plus affective entry behaviors on subsequent achievement is represented by a correlation of about +.70 (about +.80 when corrected for unreliability) and that the probable combined effect of entry behaviors (cognitive and affective) is of the order of two-thirds of the variation in achievement. That is, about two-thirds of the variation in achievement at the end of a course was determined several years before the course started.

Stated this way, it becomes evident that students in schools are to a large degree being judged more on the previous learning or achievement they bring to the course or subject than on their learning *within* the academic term or course for which the teacher's grade or achievement measure is being used. The student is being judged on his previous *history* of related learning to a larger degree than on his learning within the course. The underlying assumption of this chapter is that if all the students entered a course with equal relevant prior achievement, their variation in achievement of the course objectives and content would be much reduced. It is also assumed that cognitive entry characteristics can be *altered* to a large degree at many stages in the learning careers of individuals if appropriate learning conditions are provided.

Aptitude Tests and Subsequent Achievement in Selected Subjects
In an effort to further reduce the effect of overlap between measures of achievement as well as the effect of affective entry characteristics, we have summarized some of the relations between aptitude tests and achievement in selected subjects. The subjects selected are courses and subjects which, for the most part, are the *first set* in a new series of learning tasks. While previous learning is likely to have some relation

to achievement or learning in these courses, there are few or no courses which are usually cited as prerequisites for these courses.

Although the word aptitude does suggest the notions of "talent," "potential," and "capacity," we are here simply making use of tests which have been used to predict later learning in a school subject. Such so-called aptitude tests generally include some index of previous related learning (in the home, school, or larger environment), specific qualities which are likely to make the later learning easier, and anything else the testmaker found to be predictive of later learning in a specific subject. While we are not entirely comfortable with the use of aptitude tests as *proxy* measures for cognitive entry behaviors, they do make it clear that the history of the learner prior to the study of a subject does in part determine his learning of the subject. The aptitude tests are viewed by us as gross indicators of prior learning which have some predictive relevance to later learning of a specific school subject.

In Table 3-2 we have summarized the relations between these aptitude tests and achievement in arithmetic, mathematics, reading, and a second language. For introductory courses in these subjects the relation between total scores on aptitude measures and later achievement in these courses (either grades or achievement tests) averages about +.63 (about +.70 when corrected for the unreliability of the measures).

What these predictive relations suggest is that much of the learning in a new subject is influenced by characteristics which the students had at the beginning of the formal instruction in the new subject. In general, it is not likely that the teachers of the new subject will make special provision for those students who are very high or very low on the aptitude tests. That is, the instruction does not begin with the assumption that either the aptitudes are alterable or that the instruction should be altered to adapt to the students' entry characteristics.

Since the aptitude tests typically include a varied assortment of specific qualities and subtests which have been found to be predictive of later achievement, it is difficult to determine to what extent they include what we have termed *Cognitive Entry Behaviors*—the prerequisite learning needed for a particular set of learning tasks.

In the second column of Table 3-2 we have selected one of the subtests of each of the aptitude measures which we believe comes closer to our notion of the prerequisite learning likely to be necessary for the learning of a given school subject. The subtests we have chosen

represent previously learned behaviors which are likely to be necessary for the subsequent learning. In some instances these were developed in previous school experiences while in other instances they were
developed in the home. In this table we have shown the relations
between these subtests and later achievement on the first course in the
subject.

In first grade *reading*, the *vocabulary* already developed by the
child (prior to the first grade) is one of the most consistent predictors of
reading achievement in the 1st grade. The correlations (corrected for
attenuation) are somewhat lower than those for the total aptitude test
(see column A of Table 3-2). While it should be possible to teach first
grade reading in such a way that all children learn it well (in spite of
initial differences in vocabulary), it is likely that children with a larger
vocabulary have considerable advantages over other children in learning to read as it is presently taught in the schools.

It should be pointed out that a knowledge of the letters of the
alphabet is also a consistent predictor of later reading progress. We do
not regard this as a necessary prerequisite learning since it is directly
taught in first grade reading. This subtest is, in our view, an indicator
that some children have already been taught (or have learned) some
parts of the learning sequence usually included in 1st grade reading.
Thus, it may be a symptom of the nature of the home environment
support for school learning rather than necessary prior learning before
the 1st grade.

In *arithmetic*, the *knowledge about numbers* acquired earlier
appears to be one of the consistent predictors of achievement in 1st
grade arithmetic. While this does not appear to fully satisfy our requirement of necessary prerequisite learning (any more than prior knowledge of the alphabet for reading), it is a consistent predictor of later
arithmetic achievement. We believe that elemental notions about quantitative relations are developed in pre-school experiences (e.g., older
than, time, number of eyes, number of siblings, bigger than) and that
some knowledge of numbers is a crude but useful symptom of the extent
and quality of these experiences.

In the learning of a *second language*, the most consistent predictor
of later achievement is the ability to recognize the appropriate order of
words in sentences in the mother tongue. The task is to determine the
necessary arrangement of words to convey a particular idea. This subtest is almost as predictive as the entire language aptitude test. It would

seem to us that this subtest does get at a competence in the student's own language likely to be necessary for acquiring competence in another language.

In algebra, the consistent predictor of achievement is the individual's ability to do the *fundamental arithmetic operations*. We regard this as a likely cognitive entry behavior because these operations are required in the algebra, because teachers assume that the learners have already acquired them, and because they are used but are not directly taught in the algebra.

While we have attempted to identify specific subtests which approach what we believe to be prerequisite cognitive entry behaviors relevant for later learning, we believe that much research will be needed to identify which of these are truly prerequisite learning and which are indicators and symptoms of verbal educational development, characteristics of the home environment, motivation for school learning, or generalized learning characteristics.

It will be noted that in the prior-achievement–later-achievement studies (see Chart 3-3 and Table 3-1) the correlations average about +.80 between the two measures of achievement—even when the effect of overlap between the two measures is reduced. We believe this is too high as an estimate of the effect of cognitive entry because it is likely to include the effect of affective entry characteristics as well as the effect of the cognitive entry behaviors.

The aptitude tests, either the composite test score or the specific subtests (see Table 3-2) correlate with later achievement in the vicinity of +.50 to +.70 (+.56 to +.73 when corrected for unreliability). While these are not entirely satisfactory estimates of true cognitive entry behaviors, they suggest that the upper bound for the relation between measures of presumed cognitive entry behaviors and achievement in a subject is approximately +.70. However, it is likely that future research which identifies the "necessary" entry behaviors is likely to vary from these estimates—depending on the subject involved.

Some of the entry behaviors believed by the aptitude researchers to be relevant (and included in the aptitude tests) have such low relations with subsequent achievement as to suggest that their presence or absence have little effect on later achievement. This is illustrative of our view that not all the suggested or prescribed prerequisites are, in fact, required.

However, where suggested prerequisites based on logical and

pedagogical analyses are empirically supported by causal types of analysis as well as by the types of data included here, we believe that their absence, at least below a critical level,[1] makes it unlikely that the students who lack them will attain some degree of mastery in the set of learning tasks for which they are prerequisites. Cognitive entry behaviors, as we view them, represent causal links with learning processes and achievement criteria over selected learning tasks. If they are true causal links, then a student who lacks them to a significant degree should be unable to reach a criterion level of achievement on the task. On the other hand, such cognitive entry behaviors represent a *necessary* but *not sufficient condition* for the achievement of the learning task. That is, presence or availability of the cognitive entry behaviors does not guarantee achievement of the learning task to a criterion level.

In the research we have summarized for selected school subjects in Table 3-2, it is evident that cognitive entry behaviors account for about 50 percent of the variation in the achievement on sets of learning tasks. While we do not believe that this will be true on all learning tasks, it is likely that this is the most general case for school subjects. We represent this graphically in Chart 3-4.

The effect of hypothesized cognitive entry behaviors can be determined by studies in which entry behaviors are controlled (e.g., by comparing the achievement of students who possess them to the critical degree with those students who are below some critical point), by statistical relations between entry behaviors and achievement criteria, or by teaching all students the critical entry behaviors before beginning the learning task(s) and comparing them with a control group which varies on the measures of the entry behaviors. It is this type of research which is emphasized in the micro-studies. It is to be expected that as much as 50 percent of the variation in achievement over the learning tasks can be accounted for, controlled, or determined by educational

---

[1]We are not entirely certain in this, but we would speculate that cognitive entry behaviors are a *presence-absence* phenomenon, or a threshold phenomenon, rather than a scale phenomenon. What we mean to say is that different degrees of presence or competence in the cognitive entry behaviors should not produce different degrees of achievement of the learning task. Below some levels, the deficiencies in the entry behaviors should represent a serious handicap to the achievement of a learning task. Above some levels, differences in the degree of competence in the entry behaviors should have very little or no effect on the degrees of achievement of the learning task. This is one of the many problems for which further research is needed on the nature of cognitive entry behaviors.

Chart 3–4.
Effect of Cognitive Entry Behaviors on
Achievement Distributions

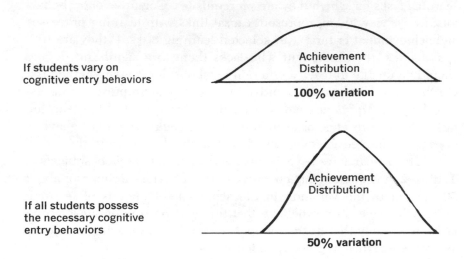

**If students vary on
cognitive entry behaviors**

Achievement
Distribution

100% variation

**If all students possess
the necessary cognitive
entry behaviors**

Achievement
Distribution

50% variation

procedures which ensure that most of the students possess the necessary cognitive entry behaviors required by the subsequent learning tasks.

GENERALIZED ENTRY MEASURES

It is likely that there are a number of common entry behaviors for the courses at the junior high school, secondary school and college levels—many of which are learned in the elementary school. That is, there is likely to be a set of *generalized* cognitive entry behaviors which is used over and over again in school learning tasks.

Reading Comprehension

Undoubtedly, one set of these generalized cognitive entry behaviors includes verbal-educational learning and especially *reading comprehension.* The reading comprehension learned in grades 1 to 6 is likely to influence much of the later learning in school and college. It is possible that this is so because most of the learning materials used in school require reading. It is also likely that being able to read the instructional material well enables many students to learn the subject *in spite* of variation in the quality of instruction. Whether or not instructional material can or should be developed which makes less use of reading comprehension is a problem for future research and curriculum development. At present, there is little doubt that much school learning does make heavy use of reading comprehension.

In Table 3-3 we have included some of the correlations between reading comprehensions and various subjects. It will be noted that the correlations are about +.70 with the subjects that depend most heavily on reading, such as literature. They are somewhat lower with mathematics and science courses. It is also clear that the relations are generally higher in the primary grades and lower at the secondary level. We speculate that the lower relations at the secondary level may be attributable to the likelihood that the most severely retarded readers may have dropped out of school before the completion of secondary education. Also, it is likely that a large portion of students still left in the secondary schools have reached at least the minimum capability in reading needed to learn most of the school subjects at this level.

In the International Study of Educational Achievement (IEA), samples of students in fifteen countries took a set of international achievement tests in science, literature, and reading comprehension (Thorndike, 1973). Each of these tests were, of course, presented to the students in their mother tongue.

In Table 3-4 we have shown the median relation between these three tests at the age fourteen level as well as in the final year of secondary education in these countries.

It is evident that reading comprehension is more highly related to achievement in literature than it is to science. It is obvious that the learning of the subject matter of the literature courses in these countries is very dependent on the reading. In countries where laboratory work is

TABLE 3-3. RELATIONS BETWEEN READING COMPREHENSION
AND ACHIEVEMENT IN VARIOUS SUBJECTS*

	Grade in school	
	6–8	9–12
Language arts and literature	.70	.70
Mathematics	.72	.54
Science	.62	.56
Median	.70	.56

*See Appendix Table 3-E.

TABLE 3-4. *MEDIAN INTERCORRELATIONS FOR LITERATURE, SCIENCE,*
AND READING FOR COUNTRIES* INCLUDED IN THE IEA STUDIES
(ADAPTED FROM THORNDIKE, 1973)†

	Students	
	Age fourteen	*Final year of secondary education*
Science vs. reading comprehension	.60	.44
Literature vs. reading comprehension	.69	.55
Science vs. literature	.41	.28
Science vs. literature (holding reading comprehension constant)	.00	.05

*The countries included are Flemish Belgium, French Belgium, Chile,
England, Finland, Hungary, India, Iran, Israel, Italy, Netherlands, New Zea-
land, Scotland, Sweden, and the United States.
†See Appendix Table 3-E.

highly emphasized in science courses, it might be expected that the
relation between reading and science achievement would be somewhat lower than in countries where science is more largely a textbook
reading course.

The relation between reading comprehension and science or literature is lower in the final year of secondary education than it is at age
fourteen, probably because in many of the countries the schools drop
the students who are less able in reading comprehension. (In the
United States, which has the largest percent of the age group still in
school at this level, the relations are about the same as at the age-
fourteen level.)

The relation between achievement in science and achievement in
literature is lower than the relations between reading and these subjects. However, it is most instructive to note that when reading comprehension is held constant (by use of partial correlation methods) the
relation between science and literature drops to virtually zero. It would
appear that the need for reading comprehension is the major common
element in both science and literature, and when this is held constant,
the two subjects are statistically independent of each other.

While we do not have similar evidence on other school subjects,
we believe it is likely that reading comprehension is the common
denominator in most school learning and that this is likely to be one of
the generalized entry behaviors required for a large portion of the
school curriculum as it is taught at present.

Another set of generalized entry behaviors probably includes the arithmetic processes which are included in many of the arithmetic tests, mathematics aptitude tests, and numerical ability tests. Basic quantitative skills are likely to be expected and are necessary prerequisites not only in mathematics and science courses but to some extent in most school learning tasks.

One could speculate about other generalized cognitive entry behaviors, such as logical reasoning processes, language development, and writing competence. Further work is needed before one can clearly identify and measure such generalized entry behaviors. Once they have been definitely established, the important educational problem is to ensure that students leave the elementary schools with these brought up to at least the minimum level required for later learning.

When general sets of entry behaviors can be identified for a large number of learning tasks (or school subjects), it is likely that a high degree of competence in these behaviors, or even an overlearning of these behaviors to a point where they are readily available to the learner when he or she needs them, will make a student's subsequent learning more effective (Gagné & Paradise, 1961).

While we have largely restricted our definition of cognitive entry behaviors to the kinds of learning which take place in particular school subjects, there are probably a great many other kinds of generalized characteristics learned throughout the school experiences which have a similar effect on later learning. These include attention skills, study skills, use of library, management of time, use of learning resources outside the classroom, and many other characteristics which facilitate school learning. Although we do not doubt their value and effectiveness, we have preferred to restrict our view of cognitive entry behavior to more specific types of learning which are clearly included in the school subjects or the manifest curriculum of the schools. However, we recognize that others may wish to emphasize these more generalized types of entry characteristics.

General Intelligence Measures

During the last half-century, teachers, psychologists, and educational researchers have given a great deal of attention to general measures of intelligence as determining or restricting the learning to be expected of children. In one sense, they have regarded general intelligence as the universal cognitive entry behavior for much of school learning at all levels from the elementary school through graduate and professional school. General intelligence and general scholastic aptitude measures have become the criteria for selection of students, they have been used for many predictive purposes in the schools, and they have been a major basis for many decisions about students.

It is our view that such measures are predictive of school learning to the extent to which they overlap with or represent indices of the more specific cognitive entry behaviors required for a particular set of learning tasks. When a specific set of cognitive entry behaviors has been identified for a course or a set of learning tasks, it should be found that tests of general intelligence or general scholastic aptitude add little or nothing to the predictive power of the specific cognitive entry behaviors. Furthermore, the predictive value of the intelligence measures for most school purposes is very limited in contrast with that of the cognitive entry behaviors.

General intelligence tests typically correlate about +.50 (±.10) with achievement over a great variety of courses and subjects (Lavin, 1965). It is likely that the correlation with school achievement measures is probably higher at the elementary school level and lower at the secondary school and college levels (in part because of the reduced range of intelligence scores to be found in the terminal years of public schooling and in higher education). In contrast, cognitive entry behaviors correlate about +.70 with achievement (and learning) of many school subjects (see pages 43 to 48).

In Chart 3-5 we have shown the relations between achievement measures in reading and arithmetic with prior measures of these subjects as well as with general intelligence measures at the elementary school level. These data are based on the Payne (1963) study, but we believe they are representative of similar longitudinal studies done by others.

It will be seen that at each grade level the correlations between intelligence score and reading or arithmetic achievement are about +.50. In contrast the correlation between measures of reading or arithmetic over adjacent years are between +.70 and +.80 during the elementary years. Thus intelligence measures account for about 25 percent of the variance while achievement measures account for 50 to 64 percent of the variance on subsequent achievement measures.

What is most instructive is to determine the effect on the correlation when one of the measures is held constant. Thus, the correlation between arithmetic (or reading) and intelligence is reduced to +.30 or less when *prior achievement* is held constant. That is, less than 10

Chart 3-5. Prediction of Achievement from Measures
of Intelligence and Prior Achievement

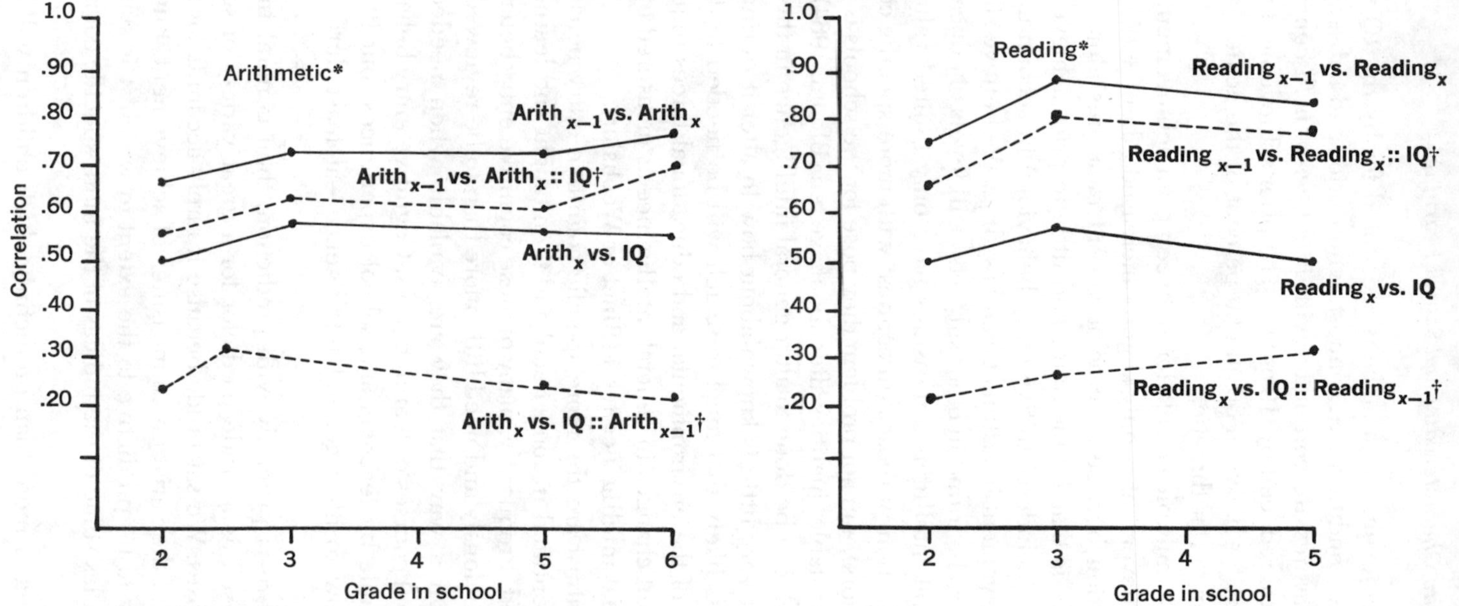

* Achievement at grade indicated (x) vs. achievement at earlier grade (x-1).
† Partial correlations.

SOURCE: Adapted from Payne (1963).

percent of the achievement variance is accounted for by the IQ measures under these conditions. In contrast, when prior and subsequent achievement measures are correlated with *intelligence held constant,* the correlations are reduced by .10 or less. The prior achievement measures still account for between 36 and 60 percent of the achievement variance in reading or arithmetic.

Similarly, the multiple correlation between prior achievement plus IQ with later achievement is only slightly increased (about +.05) over that of a correlation between the achievement measures alone. The point being made is that IQ measures add little to prior achievement measures (which include cognitive entry behaviors) in accounting for subsequent achievement in arithmetic and reading. We believe similar results are likely to be found in other subjects at all levels of education.

While general intelligence measures have only limited value for prediction or selection purposes (in contrast with more specific cognitive entry behaviors), a major problem they pose for the schools is their relatively fixed or stable qualities after about age ten (Bloom, 1964). We believe that much can be done to alter general intelligence in the preschool years, but very little is known about how to alter it during the school years. It is likely that much research will be needed to determine the nature of the environmental and educational forces required to make significant changes in general intelligence as measured by the existing individual intelligence tests (Binet or Wechsler).

Quite in contrast are the more specific cognitive entry behaviors which can be identified in some detail and then taught and learned to the level required. Frequently, many of these cognitive entry behaviors were learned previously and need little more than to be reviewed and practiced in such a way that they are available when needed for subsequent school courses or learning tasks. Cognitive entry behaviors are highly alterable by teachers and school experiences, but little is known about how to alter general intelligence—at least during the school years.

If our concern is primarily with prediction, then general intelligence may be used as a crude predictor for a great variety of school prediction purposes. We say crude because it rarely accounts for more than 25 percent of the variation on measures of achievement. Furthermore, it is likely to be predictive to the extent to which it is symptomatic of or includes some of the indices of the more specific cognitive entry behaviors.

But schooling is more than predicting which children will learn more than other children. If our primary concern is that of helping children learn in school, then we need to diagnose and treat (educationally) the student for the specific cognitive entry behaviors he needs for a particular set of learning tasks. The intelligence tests label and classify the student, while measures of the essential cognitive entry behaviors enable teachers to determine what the student needs in order to learn a particular set of learning tasks. The cognitive entry behaviors enable the teacher to relate the *history* of the learner to the current learning situation; tests of intelligence give little or no help in this process.

MICRO-LEVEL STUDIES OF COGNITIVE ENTRY BEHAVIORS

In the previous sections of this chapter we have been dealing with the relations between *initial* cognitive entry behaviors and subsequent achievement in courses, subject fields, or entire programs of instruction for one or more terms or years. We have had great difficulty in identifying and measuring these initial cognitive entry behaviors and for the most part have been using measures of previous achievement, aptitude tests, or other more generalized estimates of the cognitive behaviors with which a student entered a course or program of instruction.

In this section of the chapter we will concern ourselves more directly with particular learning tasks rather than courses or subjects which go on for an academic term or year. In the model which appears at the beginning of this chapter we have emphasized *Cognitive Entry Behaviors, Learning Task(s)*, and such *Learning Outcomes* as achievement and rate of learning. While the *initial* cognitive entry behaviors for a sequential series of learning tasks may be difficult to define and measure, it is in such a sequential series that each learning task by definition (as well as by more pragmatic analysis) includes the cognitive entry behaviors for the subsequent learning task(s) in the series. Especially should this be true for the next learning task in the series. Our concern in this section of the chapter is with the effect of cognitive entry behavior on the achievement outcomes for each task as well as on the summative achievement outcome for the entire series.

In a series of small experimental and school-based studies, some students at the University of Chicago have been contrasting a mastery learning approach to instruction with more conventional approaches to the same subject. For the most part these are sequential learning tasks in a series. Cognitive entry behaviors were measured at the beginning of each learning task (or at the completion of the previous learning task) in the series. It should be pointed out that the formative measure of achievement used at the end of a learning task was similar for the mastery and non-mastery classes. However, for the mastery class there was typically a set of corrective procedures *after* the formative test had been given. Following the corrective procedures, the mastery learning students took another parallel formative test which then constituted the cognitive entry behaviors for them for the next learning task. In contrast, the cognitive achievement over the previous learning task (without correctives) constituted the cognitive entry behaviors for the next learning task for the non-mastery students.

In Table 3-5 we have shown for the mastery and the non-mastery students the correlation between different measures of achievement on learning tasks as well as the correlation between these measures and summative-achievement measures.

In column A of Table 3-5 we have shown the median correlation between achievement on a learning task and achievement on the next learning task in the series. These correlations for the non-mastery students average +.67 (somewhat higher if corrected for unreliability). This is approximately the figure we have cited on page 47 for the macro-studies. Thus on the micro-studies for learning tasks as well as on the macro-studies for courses of a term or more, the general estimate is that cognitive entry behaviors account for about 50 percent of the variation in achievement.

It will be noted in column A that the median correlation between measures of *original* achievement on adjacent tasks is somewhat lower for the mastery students. However, it will be remembered that the mastery students received feedback plus correctives on each learning task before entering the next learning task, so that their achievement on each subsequent learning task tended to increase and their variation tended to decrease.

In column B we have included the correlations between corrected learning over each task and the original learning over the next task. Ideally, there should be little or no variation in achievement on a learning task—after correctives—and therefore the correlation between cognitive entry and achievement on the next learning task should be zero. This is approximately the case for two of the studies (Anderson; Arlin) as reported in column B of Table 3-5. It should be

TABLE 3-5. RELATIONS BETWEEN ACHIEVEMENT MEASURES IN THE MICRO-LEVEL STUDIES

Study	A Median correlation between achievement on Learning Task X and Learning Task X + 1		B Median correlation between achievement on Learning Task X (corrected) and Learning Task X + 1	C Correlation between achievement on the first learning task and summative achievement		D Median correlation between achievement on the learning tasks and summative achievement	
	Mastery	Non-Mastery	Mastery	Mastery	Non-Mastery	Mastery	Non-Mastery
Anderson (1973)	.31	.72	.06	.31	.68	.31	.68
Arlin (1973)	.32	.61	.02	.19*	.49*	.42	.50
Block (1970)	.62	.78	.32	.44	.78	.62	.78
Levin (1975)	.46	.54	.45	.59	.72	.59	.72
Özcelik (1974)	.46	.54	.45	.36†	.48†	.56	.72
Jones et al. (1975)	.72		.55			.62	
Pillet (1975)	.57		.44				
Median	.47	.67	.32	.36	.68	.57	.72

*Arlin's summative achievement is his final achievement on Learning Task 3.   †Özcelik's first learning task was not the original task in this series.

57

noted that in the three studies under regular school conditions (Özcelik; Jones; Pillet) the correlations in column B are lower than those in column A for the mastery students, but they do not approach zero. This is to be explained because it was difficult to get all the students under regular school conditions to systematically correct their errors on each learning task—although this was attained for the majority of the students.

In column C we have reported the correlations between initial achievement on the first learning task and the summative achievement test at the end of the series of tasks. Here again the median correlation for the non-mastery students is +.68, which suggests that if achievement in each learning task is not corrected, the effect of the initial (or early learning tasks) in the series is very great on the subsequent learning tasks as well as on the final achievement measure in the series. This correlation for the mastery students is much less (+.36) because achievement on each learning task was corrected; that is, the variation in learning was systematically reduced after each learning task and this is reflected in both the variation on the final summative measure as well as in the correlations between the achievement on the first learning task and the summative measure of achievement.

Finally, in column D of Table 3-5, we have shown the median correlations between the achievement measures on each learning task and the summative measures. Once again the median value of the non-mastery students is +.72, demonstrating that achievement on each learning task accounts for at least 50 percent of the variation in the summative achievement measure.

What is of special interest is the median for the mastery students. This is +.57, and it suggests that achievement on *each* of a series of learning tasks has a considerable effect on the final summative achievement measure. That is, achievement on each learning task whether uncorrected as in the non-mastery classes or corrected as in the mastery classes has a determining effect on final achievement. However, the final achievement of the mastery classes—where learning of each task was corrected—is much higher than the final achievement of the non-mastery classes—where learning of each task was not corrected (see Chart 3-6).

The general conclusion to be drawn from Table 3-5 is that achievement on each learning task is *alterable*—if feedback and correctives are used to improve student learning on each task. Furthermore, the effects of achievement on each learning task (altered or non-altered) is to

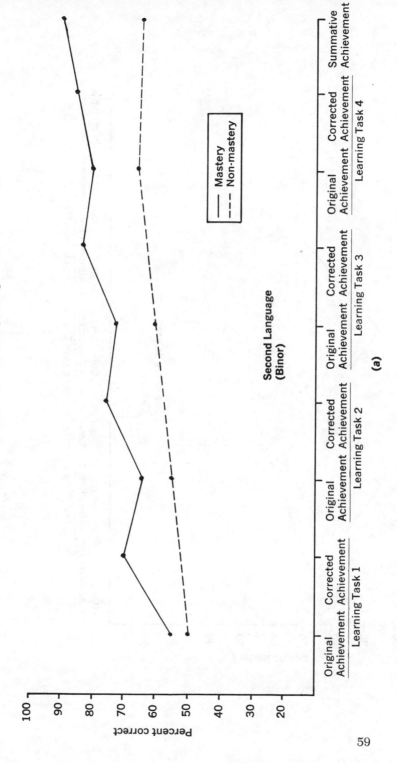

Chart 3–6. Changes in Achievement over Learning Tasks for Mastery and Non-mastery Groups

Chart 3–6 *(continued)*

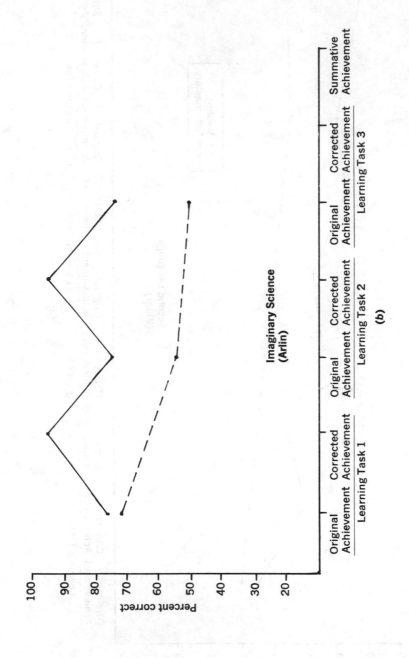

**Imaginary Science
(Arlin)**

(b)

Chart 3–6 *(continued)*

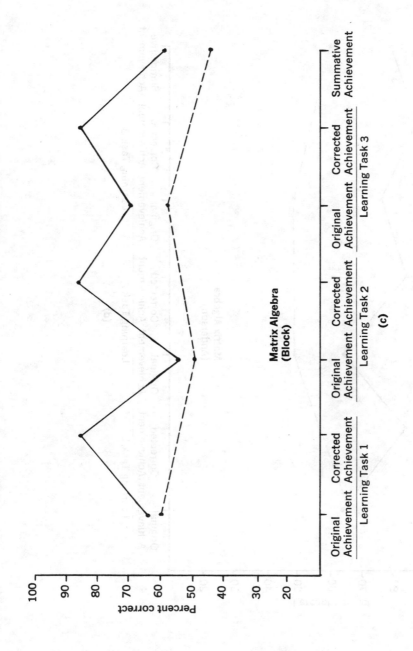

**Matrix Algebra
(Block)**

(c)

Chart 3–6 *(continued)*

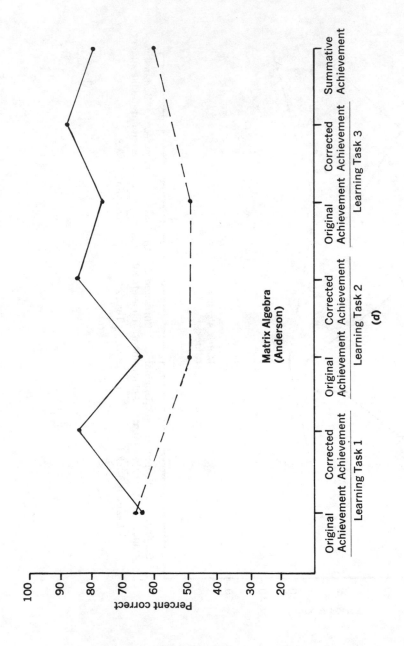

Chart 3–6 *(continued)*

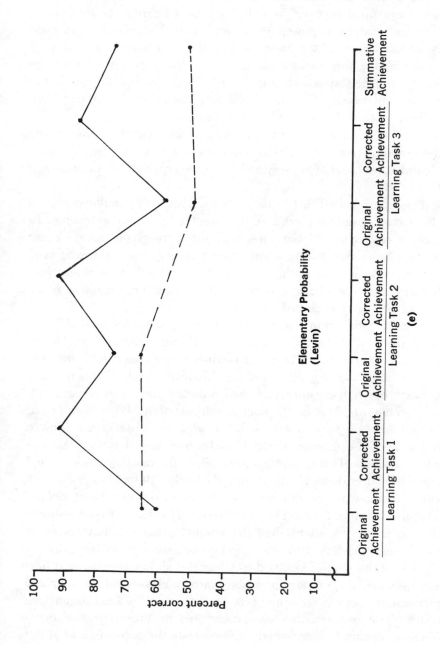

Elementary Probability
(Levin)

(e)

determine both the level and the variation on a final summative achievement measure over the entire series of learning tasks. Finally, that under mastery or non-mastery conditions, achievement on each learning task determines achievement on the next learning task as well as on the final achievement measure. Where the learning task achievement is corrected systematically for *all* students and *all* reach the criterion level on cognitive entry behaviors, then the effect of cognitive entry behavior can be reduced virtually to zero.

The generalizations about achievement and cognitive entry made in the previous paragraphs are also demonstrated in the comparison of the learning progress of mastery and non-mastery students summarized in Chart 3-6.

It will be recalled that in these studies two comparable groups of students were taught the same subject matter by the same teacher. In one class—the mastery class—the students were given feedback and corrective help after taking a formative test over each learning task, while in the other class—the non-mastery class—they were not provided with either feedback or corrective help after the original achievement measure over each task.

Ideally, both groups should have had the same level of achievement at the end of the first learning task (before correctives). This is approximately true in each of the studies summarized in Chart 3-6. However, after the formative test for Learning Task 1, the mastery students were helped until they had attained the mastery criterion, while this was not done for the non-mastery students. What is of special interest is that on Learning Task 2, the original achievement (before correction) of the mastery students is higher than it is for the non-mastery students. That is, all (or almost all) of the mastery students had attained the criterion for cognitive entry behaviors before Learning Task 2 while the non-mastery students varied in their Cognitive Entry Behaviors before Learning Task 2. The same is true of Learning Task 3—almost all of the mastery students had the cognitive entry behaviors for it while the non-mastery students varied on cognitive entry behaviors.

Each of the studies graphed in Chart 3-6 shows increasing differences between the mastery and non-mastery classes on the *original* achievement over each learning task as well as on the final summative measure. The use of corrective procedures to alter cognitive entry behaviors appears to increasingly differentiate the achievement of the mastery students from that of a comparable group of non-mastery students. In other words, cognitive entry behaviors are *alterable*. When they are altered positively, more and more of the students can be assured of higher levels of achievement over each subsequent learning task as well as over the final summative achievement measure. In these studies, learning achievement is largely determined by the extent to which students are provided with the necessary cognitive entry behaviors for subsequent learning tasks. *School learning is a highly alterable characteristic—if* appropriate learning conditions are made available to the students.

ALTERNATIVE APPROACHES WHEN NECESSARY COGNITIVE ENTRY BEHAVIORS ARE NOT AVAILABLE

In the micro-studies reported in this chapter and the many attempts to implement mastery learning (Block, 1974), the emphasis has been on ensuring that the majority of students enter successive learning tasks with the necessary cognitive entry behaviors. When this approach is used effectively at either the micro-level in the introductory learning tasks or at the macro-level in the introductory courses in the sequence, the approach is the soundest and most humane. Such an approach is essentially preventive rather than remedial. If schools did this systematically and successfully, there would be little need for some of the alternatives that will now be discussed.

If students lack or vary greatly in their possession of the necessary cognitive entry behaviors, there are a number of ways in which these *gaps* in their preparation for the new learning tasks can be approached educationally.

Perhaps the most frequent method of treating the lack of the necessary prerequisites in the past has been to advise the student *not* to take particular courses. While this may be a sound approach in some instances, it is likely to place great limits on the curriculum available to particular students. We regard this as in many ways the least desirable approach to the problem of students lacking particular cognitive entry behaviors.

It is possible in some cases to furnish instruction on the missing entry behaviors for those learners who lack them. This requires that the teacher, tutor, or learner be able to identify the elements of cognitive entry behaviors which are lacking in each of the students and that students be helped to learn them prior to or as a supplement to the learning task. This is probably a sound approach where the missing entry behaviors are limited and can be learned in a reasonable period of time.

It is also possible that some review of the essential entry behaviors, prior to the learning task, may be provided for some or all students to ensure that these prerequisites are available when they are needed. Again, the soundness of this approach depends on the extent to which they can be reviewed in the time available to the individual or group. In this and the above procedures, the emphasis is on ensuring that the students possess the essential cognitive prerequisites on which the learning task depends.

It is also possible to *alter* the learning task in various ways such that each alteration requires different entry behaviors. Thus, the students who lack the entry behaviors for one version of the learning task may possess the entry behaviors for another version or *form* of the "same" learning task.

Perhaps the most common general cognitive prerequisite for many of the learning tasks in the school after about grade 3 is reading comprehension. This is required to read the instructional materials, to comprehend the nature of the directions, and to understand problems presented in written form. It is possible to deliberately reduce the level of reading comprehension required in the instructional material, *if* this is viewed as a desirable alternative. It is also possible to present the directions for the task orally rather than in written form or to utilize pictorial, graphic, or other nonverbal methods in the instruction. The main point here is the attempt to separate the instruction and the learning of a particular task from the written context in which it usually appears.

Many other illustrations could be provided of ways in which a learning task could be altered to change the nature of the prerequisite entry behaviors. Thus, a course in science may emphasize particular mathematics prerequisites or it may reduce the mathematics required. A course in introductory statistics may have as prerequisites calculus, matrix algebra, algebra, computer programming, or arithmetic. Each way of teaching it may thus require different entry behaviors on the part of the students.

It is not entirely clear just when the alteration of the learning task to require different prerequisite entry behaviors makes it a fundamentally different learning task. It does seem possible to vary the *form* in which the learning task is taught or learned such that each *form* is equivalent in content, behaviors, and complexity. For example, logical reasoning may be taught using Venn diagrams, mathematical set theory, or in a purely verbal form. Students with different "aptitudes" (spatial ability, numerical ability, verbal ability) are able to learn logical reasoning to the same degree (or rate of learning) if provided with learning tasks in which the appropriate instructional processes are relevant to their entry skills and abilities (Pearson, 1973).

Similarly, initial reading may be taught emphasizing the look-say approach, a phonetic approach, an experience approach, a patterned-practice approach, or some other distinct approach. Each of these approaches to the teaching of reading may constitute different sets of learning tasks which require different sets of prerequisite cognitive entry behaviors. Yet, hopefully, each approach or set of learning tasks may yield approximately the same learning outcomes.

If in a particular subject or area of study it is possible to change the form such that equivalent learning tasks can be provided while each form of the task has different prerequisite entry behaviors, then the learning outcomes of each form *should be* substantially the same. A crucial test of whether this has been attained would be to construct a valid test of the essential content and behaviors and to determine whether students learning under each form achieve the same criterion level of achievement. The same test may be analyzed to determine which contents and behaviors are affected by each form of the learning task.

Thus, the philosophical and semantic question of when two or more learning tasks are the same or different may be changed to a pragmatic question of whether the learning outcomes of different forms of the same learning task are similar or not.

It is also possible to change the *objectives* and *content* of a course (a set of learning tasks) so as to alter the entry behaviors required. Thus, a course in drama may emphasize the reading of the dramatic works, the ability to empathize with the characters, or even the ability to act out a role. A course in art may emphasize reading about the history of art, sensitivity to the artistic qualities in particular art objects, or even the ability to produce particular artistic qualities. Each of these ways of teaching drama or art is likely to require different prerequisites.

Where both the *content* and *objectives* included in a learning task have been altered in order to make use of different sets of entry behaviors, it is likely that the learning tasks are fundamentally different. One is left with the question of determining the educational and social value of each alternative. This is a large curricular problem which cannot be settled here. However, the emphasis on textbooks in schools throughout the world has in all too many instances reduced each subject to the reading about the subject. Thus, the introductory psychology course is reduced to the reading of a standard textbook in the field. It is possible for the introduction to a subject like psychology to be vastly different from a reading course in the field. Science courses may emphasize reading a textbook about science or they may emphasize observation, experimentation, and first-hand experience with scientific phenomena. The humanities need not always be the reading *about* art, literature, drama, dance, or music. There are probably more useful and more direct ways of dealing with these subjects than reading about them. Whether these other ways of dealing with these subjects are more valuable depends on what are believed to be the desirable content and objectives of these subjects or fields.

SUMMARY AND IMPLICATIONS

Cognitive Entry Behaviors as Causal Variables

The evidence provided in this chapter in both the macro- and micro-studies makes it clear that there is a strong positive relation between the cognitive entry behaviors of a student and his achievement in subsequent courses or learning tasks. We have estimated that cognitive entry behavior can account for up to one-half ($r = +.70$) of the variance on relevant cognitive achievement measures over subsequent learning task(s). Relations of this magnitude are frequently found in both the macro- and the micro-studies cited in this chapter.

In this chapter we have made use of predictive studies over a year or academic term, longitudinal studies over a number of years, as well as the experimental approaches used in the micro-studies. The weight of this evidence suggests not only that there is a predictive relation between cognitive entry behaviors and subsequent achievement measures, but that cognitive entry behaviors are *causal links* in determining learning and in accounting for cognitive educational achievement.

Especially in the micro-studies it is evident that where students are helped to attain a criterion level on the cognitive entry behaviors, their subsequent achievement increasingly becomes differentiated from that of students who are not helped in this way. What is evident in these brief studies and in the longitudinal studies is that cognitive entry behaviors influence subsequent achievement, which in turn determines cognitive entry behaviors for the next course or learning task. In other words, there is a repeated cycle of cognitive entry behaviors, learning tasks, and achievement which have a long-term determinism over much of the students' school learning—unless the cycle is broken by intervention which alters the cognitive entry behaviors at strategic points in the learning. It has also been demonstrated in this chapter that students are for the most part being graded and judged not on what they learn *within* a particular course or term but on the relevant cognitive entry behaviors they possess prior to the *beginning* of the course.

History of the Learner

Cognitive entry behavior as defined in this chapter represents one aspect of the history of the learner which has relatively powerful effects on his subsequent learning. What happens to the learner at one point in his learning career has consequences, positive or negative, for subsequent stages in his learning career. The learning that takes place prior to entry into formal schooling has consequences for learning in the early years of school. These early years of school determine his cognitive entry characteristics for later years of school, and the cognitive entry characteristics produced in these later years of school have consequences for even later years of school. While we have emphasized only the *Cognitive Entry Behaviors–learning–achievement* cycle in this chapter, in Chapter 7 we will emphasize the interrelations among cognitive entry, affective entry, and quality of instruction, and their separate as well as combined effects on different learning outcomes.

Although we have emphasized cognitive entry as one form of entry behavior for cognitive learning tasks in the school, we believe there are parallel entry behaviors for psychomotor learning tasks as well as for other kinds of learning tasks. However, our concern in this book is largely restricted to cognitive learning because we believe such learning constitutes a major part of schooling.

In this chapter we have attempted to differentiate between *specific* cognitive behaviors which form the prerequisites for specific cognitive learning task(s) in the school and more *general* cognitive entry behaviors such as verbal ability, reading comprehension, and learning styles which appear to influence much of later school learning because of the *ways* in which the learning tasks are taught under group instructional methods. While both aspects of the history of the learner are under the control of the school, some aspects of the more general cognitive entry behaviors (e.g., verbal ability) are developed to a considerable extent before the student entered the school. If the school chooses to, it can do much to enable most learners to acquire the *general* as well as *specific* cognitive entry behaviors they will need for subsequent learning. The task of providing the specific cognitive entry behaviors is much easier to do than that of providing the generalized entry behaviors—partly because of the specificity of the task and partly because many of the specific cognitive entry behaviors can more readily be related to particular introductory learning tasks or courses.

Especially with regard to the cognitive entry behaviors developed in the school (both specific and general) the school has a great responsibility. If the school can assure each learner of a history of adequate cognitive entry in the first two or three years of the elementary school period, the students' subsequent history of learning in the school is likely to be more positive with respect to both cognitive and affective learning outcomes. Similarly, for each *new set* of learning experiences which start at later stages of the school program (e.g., science, social studies, mathematics, second language), providing for adequate achievement and appropriate cognitive entry behavior in the initial and early stages of the new set of learning experiences is likely to have a strong positive effect on the learning of the later sets of tasks in the series.

Alterability of Cognitive Entry Behaviors

In the micro-studies it is evident that specific cognitive entry behaviors are highly alterable, especially in the initial learning tasks in a series. In the micro-studies, some students were *helped* to acquire very adequate cognitive entry behaviors for subsequent tasks while other students were denied this help. The results were that the two groups became increasingly differentiated in their learning and their achievement over a series of learning tasks.

We believe that it is crucial to provide the help at the early stages of new learning experiences, while it is less likely that the help given at the later stages (if denied at the earlier stages of a sequential set of learning tasks or courses) will have an equal effect.

We are less certain about the alterability of cognitive entry behaviors at the later stages of a series of sequential learning tasks or courses (if nothing was done to alter them at the introductory stages). Some of the research on mastery learning at the middle school, secondary school, junior college, and university levels has demonstrated that much can be done to improve the cognitive entry behaviors even in courses or subjects which are relatively late in a sequential series. It is to be hoped that teachers and researchers will do much to attempt this alteration at every level of education and that our relatively pessimistic view about the matter will deter no one from attempting to demonstrate that cognitive entry behavior can be altered at any stage in a learning sequence and at any stage in the life of any individual. Perhaps old dogs can learn new tricks.

Each sequential set of learning tasks may be viewed as a partially new beginning. Altering cognitive entry behaviors for each new set is both possible and desirable—if the later learning of the student is to be affected.

FURTHER RESEARCH

Throughout this chapter we have pointed to particular problems for which the research evidence is limited. The importance of cognitive entry behaviors for subsequent learning in or out of the school makes it essential that we understand more about the causal processes by which cognitive entry behaviors are developed or altered and the ways in which they influence learning. A few of the questions for which new research is vitally needed are suggested below:

1. As we have tried to define cognitive entry behaviors, we believe they overlap with learning abilities and skills frequently sampled in general intelligence tests and aptitude tests. We believe that entry behaviors generally can be learned, taught, and developed by appropriate procedures and thus may be considered to be malleable and alterable. In contrast, intelligence and aptitude tests frequently emphasize more stable and less easily alterable characteristics. Research is needed to more clearly separate cognitive entry behaviors from more generalized intelligence and aptitude tests.

2. It is possible that some cognitive entry behaviors are easily learned and are highly malleable while other cognitive entry behaviors can be learned only over long periods of time or are less malleable and alterable. It would be of great value in education to understand the conditions necessary for the development and alteration of both types of cognitive entry behaviors.

3. We recognize the possibility that there are a set of cognitive entry behaviors which are frequently used in most school subjects while there may be specific cognitive entry behaviors used only in highly specialized courses and subjects. It is of importance that the common set of cognitive entry behaviors be identified and the frequency with which they are used throughout the school curriculum be determined.

4. A further problem of research is to determine the conditions under which this common set of cognitive entry behaviors is developed. Which of these are developed in early childhood education, which in the primary grades, and which are developed through general experiences? It is also important to determine the conditions in the home and school which serve to promote or are barriers to the development of particular common cognitive entry behaviors.

5. The common set of cognitive entry behaviors is regarded as so important that we must determine the nature of the curriculum and school experiences which are most likely to ensure that most learners possess these cognitive entry behaviors when they are required.

6. Finally, we must determine the conditions necessary for the maintenance or further development of the major cognitive entry behaviors. Once they are developed, what is necessary to ensure that they are available when needed? Do learners differ in the conditions necessary for the maintenance of such entry behaviors?

4
AFFECTIVE ENTRY CHARACTERISTICS

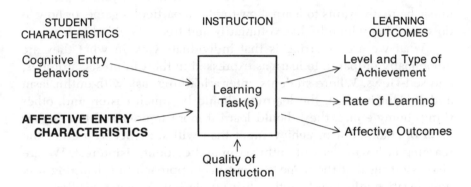

STUDENT CHARACTERISTICS	INSTRUCTION	LEARNING OUTCOMES

Cognitive Entry Behaviors

AFFECTIVE ENTRY CHARACTERISTICS

Learning Task(s)

Quality of Instruction

Level and Type of Achievement

Rate of Learning

Affective Outcomes

INTRODUCTION

If we observe a group of students beginning a particular learning unit or task, we can note a great deal of variation in the affect with which they approach the task even before they have received any instruction on it.

Some will approach it with evident interest and desire to learn the task. They appear to regard it as a relevant and desirable thing to learn. Others approach it as a duty or requirement. They expect to learn it, but with relatively little enthusiasm, joy, or delight. Finally, others approach the task with evident discomfort. They have some fear or trepidation and expect only negative things to ensue from this task and the judgments they expect from teachers, parents, and peers.

Contrast this variety of affect in a group of students toward a *required learning task* with the affect of the same students when each is beginning the *one* learning task he or she most wants to do. If this were truly possible (and it is doubtful that it could be arranged or discovered), we might expect almost every student to approach the

73

learning task of his choice with enthusiasm and, perhaps, some confidence. The student really wants to learn the task, he regards it as a good thing to learn, and he believes he can learn it and is prepared to do whatever is needed to learn it.

One may get a glimpse of such differences in initial affective characteristics when one observes an individual student approaching learning tasks in an elective subject in contrast to the same student approaching learning tasks in a required subject. Perhaps the contrast might be seen even more sharply if one observed the same individual's approach to something he wants to learn *outside* the regular school system—how to drive an automobile, how to play a piece of music he really wants to learn, how to play a particular game, or how to do something which he has voluntarily and freely decided to learn.

What we are asserting is that individuals vary in what they are emotionally prepared to learn as expressed in their interests, attitudes, and self-views. Where students enter a learning task with enthusiasm and evident interest, the learning should be much easier, and, other things being equal, they should learn it more rapidly and to a higher level of attainment or achievement than will students who enter the learning task with lack of enthusiasm and evident disinterest. We are also asserting that the same student may approach one learning task with positive affect and another learning task with negative affect.

The same notions could be put more simply and operationally, rather than by reference to such general psychological terms as interests and attitudes. For a student to learn a learning task well, he should have an openness to the new task, some desire to learn it and learn it well, and sufficient confidence in himself to put forth the necessary energy and resources to overcome difficulties and obstacles in the learning, if and when they occur.

As we view it, the student enters each new learning task with something of a history which he perceives as related to the learning task. This history and his expectations determine the initial affective characteristics as related to the specific learning task. He encounters the learning task and it may or may not perceptibly alter his initial affective characteristics. He leaves the learning task with some set of affective characteristics. We would further venture that the affective characteristics at the end of a particular learning task may become the initial affective characteristics for the next learning task which the student perceives to be related to the previous learning task(s).

Thus, we do attempt to distinguish between the affective characteristics at the beginning of a specific learning task and the affective characteristics with which the same individual *leaves* a specific learning task. These may be the same or they may be different. Both are the results of the history of the learner and the experience he has had—one prior to the task and the other within the task. In both cases, however, it is *not* the actual history of the learner. Rather it is how he has perceived this history and how he relates the particular learning task to his perception of his history.

Carroll (1963) has operationally defined motivation for a task in terms of the *perseverance* the individual brings to the task, that is, the effort he is willing to make to accomplish it. While we regard this as an excellent behavioral index of motivation, it does not help us much in understanding the affect behind this energy and effort and it does not help us in comprehending the variety of qualities of affect which may bring about the same (or different) amounts of energy and effort.

We regard the initial affective characteristics as a complex compound of interests, attitudes, and self-views. Although we prefer the term *Affective Entry Characteristics* to the term *motivation*, the two terms are not contradictory. The second term, however, is a bit too general and lacks the historical perspective and relatedness to the learning tasks that we believe is required for a useful explanatory scheme.

We have in Chapter 2 attempted to describe what we mean by a learning unit or learning task. While it is conceivable that each student may be observed entering a different learning task, we will probably secure a clearer understanding of affective entry characteristics if we concentrate on a common learning task or set of learning tasks for all students.

We begin with the major assumption that each of our learners has had a somewhat different history before beginning the particular learning task(s). Further, we may assume that each student perceives and has been affected by his history and previous experiences in a different way. Thus, even if it were theoretically possible for two individuals to have had identical learning histories, we can still conceive of them as *perceiving* these histories in different ways. Furthermore, we also assume that each individual's initial perception of the particular learning task may be different and that each individual will perceive a particular learning task in relation to his previous experiences and history.

We are not concerned with the accuracy of the individual's perceptions. The important point for initial affective characteristics is the student's perceptions and what effect they have on his approach to the learning task in question.

Macro-Micro Studies

Before reviewing the evidence on the effects of affective entry characteristics, it is essential that we distinguish the different levels at which the effects may be analyzed. We believe that the affective entry characteristics have an effect on the macro-level—on the students' learning of an entire course or program of school learning. We also believe that affective entry characteristics may have a significant effect at the micro-level—on the students' learning of a particular learning task as well as on the learning of a small number of related learning tasks.

We propose in the following section to review the relation of affective characteristics to achievement in particular courses as well as entire programs of schoolwork. Here there is a relatively large literature of studies to which we will refer. While we are primarily concerned with affective entry characteristics and their relation to *subsequent* learning, unfortunately, many of the studies we can find are studies of the relation between affective characteristics and achievement measured *concurrently*. A smaller number of the studies relate *prior* affective characteristics to *subsequent* achievement measures. It is our hope that these macro-level studies will yield generalizations about the relations between selected affective entry characteristics and concurrent as well as subsequent measures of achievement.

Insofar as possible, we will make use of relatively large-scale studies with samples of 100 or more students with carefully developed instruments for measuring the affective characteristics as well as the student achievement. We are fortunate in being able to refer to some of the results of the studies by the International Association for the Evaluation of Educational Achievement (IEA). These studies, which have been done over the past 15 years, have included carefully devised national samples in seventeen developed countries. These studies have involved seven different school subjects with varying numbers of countries participating in the different subjects. Because similar techniques were used with different age samples, these provide crude but useful developmental trends.

In addition to the macro-level studies, there are a relatively small number of micro-level studies which provide more direct evidence of the relation between affective entry characteristics and achievement over subsequent learning tasks. These studies will be used to determine the relations between affective entry characteristics and achievement outcomes. We will compare the results of these more detailed studies of the relation between affective entry characteristics and achievement outcomes with those obtained at the macro-level to determine whether similar generalizations are found at both levels. In addition, since these micro-level studies were experimental studies, we can determine the effects of related variables on *changes* in affective entry characteristics *and* the effects of these changing characteristics on subsequent achievement variables.

In short, we are interested in (*a*) the *concurrent* relation of affective characteristics and achievement, (*b*) the *predictive* relation of affective entry characteristics to later achievement, and (*c*) the *causal* relations between affective characteristics and aspects of the learning process. It is unfortunate that most of the available evidence is on the first two. Hopefully, the evidence available on (*a*) and (*b*) will stimulate educational researchers to devote more effort to the further study of (*c*)—the causal relation between affective entry characteristics and particular aspects of the learning process and learning outcomes.

MACRO-LEVEL STUDIES OF AFFECTIVE ENTRY CHARACTERISTICS

Subject-Related Affect

We began this work attempting to make a distinction between interests in a school subject and attitudes toward the subject. However, as we attempt to consider the various measures or indices used in the different studies, we can find no clear demarcation between interests and attitudes. What appears to emerge is a continuum ranging from positive views, likes, or positive affect toward a subject to negative views, dislikes, or negative affect toward the subject. These may be measured by asking the individual whether he would like to study the subject, whether he would like to continue studying the subject, what he likes or dislikes about a subject, and various questionnaire approaches which attempt to summarize different opinions, views, and preferences which may indicate some degree of positive or negative affect toward a school subject.

We believe an individual tends to like those activities which he believes he has done or can do successfully. The perception of what constitutes success is determined by the individual against the background of evidence he has received from the tasks (which he believes to be similar or related), and from the people who are in any way connected with this task or similar tasks—teachers, parents, peers. If an individual believes he has done a number of prior related tasks successfully, he is likely to approach the next learning task with some degree of positive affect. If he believes he has been unsuccessful with such prior tasks, he is likely to approach the next learning task with some degree of negative affect.

We would qualify this notion of success with the idea that the previous as well as the new task must contain some challenge and even risk taking. The student is not likely to perceive the accomplishment of a too easy task as constituting success. Similarly, he may not perceive lack of accomplishment of an obviously too difficult task as constituting failure. The main point to be made is that success (or failure) and the relatedness of the present learning task to his previous history are perceptual phenomena. In all of this, it is the student who is central in these perceptions.

The student's affect may also be in part determined by his perception of the relation between the present task and some larger set of future goals, purposes, or objectives he has in mind. If he sees the present task as contributing to these goals, he is more likely to have positive affect; if he sees the task as conflicting with or unrelated to these goals, he is more likely to have negative affect and even clear opposition to the task.

Thus, we regard subject-related affect as a resolution between perception of past history (with what the individual believes to be related tasks) and perception of the relation between the present task and future goals and purposes of the individual. Although we have been writing as though these perceptions, history, and future goals are clear and conscious, we do recognize that they may range from highly conscious and explicit perceptions to almost unconscious feelings and only dimly perceived or felt affect.

If school learning tasks in each subject were completely isolated from other subjects and voluntary in the fullest sense of the term, we would expect that subject-related affect (based on perception of past history, the present situation, and future goals) would completely determine the individual's affective entry characteristics. If, then, the individual's cognitive entry behaviors and the quality of instruction are held constant, we would expect an almost perfect relation between the individual's affect toward a subject and his achievement on the task.

We believe we can illustrate the relations between affect toward a subject and achievement most clearly by taking a few major studies in the field of mathematics. In the International Study of Educational Achievement in Mathematics (IEA) twelve countries (only ten had complete data for our purposes) participated in a cooperative study of achievement in mathematics (Husén, 1967). In each of these countries, carefully selected national samples of students were given a set of mathematics achievement tests as well as questionnaires. Many other types of data were gathered on the students, the schools, teachers, and the content and objectives of the curriculum in each country. Here we will only be concerned with the relation between the students' subject-related affect and their achievement on these tests.

The simplest method of getting at the students' affect toward mathematics was to ask each student "Would you like to take more mathematics after this year?"—yes or no. When the answer to this was related to the mathematics achievement test scores in each country, it was found that the correlation for the 8th grade students varied from +.17 to +.39 with a median of +.25 for ten of the countries. When the same question was asked of 12th-grade students taking mathematics, the correlations with achievement were from +.17 to +.38 with a median of +.30 for the ten countries (see Appendix Table 4-A).

A somewhat more complex way of getting at the students' affect toward mathematics in the IEA study was to develop an index based on several types of evidence. In this index, each of the following variables was weighted to get a final index for each student:

   a. Wishes about taking additional mathematics courses

   b. Place of mathematics in the student's desired occupation

   c. Place of mathematics in the student's best- and least-liked subjects

   d. Place of mathematics in the courses for which the student had his best and poorest grades

When this index was related to the mathematics achievement test scores in each country, the correlations for the 8th grade students varied from +.24 to +.42 with a median of +.32 (.43).[1] For the 12th grade

---

[1]Values in parentheses are corrected for unreliability of the instruments.

students, the correlations varied from +.28 to +.52 with a median of +.38 (.43) (see Table 4-1).

Thus in this set of data based on large and carefully selected samples in each of ten highly developed nations of the world, there is evidence that the correlations are higher for a more complex (and reliable) measure of affect toward the subject than for a simple measure which asks only whether the student wants to take more mathematics. Since the 12th grade students have had a longer history of learning tasks in mathematics than the 8th grade students, their affect toward the subject might be expected to be more closely related to their achievement—the difference in uncorrected correlations is small but in the right direction, about +.06 on the average. Using the reliability measure of the interest index and the reliability of the achievement measures, we have estimated the median correlation corrected for unreliability between interest and achievement to be about +.43 for both the 8th grade students and the 12th grade students. Thus, subject-related affect in mathematics as measured in this large-scale international study accounts for about 18 percent of the variance in achievement when the unreliability of the instruments is taken into consideration.

Another approach to subject-related affect measurement was taken by the U.S. National Longitudinal Study of Mathematics Achievement (Crosswhite, 1972). In this national study a twelve-item Pro-Math questionnaire was constructed including items such as:

Mathematics is boring (strongly agree—strongly disagree).

Mathematics is more of a game than it is hard work (strongly agree—strongly disagree).

I like story books (more—less) than mathematics books.

I would like to teach English (more—less) than I would like to teach mathematics.

When this measure is related to the various arithmetic and mathematics achievement tests, the median correlations for grades 6 to 8 is +.28, while the median for grades 9 to 12 is also +.28. When these are corrected for the unreliability of the instruments, the correlations are approximately +.38 (see Appendix Table 4-A). This is very close to the values found in the international mathematics study.

We have used the IEA Mathematics study and the National Longitudinal Study of Mathematics Achievement to illustrate three methods of measuring subject-related affect and the relations between these measurements and mathematics achievement. While other methods have also been used to get at subject-related affect, most of the procedures involve some expression of opinion about the subject, desires for additional experiences with the subject, or an index which combines these in some way.

We are fortunate that similar methods were used in the IEA studies in such subjects as mathematics, science, literature, reading comprehension, French as a second language, and English as a second language.[2] Although these are all concurrent studies of affect and achievement, they provide data on national samples of students in which carefully developed international instruments were used to measure both affect toward a subject and achievement in the subject. The results for the 8th grade and 12th grade students are shown in Table 4-1. Since the reader is more likely to be familiar with educational conditions in the U.S. than with conditions in the other countries, we have shown the U.S. results first, followed by the remaining highly developed nations in each of the IEA subject studies. We have also shown the median values for each subject.

At the 8th grade level where most of the countries had 90 percent or more of the age group in the schools, the results are relatively similar from country to country within each subject field. The median correlations are very similar (+.32 to +.38) for five of the subjects, while they are much lower for literature. In the five highest subjects, affect accounts for approximately 12 percent of the variance in achievement (about 20 percent when the correlations are corrected for the unreliability of the measures).

At the 12th grade level, where the countries differ widely in the percent of the age group still in school, the correlations appear to differ greatly from country to country. This may, in part, be due to the fact that some countries have a smaller and more homogeneous group of students in the final year of secondary school than do other countries, and this is likely to affect the relation between the measures of achievement and affect. Here, science, mathematics, English, and French have the highest relation between affect and achievement, while literature and reading have much lower relations. (Unfortunately, we could not obtain the results for the reading preference index at the 12th grade.) In the four highest subjects, affect accounts for 27 percent of the variance in achievement in science, 14 percent of the variance in mathematics, 12 percent in French, and 9 percent in English. In the two lowest subjects,

[2]The IEA studies were Husén, 1967; Comber and Keeves, 1973; Purves, 1973; Thorndike, 1973; Carroll, 1975; and Lewis & Massad, 1975.

TABLE 4-1. RELATION BETWEEN AFFECT TOWARD A SUBJECT AND STUDENT ACHIEVEMENT IN THE COUNTRIES INCLUDED IN THE INTERNATIONAL STUDY OF EDUCATIONAL ACHIEVEMENT (IEA)

	United States	Australia	England	West Germany	Finland	France	Hungary	Italy	Israel	Japan	Netherlands	New Zealand	Rumania	Scotland	Sweden	Belgium (Flemish)	Belgium (French)	Median	Median (Corrected)
GRADE 8:																			
Science achievement																			
–Science interest	.35	.36	.39	.27	.32		.37	.23		.49	.26	.38		.42	.35	.18		.35	(.45)
Math achievement																			
–Math interest	.24	.35	.39	.28	.32					.42	.27			.32	.38	.26		.32	(.43)
English as a second language (reading)																			
–English interest				.49	.48		.35		.28		.38				.49	.28		.38	(.47)
French as a second language (reading)																			
–French interest	.24		.38					.22			.26	.42	.22	.47				.32	(.42)
Literature achievement																			
–Hours of reading for pleasure	.34		.33		.19			.19				.29			.23	.21	.16	.23	
Reading comprehension																			
–Reading preference	.33		.49		.36			.29			.36	.36		.53	.33	.28	.28	.36	
GRADE 12:																			
Science achievement																			
–Science interest	.43	.51	.64	.40	.53	.48	.33	.27			.58	.60		.67	.53			.52	(.66)

82

Math achievement									
– Math interest	.43	.47 .29 .28 .51		.37 .52		.40 .36 .30		.38	(.43)
English as a second language (reading)									
– English interest		.27 .33	.29 .31 .27	.26		.18 .27		.30	(.42)
French as a second language (reading)									
– French interest	.35	.39		.33		.26 .43 .41		.35	(.42)
Literature achievement									
– Hours of reading for pleasure	.27	.16 .19	.13	.12		.14 .33 .15		.15	
Reading comprehension									
– Literary interest*	.20	.18 .06	.15	.16		.07 .37 .20		.17	(.23)

*Reading Preference was not available for grade 12.

TABLE 4-2. RELATION BETWEEN AFFECT TOWARDS A SUBJECT AND ACHIEVEMENT IN THE SUBJECT

	Grades 1–5		Grades 6–8		Grades 9–12	
	IEA studies	Other studies	IEA studies	Other studies	IEA studies	Other studies
Mathematics		.23 (.33)	.32 (.43)	.28 (.38)	.38 (.43)	.29 (.38)
Reading	.28	.36*	.36		.17 (.23)	
Other subjects			.31 (.45)	.23*	.32 (.42)	.40*
Medians	.28	.29	.32	.25	.32	.35

*With the exception of these cells, each value in the table is based on five or more entries.

literature and reading comprehension, affect accounts for less than 3 percent of the variance in achievement. We believe the lower correlations are attributable to the selective factors which have clearly reduced the variability of the students in both literature and reading comprehension. The reduction in variability is greatest for the countries which have the smallest proportion of the age group still in school at grade 12. In part, also, the lower correlations in reading comprehension are attributable to the shift in the measure of subject affect.

It was anticipated that the relation between subject-related affect and achievement would increase with the amount of experience with a subject. In the IEA studies this is clearly true only in science and mathematics. There is a decrease in the relations for the other subjects, which appears to be, in part, attributable to selective factors in particular countries.

In spite of considerable variation in levels of correlations between school subjects and between grade levels, as well as some variation between countries within a subject, it is apparent that the correlations between subject-related affect and achievement in these seventeen nations of the world average about +.34 (about +.10 higher when it is possible to correct the correlations for unreliability of the measures); that is, the IEA data suggest that an average of 12 to 20 percent of the variance in achievement may be accounted for by subject-related affect.

In Table 4-2 we have summarized the results of the IEA studies as well as other studies[3] of affect and achievement in mathematics, reading, and other subject fields. Where reliability data are available, we have also shown the correlations corrected for the unreliability of the measures.

The relation between subject-related affect (measured in a variety of ways) and achievement in a subject (also measured in a variety of ways) tends to be lower at the primary grade levels than at the later school levels. In mathematics, the trend for increased relations with additional experience with the subject is quite evident. The trend is present in part in the other subjects, but it is clearly not present in reading. It may well be that since reading is a distinct school subject only at the elementary school level, the relation between reading achievement and affect toward reading reaches its highest level within this period.

Although the bulk of the studies summarized in Table 4-2 involve

[3]The studies are reported in more detail in Appendix Table 4-A.

concurrent measures of affect and achievement, the results are very similar for these concurrent studies and the predictive studies, in which affect was measured at the beginning of the term and achievement was measured at its end. In those studies in which similar instruments were used (such as the National Longitudinal Study of Mathematics Achievement), we find the correlations of the concurrent measures to be of the order of +.02 higher than the pre-post measures.[4] The fact that the relation changes only slightly in a single grade or school year suggests that affect, once developed in the first few years of experience with a subject, is likely to change relatively slowly thereafter. This may in part be due to the relatively high consistency of achievement measures from one year to the next (see Chapter 3) as well as to the likelihood that once an interest or attitude has been developed toward a subject it is resistant to change. (See Chapter 6 where this idea is treated more fully.)

When we summarize the various studies reported in Table 4-2 we find that the average correlation is about +.31 (about .10 higher when corrected for unreliability) with slightly lower correlations in the primary school period and slightly higher correlations in the junior and senior high school period. That is, affect toward a subject generally accounts for between 10 and 17 percent of the variation in achievement—with a few studies, especially in the later years of school, reaching almost 20 percent of the variation in achievement.

Although we believe that more valid and more reliable measures of subject-related affect might increase the relation somewhat, we are doubtful that this type of affect would, even under improved conditions, account for much more than 20 percent of the variance on a measure of achievement. But this is a matter for future research and experimentation.

School-Related Affect

We have wondered why subject-related affect generally doesn't account for more of the variation in student achievement. We believe that this may, in part, be due to the fact that each school subject is really not a completely separable entity. For the student, each school subject is likely to be viewed as one more part of the total process of school and schooling. It is likely that children develop a general attitude toward (or interest in) schools and schooling which may influence their affective

[4]See Appendix Table 4-A.

entry characteristics for most of the learning tasks or subjects and courses within the school framework. Furthermore, school attendance is a required obligation for most children in the United States and in many other countries for a ten or twelve-year period. Legal and social requirements make it necessary for most children to be at least physically present in the school from ages six to sixteen—whether or not they like or dislike particular school subjects and whether or not they like or dislike attending school.

Subject-related affect as we have defined it is specific to a set of learning tasks that are in some way related in actuality or in the student's perception. We regarded them as specific to a subject—at least for purposes of reviewing the research. In this review, we have regarded positive or negative affect as involving some combination of interests and attitudes toward the school subject.

We now turn to a more generalized set of affective characteristics— those having to do with school and school learning. For our purposes we may call them attitudes toward school and school learning, but they may (in the literature) be termed interests, likes and dislikes, or school motivation. The main distinction we are trying to draw in these two sections is that one is *subject-specific* affect while the other is more generalized and refers to the *school and school learning.*

If we were able to measure children's attitudes toward school and school learning just before they embarked on the very first learning task provided by the school, we should find some variation, but there is likely to be relatively little variation and most of this based on what parents, siblings, and peers have communicated to the child. Hess and Shipman (1965) have reported that some children received injunctions from parents to do what they are told to do and to keep out of trouble, while other children are encouraged to learn well. Undoubtedly, all children approach school with a mixture of fear and hope, with mixtures of pride in being of school age and anxiety that they may not be able or mature enough to do what is wanted. In any case, most children have only vague attitudes toward school and school learning at their time of entry into the school. They may vary in their receptiveness to the new tasks, their ease with the new adult who is their teacher, and their feelings about the restraints which school hours and duties impose on them. But, in general, any measurement of initial attitudes toward school and school learning is the measurement of rather ephemeral human characteristics because the child has had no direct experience with the school or school learning. Incidentally, for our purposes the initial experience with the school may be grade 1, kindergarten, or even nursery school.

Let us assume that a child encounters as many as 150 separable learning units or learning tasks during the first year of school (if we assume that each learning task represents about seven hours of school work). If a child has some perceptions of success with most of these tasks, if he has received a great deal of approval for his learning of these tasks from the teacher as well as from parents and peers, and if he has generally positive relations with other children in the class or school, his attitude toward school and school learning should generally be on the positive or favorable side of whatever scale we use. School is not a bad thing in his mind and generally it is a good thing, and he is either willing to receive or even desirous of more of this kind of experience. If he is now presented with the 151st learning task (whatever it may be), he is likely to have a more firm and positive attitude toward it than he is likely to have had for the very first learning task (task number one) that he encountered in the school. If he continues to succeed, to get the approval of the teachers and others, and if all goes generally well, we may expect this generally positive attitude to be present on the 300th, the 600th, and the 1,000th learning task no matter what its content and nature. Here we are maintaining that each task is seen as having a large component of schooling and attitude toward schooling—as separate from its distinctive quality by subject matter, objectives, etc.

Contrast this positive attitude toward school and school learning, with the probable attitude of a child who has rarely been able to succeed with the 150 learning tasks in the first year of school. Such a child is unlikely to have any sense of doing anything right. He is unlikely to have received much approval for his schoolwork from teachers, from parents, and even from his peers in the class or school. Even if he has had generally good relations with the other children, he must have some sense that school is not a source of joy, success, and happiness. His attitude is likely to be generally negative or on the unfavorable side of the attitude scale toward school and school learning. School is not a good thing in his mind and generally it is a bad thing, and he is unlikely to be very eager for more of the same. If he is now presented with the 151st learning task, his attitude toward it is likely to be generally negative no matter what its content or nature. Similarly, if these generally negative results continue through several years of school, his attitude toward the 300th, 600th, and 1,000th learning tasks are likely to be increasingly negative.

Without belaboring the point too much further, we are maintaining that the student's perception of success or failure in school learning tasks and related approval or disapproval of teachers, parents, and even peers when consistent over some long period of time should result in favorable or unfavorable attitudes toward school and school learning which become generalized and apply to each new learning task, the school, and the teachers and other students in it. If the perception of failure in school is clear and consistent, the student must move from negative attitudes which involve a good deal of affect to *apathy* when he finds there is no escape from the school and its learning tasks.

We have less to say about the students in the middle who perceive that they have been successful with some learning tasks and less successful with others. There must be various ratios of success and failure perceptions which lead to a positive attitude toward school[5] while other ratios lead to unfavorable or negative attitudes. However, it is not only the ratios of actual success and failure but the individual's own perceptions and background which influence these attitudes. We believe that for this middle group the more success (and approval) perceptions the more favorable the attitudes, while the more failure (and disapproval) perceptions the more negative the attitudes.

Perhaps the most direct method of getting at students' affect toward school is to ask them whether they would like more education or not. In the International Study of Educational Achievement (IEA), students at the 8th grade level were asked how many more years of education they would like to have. When this was correlated with the achievement on the IEA Mathematics test in twelve countries (see Table 4-3), the correlations varied from +.31 to +.57 with a median of +.36. While ideally the correlations should have been with either grade-point average or a composite of achievement tests using a large part of the curriculum, it may be seen in this study involving national samples of students that achievement in a single subject is related to general attitudes toward school and schooling.

Using this rather crude index of affect toward school—the number of additional years of education desired (or expected)—we have reported in Table 4-3 the relations between this index and measures of achievement in science, mathematics, literature, and reading comprehension for each of the highly developed countries included in the IEA

[5]There may be a few exceptional students who find it so easy to be successful in most of the learning tasks that they are rarely challenged. Such students may become bored with school and develop less than positive attitudes toward it.

TABLE 4-3. RELATION BETWEEN AFFECT TOWARD SCHOOL AND STUDENT ACHIEVEMENT IN THE COUNTRIES INCLUDED IN THE INTERNATIONAL STUDY OF EDUCATIONAL ACHIEVEMENT (IEA)

	United States	Australia	England	West Germany	Finland	France	Hungary	Italy	Israel	Japan	Netherlands	New Zealand	Scotland	Sweden	Belgium (Flemish)	Belgium (French)	Median
GRADE 8:																	
Science achievement																	
–Expected years of education	.28	.38	.45	.31	.31		.38	.20		.47	.40	.34	.46	.31	.18		.36
Mathematics achievement																	
–Number of years of education desired	.35	.35	.57	.31	.33					.50	.37		.52	.35	.38		.36
Literature achievement																	
–Expected years of education	.21		.40		.36			.21						.31		.28	.29
Reading comprehension																	
–Expected years of education	.26	.44	.44		.43		.45	.30	.33		.37	.30	.46	.37	.18	.38	.37
GRADE 12:																	
Science achievement																	
–Expected years of education	.32	.20	.18	.13	.30	.23	.33	.18			.33	.20	.22	.22			.22
Mathematics achievement																	
–Number of years of education desired	.37	.23	.17	.13	.15	.06			.12	.29	.08		.17	.21	.23		.17
Literature achievement																	
–Expected years of education	.18											.09		.16		.21	.17
Reading comprehension																	
–Expected years of education	.29		.08		.18	.18	.32	.18	.24		.03	.08	.27	.26	.32	.31	.25

89

studies.[6] At the 8th grade level the median value is about +.36. (Unfortunately, it is not possible to correct these values for unreliability.)

The median values are somewhat lower at the 12th grade level (about +.19), probably because of the greater selectivity of most of the IEA countries in the last few years of secondary education. In the U.S. where over 75 percent of the age group are still in school at grade 12, the correlations are slightly higher at grade 12 than at grade 8—about +.30 versus +.27, respectively.

There are many difficulties in utilizing the amount of additional education expected or desired in the IEA studies to get at a measure of affect toward school because of the roughness of the index[7] because of the selectivity of the national school systems, and because we do not have a general measure of school achievement. In spite of these difficulties, it is evident at the 8th grade level that this index of affect toward the school may account for as much as 14 percent of the variation in school achievement in particular school subjects and perhaps more if the unreliability of the measures could be taken into consideration. We believe that higher relations would be obtained if the achievement index was based on a general measure of school achievement. Unfortunately, this was not possible for the international data summarized here.

In Table 4-4 we have summarized a number of studies showing the relation between affect toward school and school achievement. (The detailed list of studies and results will be found in Appendix Table 4-B.) Practically all the studies we could find are concurrent studies in which both affect toward school and achievement are measured at almost the same point in time. Also, in Table 4-4 (as in Table 4-2) we have included the results from the IEA studies.

The measures of affect include questionnaire studies of attitudes and feelings about school, number of years of additional education

[6]The IEA studies were Husén, 1967; Comber and Keeves, 1973; Purves, 1973; and Thorndike, 1973.

[7]Our concern here is with the attempt to relate measures of school achievement to the student's expressed desire for more education. We recognize that this index is influenced by socioeconomic status and the student's perception of the realistic possibilities of his securing additional years of school attendance. For this reason, the responses of the 8th grade students may be a better index of school-related affect than the responses of the 12th grade students in those countries where only a small proportion of the age group may be permitted or encouraged to secure some form of higher education after the completion of secondary education.

TABLE 4-4. RELATION BETWEEN AFFECT TOWARD SCHOOL AND MEASURES OF SCHOOL ACHIEVEMENT

	Grades 1–5		Grades 6–8		Grades 9–12	
	IEA studies	Other studies	IEA studies	Other studies	IEA studies	Other studies
Mathematics		.14	.36	.24	.17	.20
Reading	.23	.13	.37	.23	.25	.29
Grade-point average		.12*		.44		.42*
Composite achievement test				.46*		.48*
Median	.23	.13	.36	.34	.21	.36

*With the exception of these cells, each value in the table is based on five or more entries.

TABLE 4-5. RELATION BETWEEN ACADEMIC SELF-CONCEPT AND MEASURES OF SCHOOL ACHIEVEMENT

	Grades 1–5	Grades 6–8	Grades 9–12
Specific achievement test –Specific academic self-concept*	.31	.30	.25
Course grade –Specific academic self-concept*	.35	.45	.43
Achievement test composite –General academic self-concept	.30	.52	.30†
Grade-point average –General academic self-concept	.23†	.57	.51
Median	.30	.49	.37

†With the exception of these cells, each value in the table is based on five or more entries.

*Data on specific academic self-concept largely based on mathematics data.

expected or desired, and other general attitudes toward education, schools, and teachers.

Ideally, affect toward school should be related to grade-point average or total scores on an achievement test battery. Where we could find such studies, we have included them in Table 4-4. However, we believe that reading and mathematics are so much a part of most years of school that they should also relate to general affect toward school.

The correlations between affect toward school and achievement tests for particular subjects are relatively low in grades 1–5 but are higher at the junior and senior high school levels. After grade 5, the median correlation is about +.25. In contrast to these correlations with specific school subjects is the much higher relation between general measures of school achievement (grade-point average or composite achievement tests) and affect towards school. Although very low in grades 1–5, these relations average about +.45 at the junior and senior high school levels. The trends in this table support our general view that the relation should increase with the amount of experience with school and school learning. However, the number of studies available is not sufficient to establish the detailed development of school affect with each additional year of school experience. Further research is needed to determine just how school affect develops and its causal relation to school learning.

There is enough data in Tables 4-3 and 4-4 to indicate that affect toward the school, under good conditions of sampling and measurement, will account for as much as 20 percent of the variation in school achievement. Whether or not future research will support this generalization remains to be determined.

Academic Self-Concept

Closely related to attitudes toward school and school learning are the *attitudes toward the self* about school learning. In our discussions of affect toward school and school learning we maintained that a schedule of success and approval or failure and disapproval over a large number of learning tasks and over relatively long periods of time would lead to a generalized attitude toward the school and school learning.

Similarly, a schedule of success and approval or failure and disapproval over a number of years will lead to the student's generalizing about *himself* as a learner or student. Eventually, he must shift from blame directed to the school or the teachers for his lack of success in school to blame directed toward the self. Or, he will shift from approval of the school and the teachers for his success in school to approval of the self. Especially by the end of the primary school (grades 4–6), the student who consistently succeeds in school must generalize to approval of the self and a generally positive concept of the self as a learner. Also, by this period the student who has consistently failed (and is reminded of this by his teachers and parents) must come to view himself with a generally negative self-concept as a learner.

There have been a number of methods of measuring the academic self-concept (Brookover, Shailer & Paterson, 1964; Sears, 1963; Farquhar & Christensen, 1967; Feather, 1965). In general, these are all based on the student's reporting something about how he views himself in relation to learning, the school, and teachers, and how he views his learning in relation to the learning of other students in his class or school. In the Brookover Self-Concept of Ability measure, for example, the student is asked questions like the following:

How do you rate yourself in school ability compared with your close friends?

What kinds of grades do you think you are capable of getting?

How do you feel if you don't do as well in school as you know you can?

How important to you are the grades you get in school?

We have summarized the studies we could locate which relate measures of academic self-concept to measures of achievement—either grade-point average or composite achievement scores. We have also included a number of studies where the academic self-concept in a specific subject is related to achievement in particular subjects.

In the studies summarized in Table 4-5[8] it will be noted that academic self-concept in a particular subject (mathematics, science) has a lower correlation with measures of achievement in the particular subject than is true of a more general academic self-concept in relation to overall measures of school achievement. We believe that the higher relation for the more general academic self-concept is attributable to the greater number of school experiences and judgments on which it is based. In addition, the reliabilities of general measures of academic self-concept and achievement are likely to be somewhat higher than the reliabilities of the more specific measures. In some ways subject-specific academic self-concept may be viewed as another measure of subject-related affect rather than as a self-concept measure.

It will also be seen in Table 4-5 that academic self-concept (specific or general) correlates more highly with teachers' grades than with achievement test scores. This phenomenon has been studied more

[8]See Appendix Table 4-C for the detailed studies.

directly at the 5th grade level by Torshen (1969) who found that academic self-concept (general) correlated +.46 with overall teachers' grades while for the same students it correlated +.33 with overall achievement test scores. This difference is somewhat greater than those summarized in Table 4-5, but the general trend is apparent.

It is believed that the higher relation between academic self-concept and teacher grades is attributable to the fact that teachers' judgments (and grades) are communicated to the student almost daily in the classroom, while standardized tests may be used rarely during an academic year. Furthermore, teachers' judgments tend to emphasize the student's relative standing in the class or school. This is the peer group against which the student typically compares himself, especially in reporting on his academic self-concept. The standardized test scores refer to a larger population (typically the national distribution) and this is only rarely the group against which the student judges his own progress. Thus, the student's view of himself is likely to be most directly influenced by the frequent judgments about himself as a learner that he receives in school and especially those judgments made by teachers and peers in the school and his parents and siblings in the home. These tend to be relative judgments in that each student's learning is compared with the learning of other students in the same class or school. It should also be noted that academic self-concept questions do emphasize the student's relative standing in his class or group and are thus parallel in structure to achievement measures which emphasize relative standing in the classroom group.

In the studies reported in Table 4-5 on the relations between academic self-concept and *composite measures of achievement* (either test scores or grade-point average), it will be seen that the correlations are relatively low at the primary school level while they are much higher after grade 5. The most frequent estimate of the relation after grade 5 is of the order of +.50.

This contrast between the relations in the early years of school with those in the later years suggests the cumulative effect of school achievement on the academic self-concept of the student and is in keeping with our point of view about the way in which the history of the student influences his affective entry characteristics.

The cumulative effect of achievement on academic self-concept was directly studied by Kifer (1973) who followed the relation between academic self-concept and teachers' marks over grades 1 to 8. Kifer selected students who were in the upper fifth of their classes in teacher marks in grades 1 to 2, 1 to 4, 1 to 6, and 1 to 8. He also selected other students in the same classes who were in the lowest fifth of their classes in marks in the same grades. Each of these students was given the Brookover Self-Concept of Ability measure.

The results of this study are summarized in Chart 4-1. It will be noted that only slight differences in academic self-concept between the successful and unsuccessful students are apparent at the end of grade 2. Somewhat greater differences are apparent at the end of grade 4, while the differences at the end of grade 6 and at the end of grade 8 are very great. The academic self-concept of students is clearly influenced by the number of years in which the students have been judged and marked by the schools, and this is most clearly apparent for the extreme students.

In addition to studying the extreme students, Kifer also studied the relation between academic self-concept and teachers' marks for the entire group of students in grade 5 and grade 7. The correlation between teachers' marks and academic self-concept at grade 5 was $+.23$ while at grade 7 it was $+.50$—a result which is similar to that summarized in Table 4-5.

Thus academic self-concept is the strongest of the affect measures in predicting school achievement. Under appropriate methods of measuring it and general school achievement, it accounts for about 25 percent of the variation in school achievement after the elementary school period.

We should keep in mind that the academic self-concept is an index of the student's perception of himself in relation to the achievement of the other learners in his school class. It is, undoubtedly, based on the feedback he receives from grades, tests, teachers, parents, and peers about his schoolwork. The more evidence the student receives, the more likely it is that his academic self-concept will be predictive (and determinative) of his future academic achievement—unless some major change takes place in the student or the school. While academic self-concept is likely to be based on the student's perception of his previous school history, it should be remembered that our concern with academic self-concept is primarily as an *affective entry characteristic* likely to affect achievement over *subsequent* learning tasks.

Subject-Related Affect, School-Related Affect, and Academic Self-Concept

In the preceding sections we have been viewing affective entry characteristics as being restricted to a single dimension and as separable characteristics. Affect toward a subject is the most narrow, attitudes

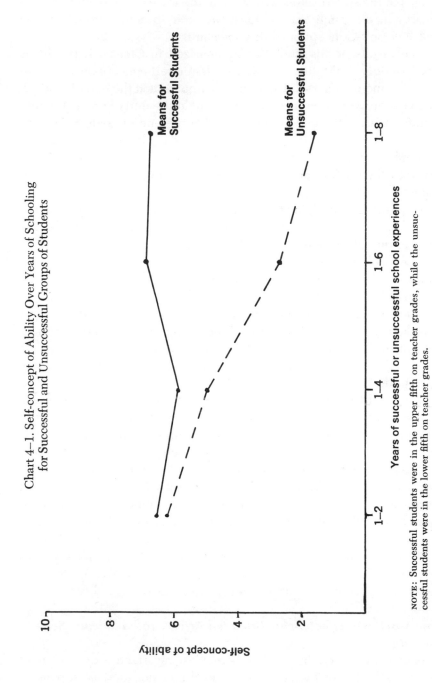

Chart 4–1. Self-concept of Ability Over Years of Schooling for Successful and Unsuccessful Groups of Students

NOTE: Successful students were in the upper fifth on teacher grades, while the unsuccessful students were in the lower fifth on teacher grades.

SOURCE: Adapted from Kifer (1973).

toward school are somewhat more general, while attitudes toward the self appear to us to be the most general characteristic. We regard all three of these dimensions as making up what we are terming affective entry characteristics for each new learning task or set of learning tasks.

It is our belief that these may be separable in the early years of school but that gradually they become a highly interrelated system, so that distinctions among these three subcharacteristics may be useful only for analytic purposes and that for all practical purposes they become a single generalized characteristic.

We have found very few studies which interrelate these three aspects of affective entry and which relate them to measures of concurrent or subsequent achievement. In general we find that combining two or three of them to predict school achievement yields no higher relation than the highest of the two or three (Dolan, 1974; Malpass, 1953; Crosswhite, 1972). Thus, Dolan (1974) combined subject affect, school affect, and academic self-concept and found the composite relation with school achievement to be +.50, the same as for academic self-concept alone. Similarly, Malpass (1953) combined school affect with academic self-concept and found the correlation with school achievement to be about +.50, the same as academic self-concept alone. More research is needed on this problem, but we believe that further study is likely to show much the same trends as the few studies we have been able to find.

Thus for most practical purposes, academic self-concept is likely to be the one best index of affective entry characteristics—at least for prediction purposes.

Quite in contrast is the use of affective entry characteristics for diagnostic purposes. The teacher who teaches a particular subject (and the particular learning tasks of that subject) is concerned with determining the extent to which students have developed interests or attitudes toward the subject which are in contrast to their attitudes and views about school or themselves. If the student's school attitudes are generally positive, but his interests in the subject are negative, presumably the teacher would approach the problem in a different way than if both are negative. The patterns of attitudes and interests also are useful in determining whether the problem can be attacked in a single subject or must be a schoolwide solution.

The study of varying patterns of subject-specific, school-related, and self-related affect may also be of value in determining whether curriculum changes as well as new instructional approaches may be recommended as ways of reducing negative affect and perhaps of increasing positive affective entry characteristics.

MICRO-LEVEL STUDIES OF AFFECTIVE CHARACTERISTICS

In the previous sections of this chapter we have been dealing with the relation between affective characteristics and concurrent or subsequent achievement in courses, subject fields, or entire programs of instruction for a term or more. This is a far cry from our attempt to relate affect to particular learning tasks. In this section we will deal more directly with affect and its relation to achievement over smaller units of learning, that is, something approaching a learning task.

In a series of small, experimental, and school-based studies, some students at the University of Chicago have been contrasting a mastery learning approach to instruction with more conventional approaches. The affective measures they have been using are limited to subject affect. They did not make use of school-related affect or general self-concept of ability because they did not believe there would be detectable changes in these characteristics within the school term or shorter time periods involved in these studies. They were interested in both the effect of affect on achievement as well as the effect of achievement on affect.

In Table 4-6 we have shown the relations between a measure of interest in the subject and achievement over one or more learning tasks. In these studies, the mastery and non-mastery students have been combined. In general, it will be seen in column A that interest at the beginning of a learning task and achievement at the end of the task correlates about +.30 (.38).

In contrast is the relation between achievement at the end of *one* learning task and interest at the *beginning* of the next learning task. In Table 4-6 (column B) it will be seen that these average about +.30 (.38)—the same as the relation between interest and achievement on the subsequent learning task. It should be pointed out that this way of viewing the problem is that prior achievement influences subsequent affect (but it also is indicative of the fact that the measures of achievement and interest are approximately concurrent). The small differences between columns A and B in the particular studies are suggestive of

TABLE 4-6. CORRELATIONS BETWEEN INTEREST AND ACHIEVEMENT IN THE MICRO-LEVEL STUDIES

	A *Median correlations between interest at the beginning of a task and achievement at the end of the task*	*B* *Median correlations between achievement at the end of a task and interest for the next task*	*C* *Correlation between interest at the beginning of a series of tasks and achievement on a summative test at the end of the series*	*D* *Correlation between interest at the end of a series of tasks and achievement on a summative test at the end of the series*
Achievement in an imaginary science (Arlin, 1973)				
–3 learning tasks	.40	.34	.07	.42
Achievement in matrix algebra (Anderson, 1973)				
–3 learning tasks	.23	.28	.06	.19
Achievement in college biology (Özcelik, 1974)				
–4 learning tasks	.29	.30	.31	.30
Achievement in matrix algebra (Block, 1970)				
–3 learning tasks	.32	.30	.06	.31
Achievement in elementary probability (Levin, 1975)			.02	.37
Median	.30 (.38)	.30 (.38)	.06 (.08)	.31 (.40)

small changes in subject affect in relation to perceived achievement over prior tasks.

The correlations between subject-related affect and achievement over particular learning tasks in these micro-level studies are of about the same magnitude as the relations between subject-related affect and achievement over entire courses or subjects as reported in Table 4-2 for the macro-level studies. In other words, subject-related affect as reported by countries for entire programs of courses in a subject, as reported for particular courses in the other studies, and as reported for particular learning tasks in the micro-level studies all yield similar generalizations about the magnitude of the relation between subject-related affect and measures of subsequent or concurrent achievement.

Quite another level of relation may be found between affect at the beginning of a *new* series of learning tasks and achievement at the end of the series of learning tasks (column C). With the exception of the Özcelik study, the initial affect is for a new set of learning tasks for which the student is unlikely to have had previous experiences. (In the Özcelik study, college biology is a subject with which the students have had some experiences or at least have taken some science courses before this one.) With this exception, subject-related affect at the beginning of a *new* series of learning tasks has almost no relation with the final summative measure of achievement at the end of the series (+.06). The Özcelik study produces the familiar correlation between affect (where the student has had some history) and the final summative test at the end of the series (+.31).

For purposes of contrast, we have put in the final column of Table 4-6 the correlation between affect at the end of the series or learning tasks (presumably dependent on the students' history with the tasks) and the summative test. These correlations average +.31 (.40), again about the same level as the macro-level studies reported in Table 4-2. These two columns (C and D) suggest that subject affect emerges from the student's perception of his history of achievement over a series of learning tasks even in such *short time periods* as represented in these micro-level studies.

However, these correlations do not fully reveal the ways in which achievement influences affect. Where we have mastery versus non-mastery learning groups, it is possible to note the ways in which the two groups of students diverge in subject-related affect as the groups attain different levels of achievement over the learning tasks in the series. In Chart 4-2 we have plotted these results for five studies. While the

Chart 4–2. Changes in Subject-related Affect* Over Learning
Tasks for Mastery and Non-mastery Groups

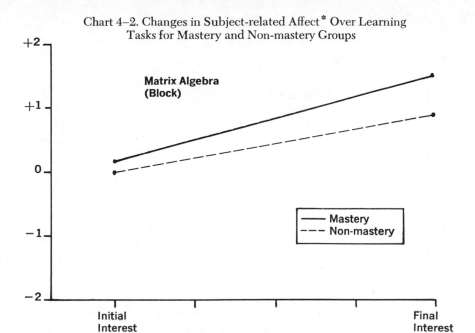

**Matrix Algebra
(Block)**

Mastery
--- Non-mastery

Initial
Interest

Final
Interest

(a)

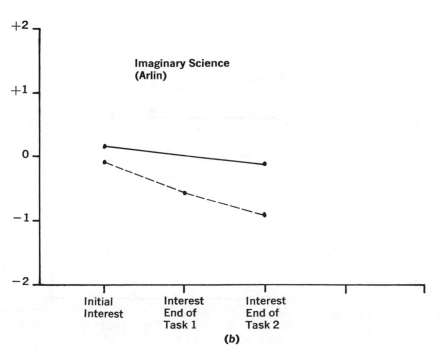

**Imaginary Science
(Arlin)**

Initial
Interest

Interest
End of
Task 1

Interest
End of
Task 2

(b)

*Affect scores are in standardized units from the mean.

Chart 4–2 *(continued)*

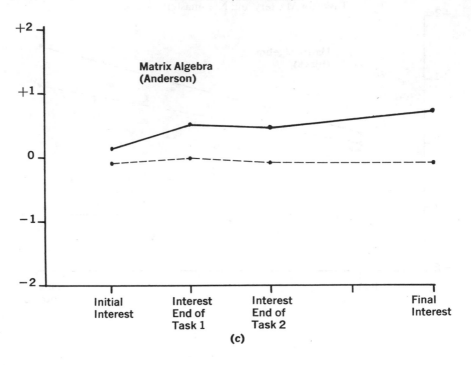

(c)

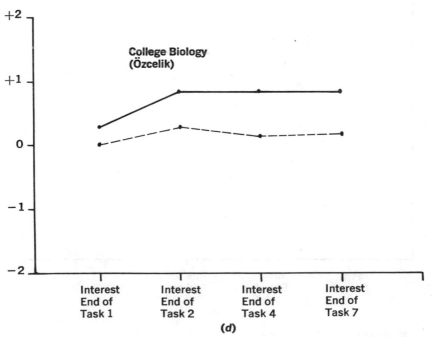

(d)

Chart 4–2 *(continued)*

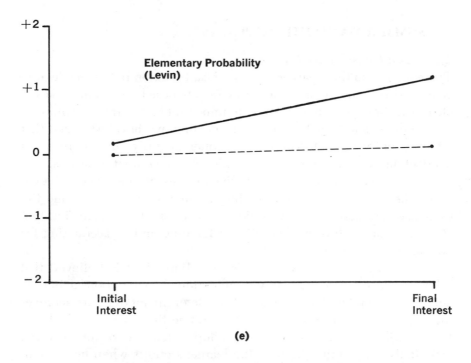

(e)

results are not always dramatic, it is evident that over the short periods of time involved in these studies (1 week to 3 months), the mastery group tends to increase in interest in the subject while the non-mastery group tends to remain the same or decline in interest. The two groups diverge in affect toward the subject as one experiences successful achievement while the other group remains the same or declines in relative achievement.

What these micro-level studies demonstrate is that achievement and subject affect are interrelated and that one influences the other in a kind of spiral effect. Thus, high achievement (or perceived high achievement) increases positive affect, which in turn influences further high achievement, and this, in turn, influences further positive affect. Similarly, low achievement decreases positive affect, which in turn depresses further achievement, and this further decreases positive affect. Although the effects in these brief studies are relatively small, the trends are fairly clear. It is to be hoped that further research at both the micro-level and macro-level can be done to determine the conditions under which similar results are to be found as well as the special conditions under which such effects do not appear.

103

SUMMARY AND IMPLICATIONS

Affect as a Causal Variable

The evidence in this chapter of a significant relation between affective characteristics and related measures of school achievement makes it clear that affective characteristics are important in determining or influencing the student's achievement. In general, we have estimated that affective entry characteristics can account for up to one-fourth ($r = +.50$) of the variance on relevant cognitive achievement measures. The evidence in concurrent and predictive studies of affect and achievement, the limited evidence available in longitudinal studies, and the evidence reported in micro-studies are consistent in suggesting that affect is a causal link in determining learning and in accounting for educational achievement.

While the process evidence is very limited, it is believed that relevant affect is determined by the individual's perceptions about his achievement and that, in turn, affect is a determinant of future achievement. Affect, in our view, helps to determine the extent to which the learner will put forth the necessary effort to learn a specific learning task. It also determines, in part, the learner's efforts when he encounters difficulties and frustration in the attempt to learn something. In turn, the student's effectiveness in learning a particular task will affect his motivation or effort on a subsequent learning task which he perceives as related to the previous task or tasks.

History of the Learner

Affective entry characteristics, as defined in this chapter, are relatively weak and unformed early in the individual's school learning career but become more structured and effective as the individual accumulates a history of learning. We have made much of the learner's perception of his success or failure with previous learning tasks as a determinant of his affective entry characteristics for subsequent learning tasks. By this we meant that the student interprets evidence and feedback provided in the school as an indication of whether he has learned well or poorly and that he then relates the evidence to what he perceives to be related learning tasks encountered subsequently. However, we do not believe there is a single ratio of success and failure which will determine a particular affective characteristic since individuals with equal levels of success or failure will vary in their perceptions of their effectiveness.

In considering affective entry characteristics we have attempted to distinguish between affect which is related to a particular class of learning tasks, such as reading, arithmetic, or science and which we have termed subject-related affect; affect which is more general and

chool learning; and finally affect which is
he patterns of subject-related affect, school-
self-concept are likely to be highly varied
but appear to form a single generalized di-
hough we can measure these separately and
consequences for the individual, we regard
em of affect which becomes more structured
h increased history of the learner.
ner as we view it is largely a history of his
te learner is not born with a view about
natics. Rather, the student acquires it during
he school can assure a history of successful
trning, especially during the elementary
s subsequent school history is likely to be
h cognitive achievement learning outcomes
characteristics and affective outcomes (see
schools have great responsibilities for both.

While affective entry characteristics are likely to become resistant to change after the individual has accumulated a long history of experiences with particular types of learning tasks, there must be a variety of means which may be effective in increasing the effort a student will devote to a particular new learning task. If these means are effective in enabling the student to view himself as relatively successful with that learning task, he may bring equal or greater effort to a subsequent learning task he regards as related to the previous one. One means for doing this is to improve the quality of instruction so that a larger proportion of the students attain some sense of accomplishment or mastery. Still another method is to both help the student and reward him in such a way that he gains satisfaction from the task and his achievement in it. Put slightly differently, teaching, curriculum, and grading policies in the school which stress high ratios of success experiences to failure experiences should result in increased amounts of positive affective entry characteristics for subsequent related learning tasks.

For a new series of learning tasks (new subjects, new curricula) success on the learning tasks which are early in the series are likely to have more productive consequences than failure on the early tasks followed by success on the later tasks—if this is even possible. It should also be pointed out that if students perceive the learning tasks as new and different or as unrelated to previous learning tasks, they are likely to begin with relatively neutral or even positive affective entry characteristics in spite of their previous experiences. This was especially stressed in the micro-level studies reported in this chapter.

If students enter a series of learning tasks with negative affective entry characteristics, they are likely to need a higher quality of instruction to attain a particular criterion of achievement than do students who enter with more positive affective entry characteristics.

Who Can Learn?

Affective entry characteristics are effective in determining subsequent learning, but we do not believe they completely determine such learning. Individuals can learn in spite of relatively negative affective entry characteristics and individuals with very positive affective entry characteristics may fail to learn if they lack the essential cognitive entry behaviors.

As we view it, positive affective characteristics, when combined with appropriate cognitive entry behaviors, enable the individual to learn with less than optimal qualities of instruction. Negative entry characteristics pose difficult problems for learning which, in part, may be overcome by very good qualities of instruction which are especially sensitive to the individual's needs and difficulties.

The relatively high relation between cognitive behaviors and affective characteristics under most school conditions suggests that instruction must take these into consideration in determining what is necessary to develop both high cognitive learning outcomes as well as more positive affective characteristics. Favorable school conditions can enable most students to learn well and to get satisfaction from their learning.

Further Research

Throughout this chapter we have pointed to particular qualities for which the research evidence is limited. The importance of affective entry characteristics for subsequent learning in or out of the school makes it essential that we understand more about the *causal process* by which affect is developed and the *ways* in which it influences learning.

A few of the questions for which new research is vitally needed are suggested below:

1. How do individual temperament and home environmental conditions determine the ratios of success and failure experiences needed to provide positive affective entry characteristics?

2. Under what conditions is individual subjective perception of success or failure similar to or different from objective evidence of success or failure?

3. What are the special learning and environmental conditions which can drastically alter previously acquired affective characteristics relevant to school learning?

4. How do the conditions for the maintenance of particular affective entry characteristics differ from the experiences and conditions which were critical in developing these affective characteristics?

5. After affective entry characteristics have reached a particular level of stability, can the individual maintain them with different ratios of perceived success and failure than were needed at earlier stages in the development of these characteristics?

5
QUALITY
OF INSTRUCTION

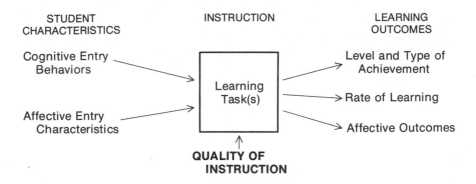

| STUDENT CHARACTERISTICS | INSTRUCTION | LEARNING OUTCOMES |

There is little doubt that under normal school conditions the characteristics of students at the beginning of a series of learning tasks have far more effect on what they will learn than does the quality of instruction they receive. Coleman (1966a), the Plowden Report (1967) in England, Dave (1963), and Wolf (1966), and the IEA[1] Studies give ample evidence that the characteristics of children and their home environments account for the largest proportion of the variation in the measured achievement of students at particular points in their educational careers.

In Chapters 3 and 4 we have emphasized that cognitive entry behaviors can account for about 50 percent of the variation in achievement, while affective entry characteristics alone can account for about 25 percent. We have estimated in Chapter 7 that, in combination, these entry characteristics could account for about 60 percent of the achievement variation on a new set of learning tasks.

---

[1]The IEA studies were Husén, 1967; Comber & Keeves, 1973; Purves, 1973; Thorndike, 1973; Carroll, 1975; and Lewis & Massad, 1975.

We doubt that the Quality of Instruction can overcome the effect of lack of the prerequisite cognitive entry behaviors unless the instruction is directly related to remedying these deficiencies or unless the nature of a learning task is sufficiently altered to make it appropriate for students in terms of the entry behaviors they bring to the task. In other words, the lack of the necessary prerequisite cognitive entry behaviors for a particular learning task should make it *impossible* for the student to master the learning task requirements no matter how good the quality of instruction for that task. This is, in part, a problem of definition. If a learning task is carefully defined, analyzed, and evaluated, it is what it is, and the lack of requisite cognitive entry behaviors should make it impossible for a student to learn it to some criterion of mastery—no matter how good the quality of instruction on *that* learning task or how much time and perseverance the student gives to *that* learning task. If on the other hand, the learning task can be altered in a number of ways such that each alteration in the learning task requires different entry behaviors, then it is quite possible that students who lack cognitive entry behaviors for one form of the learning task may possess the entry behaviors for another form of the learning task. In such cases, students who can't learn under the one form may be able to learn under another form—if they possess the necessary entry behaviors for that form of the learning task.

Furthermore, it is possible that if the student acquires the necessary entry behaviors on his own—by special tutoring or help, or by the instruction initially shifting from the *original learning task* to the *prerequisites for that task*—the student may eventually learn the original learning task.

Thus, the securing of the necessary prerequisites and the redefinition, redesign, or restructuring of the learning task or some combination of the two may overcome the initial lack of cognitive entry behaviors. Since we have approached quality of instruction as though it deals with one or more learning tasks defined in a particular way, we are maintaining that quality of instruction on a particular learning task (defined in a particular way) cannot overcome the lack of the prerequisite cognitive entry behaviors for *that* learning task (see Chapter 3).

In contrast to initial Cognitive Entry Behaviors—defined as the prerequisite subject content and other prerequisite cognitive skills for the particular learning task—are the initial affective characteristics (see Chapter 4) which include the individual's interests, attitudes, and motivations for the particular learning task. Here, we are convinced that very good quality of instruction may overcome negative initial affective characteristics, so that the student can learn the particular learning task(s) to a high level. However, this can be done more easily when the individual has had fewer frustrating and negative experiences with similar or related school learning tasks than when he has had a long history of negative experiences and few rewarding experiences in the school with similar or related tasks.

In spite of these views about the determinism imposed by the effects of initial cognitive entry behaviors and affective entry characteristics, we have become more and more certain that the quality of instruction can have powerful effects on learning over particular learning tasks. However, before attempting to define what we mean by the *Quality of Instruction,* it is necessary to deal with the great amount of research which has been done on the characteristics of teachers, characteristics of the class or classroom, and the characteristics of the school.

RESEARCH RESULTS ON CHARACTERISTICS OF TEACHERS, CLASSROOMS, AND SCHOOLS

Much research on these characteristics has been done over the past four decades. Some of these studies have been designed to determine the relation between student achievement or other measures of learning and such teacher characteristics as age, length and type of pre-service training, amount of experience, teacher attitudes, and salaries. Much of this research has been summarized by Barr (1948), Domas and Tiedeman (1950), and Morsh and Wilder (1954). In addition, large-scale national studies such as Coleman (1966a) in the United States, the Plowden Report (1967) in England, and the IEA multinational studies in mathematics, science, reading comprehension, literature, French as a second language, and English as a second language have reported on the relation between student achievement in particular subjects and some of the above teacher characteristics. In general, the relations are relatively low. So much so that the *characteristics of teachers* rarely account for more than 5 percent of the achievement variation of their students—and usually much less.

Similarly, many studies have been done on the *characteristics of the classroom or school* including such variables as number of students, equipment and facilities available, expenditures per student, and school organization and administration. Here again the relation

trying to provide the student with the *cues* as to what he is to learn. He may do this by talking to the student and explaining what he is to do, by using his own body to demonstrate what is expected, or by getting the student to stand, hold the racket, or swing in a particular manner. If the tutor is a very able one, he will provide a variety of cues to help the student understand what he is to do. The same task can be explained and/or illustrated in a variety of ways, and the tutor will search for the cues which will be best understood or grasped by the particular learner. The good tutor is likely to have a variety of ways of explaining or illustrating what is to be learned, and he will use one or more ways of presenting the cues which he believes will work best for the particular learner. He observes the student's responses to these cues, gives additional cues, or shifts the form of the cues until the student apparently grasps what he is to do.

During the learning process, the tutor will have the student actually do the various stands, holds, and swings, and he will provide further cues to correct these to some standard as the learning proceeds. He is getting the student to actively *practice* or *participate* in the process. Although it is relatively easy to secure and observe the practice efforts in a skill like serving a tennis ball, such practice or participation is necessary and must be present as a part of any kind of learning process—whether it be a highly abstract and complex cognitive type of problem solving, a less complex cognitive skill, or a more concrete psychomotor type of skill learning.

The good tutor recognizes that the amount of participation or the amount of practice of the specific learning elements needed will vary from learner to learner. Some students will acquire it with a minimum of overt practice while others will need much more practice until they get it correct. Some learners can learn the entire operation in a few practice efforts while other learners must practice parts of the operation separately until they get each one to the proper level before they can practice the whole operation.

We further may note that the tutor makes many little expressions of encouragement—usually when the student does something right or something nearly right. Sometimes these encouragements are expressed in words, sometimes in a smile, sometimes in a look or gesture. These encouragements seem to be most frequent at the beginning of the learning activity, and they appear to be reduced in frequency as the tutor notes the learner responding with smiles, gestures, nods, or monosyllables as he (the learner) does something that seems to work and he believes is good; or with frowns, grimaces, or expressions of dismay, as he does something that he regards as wrong or ineffective. The good tutor varies the types of encouragement or reinforcement with the learning situation, the stages in the learning activity, and the learner. Furthermore, he attempts to create a situation (as suggested above) in which the learner becomes his own source of reinforcement. Essentially, the tutor manages the student's learning to ensure that the learner secures the necessary *reinforcement* or *rewards* to motivate his participation and perseverance in the learning as well as to signal when parts of the learning are going well.

At various stages in the learning, the tutor checks on the learner to note what he has accomplished and to determine where or when he needs additional correction and support. This is what we have termed *feedback and correction.* Here the tutor may alter the instruction to help the learner over particular difficulties. He may get the learner to practice a particular aspect of the learning to strengthen particular correct procedures or to eliminate specific incorrect ones. He may also alter the reinforcements to make them more appropriate to the learner.

What we have done in this semifictional abbreviated account of a tutor-student learning situation is to highlight some of the aspects of quality of instruction. A fuller and more abstract development of these aspects will be presented in the following material. We have, by the choice of a situation with a single learner, attempted to emphasize the *management of learning.* In the classroom situation the teacher is constantly shifting from the *management of learning* to the *management of learners.* We believe that the teacher is frequently distracted from the first by the need to manage the learners so as to avoid the wrath of the administration and others or to feel that he is in control of the situation. If the management of learning is effective, it is likely that the teacher will need to give relatively little attention to the management of the learners.

There is no doubt that a teacher with a group of students must find ways of securing the attention of the students and getting them to focus on particular learning tasks. This management of learners is a necessary prelude to any learning. Although the tutor has the same problem with a single learner, it is likely that the numerical difference in learners complicates the problem very much for the teacher. Even the tutor who attempts to tutor three students at once will find the problem much more complex than tutoring a single student. But these are problems of the management of learners. A theory such as we are proposing in this book does little to help teachers with problems of this kind other than to register the belief that management of learning is what is at the center of teaching and that if this is done well, it should reduce the amount of effort and emotion needed to control the learners.

While we are emphasizing the relations between a teacher and a group of learners, the quality of instruction also has to do with the materials of instruction, the organization of the content and objectives of the instruction, and the availability of time and resources to accomplish the instruction.

COMPONENTS OF QUALITY OF INSTRUCTION AND RELEVANT MACRO-LEVEL STUDIES

Stripped to its essentials, the *Quality of Instruction* as we define it here has to do with the *cues* or directions provided to the learner, the *participation* of the learner in learning activity (covert or overt), and the *reinforcement* which the learner secures in some relation to the learning. Because much of school instruction is group instruction and because any attempt at group instruction is fraught with error and difficulty, a *feedback and corrective* system must be also included in the quality of instruction. It is these four elements of instruction—*cues, participation, reinforcement,* and *feedback/correctives*—which we will consider next.

Cues

Any learning includes some elements to be learned and some method of communicating cues to the learner as to what the elements are and what he is to do about them. These cues may be relatively simple such as a sound or word to be related to a particular object, event, or activity; the relating of a particular action to a particular signal; the demonstration of a sequence of physical activities; or the directions for a complex set of cognitive processes. Although we appear to be suggesting that the cues begin the process, it should be obvious that instruction is not a simple progression from cues to each of the other aspects of instruction. The cues may be provided at many stages in the learning process, and the elements of instruction suggested in the previous paragraph may be arranged in many different sequences; we can even imagine situations where they may occur almost simultaneously.

The cues include instruction as to what is to be learned as well as the directions as to what the learner is to do in the learning process.

There are many forms in which the cues can be presented. In most group instruction in the schools the major cues tend to be *verbal* in nature; that is, the student is directed by the teacher or by the materials of instruction to do certain things, to call something by given terms, to remember particular things in the form of words or sets of words, or to perform some complex cognitive or psychomotor process.

Not all cues need be in verbal form. Some may be in the form of *visual* stimuli and patterns which are to be remembered or responded to in an appropriate way. Others may make use of other senses—tactile, kinesthetic, olfactory. Cues may take the form of models, observations of self or others, or demonstrations which the student is to reproduce in some way.

Cues differ not only in the form in which they are presented but also in their strength. The strength of a cue or set of cues may be determined by the salience with which it is presented. Size, shape, color, and volume are only a few of the ways in which a cue may be distinguished from a background or from other cues. A cue may also become stronger by repetition, by making it more concrete or observable, by adding dramatic intensity to it, and by other arrangements which bring it to the attention of the learner and which get the learner to focus on the cues to be learned as against the many other competing aspects of the particular environment. The strength of a cue is subject to many of the Gestalt laws of *pragnanz* (Hilgard & Bower, 1966, pp. 233–235) by which a figure is separated from a ground.

Still another aspect of cues has to do with their meaningfulness. If the cues are familiar and have been encountered and used before, they are more likely to be easily learned in a new context and arrangement than if they are all new and strange to the learner. The cues must be understood or comprehended if the student is to make use of them in his learning. It is likely that cues which are easily understood in one form by some students may need to be expressed in other ways before they become meaningful to other students.

The important point to be conveyed is that learners may differ in the extent to which they can learn from particular cues. If the only form in which cues are presented are verbal, then it is likely that students who are most proficient or comfortable with verbal cues will learn most easily, while students who learn in other ways will be at a disadvantage (Cronbach & Snow, 1976; Kim, 1968; Pearson, 1973). Similarly, if students who can learn best through mathematical, graphic, or other nonverbal ways are presented with appropriate forms of cues, they are likely to learn more easily than they will with other forms.

In general, much attention in instruction and curriculum development has been spent on finding the *one* best form of presenting cues, specifying directions, and determining the size of step, or amount of detail to be presented to a *group of learners*. Only recently have we become more aware of the variety of ways in which cues can be presented and the variety of ways in which individuals may learn. Also, the technology of instruction has more recently produced a large variety of ways in which the same ideas or procedures can be taught. No longer is the only way in which something can be taught confined to a single textbook or verbal presentation by the teacher. A great array of learning materials, forms for presenting the learning to be accomplished, and instructional procedures have been devised and used. In general, we believe that the greater the variety of instructional materials and methods used within a classroom, the greater is the likelihood that each student will secure the cues he needs for his learning. What remains is to determine sounder procedures for relating individual differences in learners to differences in the ways in which the learners should encounter the cues.

In Table 5-1 we have summarized the studies we could locate on the relation between the cues provided a class and the achievement of the students. Most of the studies we could find involve an observer rating the instruction in terms of its *difficulty* for the students to understand, the *clarity* of the ideas and concepts as presented, and the extent to which the instruction was *interesting* or dynamic. We could find only eight studies which made observations of the cues (as we have defined them), and most of these made use of correlations between the qualities of the cues and the *final* learning level of *groups* of students. Much more evidence is needed before the importance of the cues can be established with greater definitiveness than is presently the case. What is especially needed are studies of the relation between the quality of the cues and the learning gains of individual students. However, in the studies which we could find, the relation between the quality of the cues and the final achievement of *groups* of students is about +.38. Only a few studies were available which reported on the relation between the quality of the cues and the *gains* in achievement of groups of students. Here the median correlation was +.53—somewhat higher than the correlations with final achievement. In general,

TABLE 5-1. MEDIAN CORRELATIONS BETWEEN COMPONENTS OF THE QUALITY OF INSTRUCTION AND MEASURES OF ACHIEVEMENT

Components of the Quality of Instruction	Group Measures		Individual Measures	
	Final Achievement	Gain in Achievement	Final Achievement	Gain in Achievement
Cues	.38 [19]*	.53 [4]		.58 [10]
Reinforcement	.26 [12]	.24 [13]		
Participation	.26 [7]	.28 [11]	.42 [34]	.47 [8]
Feedback/Correctives†				

*The numbers in brackets refer to the number of entries included in the studies reported in Appendix Tables 5-A, 5-B, 5-C, and 5-D.   †Based on the micro-level studies reported in Table 5-2.

we estimate that about 14 percent of the variance in the achievement of groups of students is at present accounted for by the qualities of the cues.[2] We suspect that more careful studies in the future are likely to make the quality of the cues more central in learning than now appears to be the case with the few studies available. Furthermore, it is likely that the future research on cues will be more concerned with their strength and meaningfulness to individual students than with their effect on groups of students. This type of research will be especially important in determining the extent to which individuals differ in their ability to make use of particular cues—a point which has been repeatedly stressed in this section of the chapter.

Reinforcement

Most learning theories (Hilgard & Bower, 1966; Dollard & Miller, 1950) are in agreement that learning is effective only when it is accompanied by reinforcement. While there is some question about the relative effectiveness of positive versus negative reinforcement, there is little question that reinforcement of some type is needed during or after each part of the learning process.

Teachers have long recognized the need for rewarding or reinforcing learning, and almost every teacher will be observed to use reinforcement during most learning sessions. However, teachers differ greatly in the variety of reinforcements they use, in the frequency with which they use reinforcements, and in the amount of reinforcement they give to different individuals in their classes.

In the early years, teachers make relatively effective use of their own approval or disapproval of the child and of his learning. These tend to be largely verbal expressions by the teacher directed to a particular child. What many teachers need to learn is the great variety of ways in which approval or disapproval may be expressed, including simple recognition of the child, giving attention to the child, close physical proximity to the child, gesturing, smiling, or frowning.

The teacher may also recognize that food, toys, or objects are also powerful reinforcers when used appropriately. While some reinforcements may be related to primary drives for food, warmth, or rest, most of the reinforcers used in the school are likely to be learned. These learned reinforcers include social approval and acceptance by the

---

[2]These studies are reported in Appendix Table 5-A.

teacher, parents, and peers. They may also include objects which are in some ways related to social approval—such as stars or points.

Reinforcers may also be related to the individual's need for self esteem. That is, the student must approve of himself, and any device, object, or expression which helps him to maintain or enhance his self esteem can serve as a reinforcer.

Reinforcers need not be administered always by the teacher. They may be supplied by the social group or class of which the student is a member, by his peers, and by other adults, including parents. Eventually, the student may be his own source of reinforcement. Also, the task to be learned can, under some conditions, become a source of feedback and reinforcement.

What is a reinforcement to one student may not serve in the same way for another student. And it is even possible under some conditions that what is perceived to be a positive reinforcement by one student may be perceived as a negative reinforcement by another. Perhaps the importance of this is that reinforcements are likely to be differentially perceived by students and that the teacher who operates with a limited amount and variety of reinforcements may not be adequately reinforcing some of the students in the class.

Studies of the variety of reinforcements and the conditions under which they are effective (Havighurst, 1970; White, 1959; and McClelland, 1965) make it clear that this is one area in which teachers need much help—especially when they attempt to provide good quality of instruction for learners who come from a variety of social and cultural backgrounds.

In any case, it is likely that individual learners may need different types of reinforcers and even different amounts of reinforcement at various stages in the learning process.

In Table 5-1 we have summarized the relation between the rewards or reinforcement provided by the instructor and the achievement of students. These are based on ten studies of the frequency, variety, and types of rewards provided the *class* (see Appendix Table 5-B). About one-half of the correlations (12) reported in these studies relates qualities of the reinforcement to *final achievement of groups* of students. Here the median correlation is +.26. Another half of the correlations relates qualities of reinforcement to *gains in achievement of groups* of students. Here the median correlation is +.24. All these were studies at the primary and middle school level. The relations we find indicate that only about 6 percent of the achievement variation between classes can be related to the rewards available. Here again, our evidence is so limited that the full effect of classroom rewards on student achievement can not be said to have been established.

What is especially needed are studies where the rewards are related to *individuals* in the class, since the frequency and variety of rewards available to the class does not indicate anything about which students receive the reinforcements and what effect it has on their learning. This type of research is especially important since the work of Dahlöff (1971) and Brophy and Good (1970) make it clear that being in the same classroom with a particular teacher does not guarantee that all students in the group are treated equally with regard to reinforcement.

Participation

A learner must do something with the cues to actually learn. The simple presentation of a set of cues to a passive learner is not likely to produce much in the way of learning. The student must participate or practice, either overtly or covertly, in remembering or using the cues, attempting to make the appropriate responses, or performing the acts, behaviors, or responses specified by the cues until they have become a part of his repertoire. Although learning theorists may differ in the terms used, we have chosen to use terms such as *practice, response,* or *participation* to indicate that some active involvement of the learner is required if learning is to take place.

Teachers develop a variety of strategies for ensuring participation. They may focus on one child at a time, break a large group of students into smaller groups where each member of the small group must do something observable by the others in the group, have each child go through selected steps in a process so that it can be observed, secure evidence in the form of oral or written materials in some problem-solving situation, or have each student complete homework or other assignments on a set of tasks to be performed. Unfortunately time and other limitations involved in teaching a group of learners make it difficult for the teacher to observe or ensure that each of the learners is actively participating in using the cues in the desired ways.

However, not all participation must be overt and observable. If the students are actively participating in a covert way, this may be as effective under some conditions as overt participation (Bloom, 1954). It is likely that overt participation may be especially needed for young children to learn, while covert participation—if it can be ensured—is highly effective for older learners.

The problem of participation is rarely a problem for the tutor with his one student. He can get so much evidence on the learner's participation that he can, if he is sensitive, determine whether the amount of participation needed by the particular learner has been secured. In group learning situations it is much more difficult to ensure that each learner is actively participating.

Individual students do differ in the amount of participation they may need to learn something. In studies of learning in the laboratory it is evident in simple memory studies that some students may need to repeat or practice the material to be learned more times to reach criterion performance than do others. In studies of the amount of time and practice needed to learn more complex material it is evident that the slowest 10 percent of students may need about five to six times as much rehearsal, practice, or participation in the learning activity as the most rapid 10 percent of students. These are rough orders of magnitude, but studies on computer-assisted instruction (Atkinson, 1968) and studies on Individually Prescribed Instruction (Glaser, 1968) suggest these figures are good rough approximations of the range of time and practice required for extreme groups. Individuals may fall outside this range and extreme students may differ by as much as 10 to 1.

Evidence is accumulating that when students enter a learning task with the necessary cognitive entry behaviors and similar levels of affective entry characteristics the amount of participation and practice required to reach a criterion level of achievement becomes very similar from student to student (Bloom, 1974b). Especially does this appear to be the case in the later tasks in a sequential set of learning tasks. That is, while students may vary considerably in the amount of participation and practice (and help needed) in the early learning tasks in a sequential series, in the later learning tasks in the series—if they have thoroughly mastered the initial tasks—they will approach equality in the amount of participation (or time and practice) needed to master the task (Bloom, 1974b). Much research is needed to determine the conditions under which equality is true of participation needed. Under conventional school group instructional conditions (where there is little feedback and corrective procedures), this is unlikely to be true. However, it should be noted that teachers (and school schedules) typically proceed in their teaching and instructional assignments as though all students should learn with approximately the same amount of practice or participation.

We are fortunate that about twenty studies of classroom situations have included measures of participation. These are available at all levels of education and include very precise counting of the amount of participation and practice of groups of students as well as efforts to observe and record the interest, attention, or time devoted directly to the learning by individual students (see Appendix Tables 5-C and 5-D).

These studies have been summarized in Table 5-1. Where the class group was the unit of study for *participation,* the correlation with either final achievement or gain in achievement is very similar—about +.27. In contrast, where the individual's participation was observed or measured, the correlation with final achievement was +.42, while the correlation with gains in achievement was +.58. The overall correlation between the level of participation of individuals and their achievement is slightly higher for the secondary school studies than it is for the primary school studies included in Appendix Table 5-D.

In general, about 20 percent of the variation in achievement of *individuals* is accounted for by their participation in the classroom learning process. It is of interest to note that the amount of active participation in the learning (overt or covert) is an excellent index of the quality of instruction for the purpose of predicting or accounting for individual student learning. Undoubtedly this is true because the amount of participation can approach some maximum value only when students are being adequately reinforced, and it is likely that students can participate actively only when the cues are interesting and meaningful to them.

We believe that a crude but effective method of estimating the quality of instruction for a group or individual is to note the extent of overt or covert participation of students in the learning process. Where the overall quality of instruction is poor, only a few students will be actively participating in the learning. And as active participation in learning decreases, we would expect discipline and student management problems to increase.

More research is needed on ways of measuring student participation both quantitatively as well as qualitatively. Also, we need to determine how participation changes under favorable learning conditions as well as under less favorable and less effective qualities of instruction with respect to cues and reinforcement. We will summarize some of the recent research on this in the micro-level section of this chapter as well as in Chapter 7.

Feedback/Correctives

When one student is being taught something by a skilled tutor, there are many adjustments made in the teaching-learning process. The tutor quickly adapts the *cues, amount of participation or practice,* and the use of *reinforcement* to the learner's characteristics and needs. The process is likely to be so simple and natural that in many instances the tutor makes the adjustments to the learner's needs without being fully conscious of when and why he is doing it. The feedback about the learning is so direct that both the student and tutor may communicate the needs and adjustments by other than verbal means. Gestures, frowns, smiles, the manner of sitting and working, and other nonverbal signals may play as large a role in the communication between student and tutor as other, more verbal behavior.

Thus, while feedback and correctives are constantly taking place in the interactions between a tutor and one student, the process is subtle and takes place in a nonformal way. Under excellent tutor-student conditions, the feedback and correctives are likely to account for the relatively high level of achievement of the student or the relatively rapid rate in which the learner reaches the criterion of mastery set by the tutor.

But in most school learning, instruction is provided to groups of students—usually about thirty students in a group. Under these conditions, even the best use of cues, participation, and reinforcement must be differentially effective for individual learners. What is an excellent set of cues for one student may be less than ideal for another. The amount of participation and practice that is adequate or optimal for one student may be far from optimal for another, and the amount and type of reinforcement that is about right for one student may be inappropriate for another. While the sensitive and very competent teacher may make adjustments for each child as he or she comes to know the students in the class, even here a teacher may have many difficulties. Whatever we do in providing group instruction—the use of excellent instructional material and the use of highly trained and capable teachers—we are likely to provide well for some children and less well for other children (S. Bloom, 1976).

Some provision must be made for a way of determining the adequacy and appropriateness of cues, participation, and reinforcement for each learner and for *altering or correcting* these as needed for each individual student. Ideally, this should be an integral part of the teaching-learning process, and it should be consistently used for each new learning task or learning experience. We doubt that this ideal can be fully attained except where the teacher is dealing with one student at a time, or where there are only a few learners for whom the teacher is responsible.

While it is possible to analyze the literature for the relation between student achievement and cues, reinforcement, or participation, there is almost no evidence in the research literature which deals directly with feedback and correctives. The only evidence we can find that relates learning to the effects of feedback and correctives is based on the developing literature on mastery learning.

In much of the literature on mastery learning strategies summarized by Block (1971, 1974), control and mastery learning classes, frequently taught by the same instructor, are compared with respect to achievement outcomes at the end of the course. The major difference between the two classes is the use of feedback-corrective procedures.

The feedback procedures typically consist of brief formative tests, at the end of each learning task, which indicate what the student has learned and what he still needs to learn to attain mastery of the task. Mastery is frequently defined as something approximating 80 to 85 percent of the items on a criterion-referenced test.

The correctives are the suggestions as to what each student should review in the original or new instructional material, programmed instruction, special explanations in the form of sound cassettes, and additional workbooks and practice exercises. Additional instruction on particular ideas missed by the student are frequently given by other students, aides, and even by the teachers in some instances.

Stated another way, the primary emphasis in the corrective procedures is on *alternative cues* and *additional time and practice*. It is possible that the corrective procedures may include additional reinforcement, but how much of this takes place is not clear.

While the feedback and corrective procedures used in mastery learning classes do not have all the qualities stressed above in the tutor-student relation, they are quite effective in altering the learning achievement of students.

In one study by Block (1970) it was found that in the control class the average student attained about 50 percent of the possible score on the formative test for each learning task. In contrast, the feedback and correctives for each student in the mastery class brought the average student up to 90 percent of the possible score on the same tests.

Most of the results of the mastery teaching-learning strategies reported by Block (1971, 1974) are dependent on the use of these feedback and corrective systems. Under such conditions, a large number of mastery learning studies report that while about 20 percent of the students in the control classes attain the criterion of mastery, approximately 80 percent of the students in the mastery classes attain the same criterion of mastery on a summative test at the end of a series of learning units. Under more ideal use of feedback and correctives, the shift is from about 20 percent of the control students attaining the mastery criterion to approximately 90 percent of the mastery students reaching the same criterion of mastery. In the micro-level studies reported later in this chapter, we find the median correlation between individual student achievement on the last learning task in a series and the *use* versus *absence* of regular feedback and corrective procedures to be about +.47. This has been summarized in Table 5-1. (The results for each of the studies are reported in Table 5-2.)

We treat this in more detail in the micro-studies. However, it is evident that one of the most powerful set of features in the Quality of Instruction, as we define it here, is the feedback-corrective procedure. This apparently accounts for the major differences in the distribution of achievement in the control versus mastery learning classes. Although such procedures may be found in conventional classroom instruction, we do not think that they are likely to be used regularly and systematically as is the case with mastery teaching-learning strategies.

Cues-Reinforcement-Participation-Feedback/Correctives

In the preceding sections of this chapter we have been dealing with these four qualities of instruction as separate entities. We can find no studies in the literature which deal with them in a combined way. However, some use of the first three is included in the Walberg (1969) and Anthony (1967) studies of classroom environments. These studies indicate that the correlation between the quality of the classroom environment and gains in student achievement (by classes) is as high as +.64 for the Anthony study while it is +.37 for the Walberg study. The difference between the results of the two studies may be attributed largely to the differences in the methods of studying these variables.

Since, as was pointed out on page 123, we regard the level of student participation as a crude index of the presence of good cues and reinforcement for the individual, we may regard 20 percent of the achievement variance as the probable lower bound of the effects of quality of instruction. The use of feedback/correctives suggests that a better estimate of the effects of quality of instruction may be about 25 percent of the achievement variance.

In contrast is the Anthony study for groups of students which account for as much as 40 percent of the achievement gain variance between groups of students. If the quality of instruction includes all four qualities of instruction, it is likely that quality of instruction may be even more effective than the estimates suggested here.

Obviously, much further research is needed to account for these qualities of instruction separately as well as in combination. We regard this as one of the most fruitful areas of research for the improvement of instruction.

MICRO-LEVEL STUDIES OF QUALITY OF INSTRUCTION

In the studies done at the University of Chicago, it is possible to observe the effects of quality of instruction on the learning level of students as well as the effects of quality of instruction on other aspects of the learning process. In these studies, the instruction was done in two phases. The original instruction for the students in the mastery and non-mastery classes was as similar as the researcher could provide. In some cases, the instructor and the instructional material were the same for the two groups while in other studies the instructional materials were identical for the two groups.

Following the original learning for the two groups under similar conditions in each learning task, a formative test was given to both groups. For the mastery group, the results of the formative test were the basis for corrective instruction to ensure learning of these students to the criterion level (usually about the 85 percent level of mastery). In this corrective learning instruction, aides, tutors, and/or materials were provided the students to ensure more adequate cues, additional practice, and, to some extent, additional reinforcement of the student learning. The extent of success of the corrective instruction was determined by having the students take a second form of the formative test over that unit of learning. In a few cases, further additional instruction was provided and a third set of formative test questions was used. In these studies, there was little doubt that the majority of students reached the criterion level of mastery before going on to the next learning task. In the case of the non-mastery or control students, no corrective instruction was given the students after the taking of each formative test. Thus, the major difference in quality of instruction in these micro-studies was

TABLE 5-2. CORRELATIONS BETWEEN QUALITY OF INSTRUCTION AND ACHIEVEMENT IN THE MICRO-LEVEL STUDIES

	Correlation between the Quality of Instruction and the Original Achievement on Learning Task (LT)			Correlation between the Quality of Instruction and Summative Achievement
	LT-1	LT-2	LT-3	
Achievement in Matrix Algebra (Anderson, 1973)	−.02	.33	.52	.52
Achievement in Matrix Algebra (Block, 1970)	.19	.23	.38	.32
Achievement in Elementary Probability (Levin, 1975)	−.06	.22	.23	.55
Achievement in Imaginary Science (Arlin, 1973)	.19	.43	.58	
Achievement in Second Language (Binor, 1974)	.24	.45	.55	.65
Achievement in Second Language (Pillet, 1975)		.15	.33	
Achievement in College Biology (Özcelik, 1974)		.38	.66	
Achievement in College Math (Özcelik, 1974)		.51	.43	
Median	+.19	+.35	+.47	+.53

NOTE: Quality of instruction is the use of feedback and correctives in all the studies except the Özcelik study where students' perceptions of quality of instruction are used.

that the mastery students were given *feedback and corrective instruction* after the original learning of a task while the non-mastery students were not.

Effect of Quality of Instruction on Achievement

The effect of quality of instruction (mastery versus control procedures) on the final critical learning task and on the summative achievement measures is shown in the correlations in Table 5-2. The median correlation between quality of instruction and achievement on the final critical task (before feedback and correctives) is +.47, while the median correlation between quality of instruction and achievement on the summative achievement measure is +.53. Thus the relation between quality of instruction and the students' performance on a final formative test or overall measure of achievement is approximately +.50. This is slightly higher than the lower-bound estimate of the effect of quality of instruction reported for the macro-studies on page 126. Perhaps the slight differences in the correlations may be attributed to the greater control of quality of instruction (especially the feedback and correctives) in these micro-studies than is possible in the more naturalistic school-based studies represented in the macro-studies.

    Some of the symptoms of the underlying processes of quality of instruction and their effects on the increasing differences in the achievement of the mastery versus non-mastery group of students may be seen in Table 5-2. On the first formative test (before corrective instruction) the median correlation between quality of instruction and achievement is approximately +.19. This low but positive correlation may be attributed to slight differences between the two groups at the beginning of the instruction. At the end of the second learning task, the median correlation between quality of instruction and achievement is +.35, while it is +.47 at the end of Learning Task 3 and slightly higher on the final summative achievement measures. What this makes clear is that the *feedback and corrective* procedures for the mastery group and the lack of these procedures for the non-mastery group produce increasing differentiation between these two groups, and this is reflected in the pattern of correlations. This may be seen even more directly in Chart 5-1 where only slight differences are present in the mean achievement of the two groups at the end of Learning Task 1, greater differences are present at the end of Learning Task 2, and much larger differences may be seen in the achievement at the end of learning task 3 as well as on the final achievement measure.

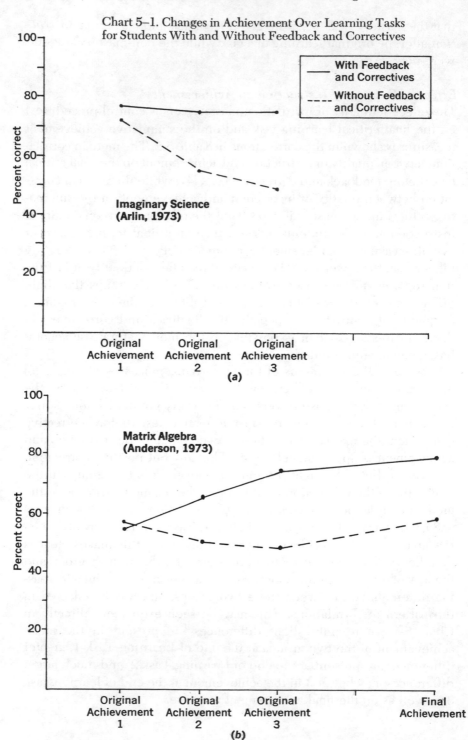

Chart 5–1. Changes in Achievement Over Learning Tasks
for Students With and Without Feedback and Correctives

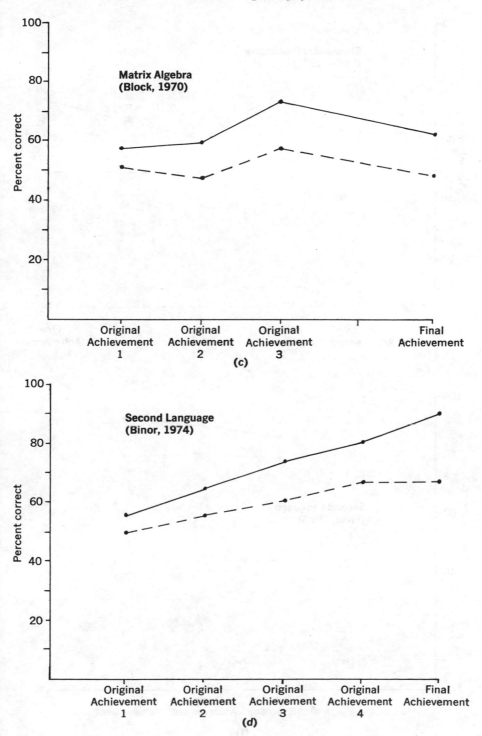

Matrix Algebra (Block, 1970)

(c)

Second Language (Binor, 1974)

(d)

Chart 5-1 *(continued)*

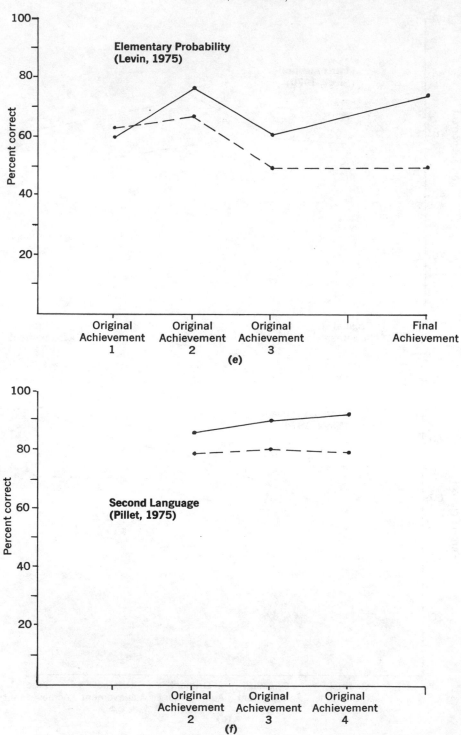

Elementary Probability
(Levin, 1975)

Percent correct

100

80

60

40

20

Original
Achievement
1

Original
Achievement
2

Original
Achievement
3

Final
Achievement

(e)

Second Language
(Pillet, 1975)

Percent correct

100

80

60

40

20

Original
Achievement
2

Original
Achievement
3

Original
Achievement
4

(f)

Effect of Quality of Instruction on Learning Processes

In Table 5-2 and Chart 5-1 there is evidence of the increasing differentiation of the mastery and control groups in achievement. Thus on the
first learning task (before feedback and correctives) the two groups are
approximately equal while on the *third learning task* (again before
feedback and correctives) the two groups are very different in their
achievement. It is clear that the mastery group was provided with
additional time and help after the first and second learning tasks while
the control group was not.

We may regard the achievement on the first and third learning
tasks (before feedback and correctives) as an indication of the *amount
learned* in a given period of instruction where both groups were given
approximately the same amount of time in the original instruction. If we
view it in this way, it is evident that the amount learned per time (rate
of learning) was approximately the same on the first learning task but is
very different on the third learning task. That is, the two groups became
more and more different in the amount they learn in a given time
period or in the proportion of students who reach a given criterion of
achievement (the mastery level) in a particular amount of time.

It is difficult to explain exactly why this happens—that is, why the
students under the mastery approach appear to increasingly learn more
effectively as they move from one learning task to another. We believe
this may, in part, be explained by the changes in the way in which they
participate in the learning of each task (before feedback and correctives).

In the Anderson (1973) study he reports the correlation between
time on task (the overt and covert participation) in the original learning
of each task and the quality of instruction. On the first task the correlation between quality of instruction and time-on-task is $-.08$; it is $+.36$
on the second task and $+.50$ on the third learning task. In other words,
the mastery and non-mastery students became more and more different
in their use of the time in the original instruction.

In the Anderson (1973), Özcelik (1974), Arlin (1973), and Block
(1970) studies, it is evident that indices of involvement, participation,
and *time-on-task* are predictive of the achievement (the correlations
average about $+.60$). Thus, an index of *participation* appears to account
for student learning, and this index is altered drastically for the mastery
and non-mastery students. We will deal with this in greater detail in
Chapter 7. The point to be made here is that the quality of instruction in

the micro-level studies has major consequences for *achievement* as well as the *learning processes* used by students.

Further research is needed to determine the extent to which quality of instruction has long-term effects on both achievement and the learning processes of students.

SUMMARY AND IMPLICATIONS

We have defined Quality of Instruction in terms of particular characteristics of the interaction between *instruction* and *students*. We have stressed *cues-participation-reinforcement* as the major characteristics in the instruction (or instructional materials) and their effects on student learning. Because group instruction tends to be differentially sensitive and responsive to the students in a class, we have emphasized the use of *feedback and corrective* procedures as one means of ensuring that each student gets as good quality of instruction as he needs.

In the macro-studies there is evidence that the qualities of *cues, participation, and reinforcement* can account for at least 20 percent of the variation in student learning, while in the micro-studies the evidence indicates that about 25 percent of the variation in student learning can be related to the improvement of the cues and participation through *feedback and corrective* procedures for each student.

The one quality that appears to be the strongest symptom of the entire quality of instruction is the level of participation. The literature on both the macro- and micro-studies suggests that this is the clearest indicator of the effectiveness of instruction. Thus the extent and type of participation in the learning process—an observable symptom that teachers, inspectors, and school administrators have been using from time immemorial—turns out to be the best single indicator of quality of instruction. Whether it is a resultant of the effectiveness of the cues and reinforcement or just one more variable in the quality of instruction matrix may be little more than a matter of definition.

In general, we find that students who have developed effective learning and study procedures will be less affected by variations in the quality of instruction than students who have developed less effective learning procedures. Similarly, more mature and capable learners will be least influenced by varying qualities of instruction while less mature or less capable learners will be most influenced by quality of instruction.

Stated another way, if maximum quality of instruction is provided in the early learning tasks in a series and most of the learners attain mastery of these learning tasks, something less than maximal quality of instruction appears to be needed in the later learning tasks in the series to ensure mastery of these later tasks. Thus, the generalization appears to be that students can acquire learning procedures which will enable them to learn well under less than ideal qualities of instruction.

Quality of Instruction as a Causal Variable

The evidence in this chapter of a substantial relation between quality of instruction and measures of school achievement makes it clear that instruction as we have defined it here is important in determining and influencing the students' achievement. In general, we have estimated that quality of instruction can account for at least one-fourth ($r = +.50$) of the variance on relevant cognitive achievement measures. The correlational evidence in the macro-studies supported by the experimental evidence in the micro-studies suggests that quality of instruction is a causal link in determining learning and in accounting for educational achievement.

Although the process evidence is very limited, it is believed that quality of instruction, and especially the use or absence of feedback/corrective procedures, is effective in determining the extent to which two comparable groups of students will learn well or poorly in a given set of learning situations. Thus, in the micro-studies, students who were similar at the beginning of instruction but were placed by *chance* in a mastery or non-mastery class (taught by the same teacher) became more and more differentiated in their achievement over each successive learning task as well as on the final summative achievement measures. The increasing differentiation between the two groups is suggestive of the causal effect of the instructional procedures on the student learning outcomes.

There is limited evidence in the micro-level studies on the ways in which the two groups of students became differentiated with respect to rate of learning and involvement in the learning. This evidence plus the macro-level studies on *participation* gives support to a strong inference that quality of instruction has an effect on the learning processes of students as well as on their learning outcomes.

Further research is needed to understand the causal effects of quality of instruction on cognitive development, learning processes, and affective development of students.

History of the Learner

We have suggested in Chapters 1 to 4 that we may view the history of the learner in terms of the characteristics the student brings to a particular learning task or set of learning tasks. We have also suggested that what happens to the learner within the learning task(s) also becomes part of his history—especially as it influences subsequent learning tasks. Quality of instruction as we view it is a major variable in determining the history of the learner within a particular set of learning tasks. Quality of instruction at any given time period also determines much of the future history of the learner within the schools as well as in the post-school years.

The previous history of the learner does set some limits on what he can learn in a particular set of learning tasks. However, there is evidence in this chapter that we can only determine the full limits of what the student can and will learn when we have provided qualities of instruction which are optimal for the individual learner. As we view it, it is extremely rare in schools throughout the world that an individual learner is provided with such optimal qualities of instruction. Group instruction, as presently used in most countries of the world, may approach optimal qualities of instruction for only a small proportion of students in a given class. Even when this is the case, it is likely that the majority of students in the class are paying a heavy price for the ways in which the different qualities of instruction serve the special needs of a few members of the class.

It appears to the writer that it should be possible to increase greatly the proportion of students who can be provided with optimal qualities of instruction if group instruction can make use of a feedback/corrective system which constantly corrects for the learning errors under group instruction. In effect, an individualized approach to quality of instruction must accompany group qualities of instruction if most of the learners are to learn more effectively than at present appears to be the case in countries throughout the world.

Alterability of Learning

Although entry characteristics (cognitive as well as affective) are likely to become resistant to marked change after the individual has accumulated a long history of experience with particular types of learning tasks, it is evident in this as well as in the previous chapters that there is almost no point in the individual's history when his learning character- istics cannot be altered either positively or negatively. The quality of instruction can be improved so that a larger proportion of students attain a level of mastery with consequent changes in their subsequent cognitive entry behaviors and affective entry characteristics. Similarly, very poor qualities of instruction can have negative effects on current as well as subsequent learning.

The proportion of students whose learning characteristics can be altered in a positive way is likely to be highest on the early learning tasks in a series and to be somewhat reduced the later the optimal qualities of instruction are introduced in the series. It should be stressed that each learning series does not start at the beginning of school. A new series of learning tasks may begin *each time* a fundamen- tally new school subject is introduced in the learning career of an individual student.

Who Can Learn?
We have determined who can learn (as well as who cannot learn) largely by the use of qualities of instruction which are far from optimal for the majority of learners. The previous history of the learner has been the major determiner of the learning that takes place in a given set of learning tasks. Where the quality of instruction approaches the optimal for a given learner, we would expect that the limiting effects of the previous history could be decreased while the effects of the current history (the quality of instruction provided in a particular set of learn- ing tasks) could be greatly increased.

Where "good" or optimal qualities of instruction are provided in the early learning tasks in a series, we expect that most learners would learn well—not only on these early learning tasks but also on the related subsequent tasks in the series. Such a series may, as in reading, mathematics, and other subjects, continue for a number of years of school. This expresses the view that good quality of instruction can have very powerful effects, especially when used at the beginning of a series of learning tasks. If this is provided, it is likely that a high propor- tion of the students will be able to learn well in subsequent learning tasks with less than optimal qualities of instruction.

However, even where students were not provided with such ideal qualities of instruction at the beginning of a learning series, it is highly probable that optimal qualities of instruction even at later stages in the learning series may change the affective entry characteristics as well as cognitive entry behaviors for subsequent learning tasks in the series. Where the instruction is sensitive to the student's previous history, it is likely that favorable school conditions can enable *most* students to learn well, to develop more effective learning processes, and to get increased satisfaction from their learning.

Who can learn in the schools is determined to a large extent by the conditions in the school; the quality of instruction is a major determiner of who will learn well—*the few or the many.*

6
AFFECTIVE OUTCOMES OF SCHOOL LEARNING

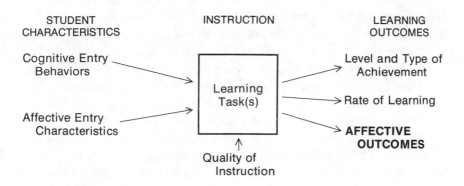

| STUDENT CHARACTERISTICS | INSTRUCTION | LEARNING OUTCOMES |

Cognitive Entry Behaviors → Learning Task(s) → Level and Type of Achievement

Affective Entry Characteristics → → Rate of Learning

↑ Quality of Instruction → **AFFECTIVE OUTCOMES**

INTRODUCTION

In the model which has been emphasized throughout the book, we have attempted to distinguish between entry characteristics and learning outcomes, at both the macro-level and the micro-level. For the most part, at the macro-level we have emphasized *achievement* as the major measurable learning outcome. At the micro-level we have emphasized *achievement,* but we have also referred to *rate of learning* and at least one type of affective outcome—*subject-related affect* (interests in and attitudes about a specific school subject and further learning of the subject).

In Chapters 4 and 7 we emphasized the role of *affect* as an entry characteristic and have shown the way in which affect as an entry characteristic changes positively with favorable learning conditions and

Note: An earlier version of this chapter was included as chapters in Block, J. H. (ed.), *Mastery Learning: Theory, and Practice.* New York: Holt, Rinehart and Winston, Inc., 1971; and Pringle, M. K. and Varma, V. P. (eds.), *Advances in Educational Psychology 2.* London: University of London Press, Ltd., 1974.

learning results. Similarly, we have shown how affect changes negatively with unfavorable learning conditions and learning results. In this chapter we propose to emphasize the affective consequences of school achievement—especially at the macro-level—because we believe they are so important in terms of their long-term consequences for both the individual and society.

We believe it is likely that some of the affective consequences develop relatively slowly. However, once they have developed, they are not easily altered in short time periods, such as those represented by the micro-level studies reported in this book. It is quite possible that especially powerful positive or negative experiences may have detectable and rapid effects on some of the affective outcomes. However, other than the detectable changes in subject-related affect, which we discuss in Chapters 4 and 7, we have no evidence in the micro-level studies of the other types of affective outcomes. Perhaps the research of the future will demonstrate that some of these more stable affective outcomes can be altered even though it may require more time and patience than we have found to be the case in affect about a new school subject.

Nevertheless, we believe the subject of the affective outcomes of school learning is important enough to justify separate treatment in a chapter by itself. While we are certain that affect as we have defined it in Chapter 4 and later in this chapter can be altered by many factors, we believe that the major factor influencing affect in the school is the student's *perception* of his competence in school learning. Since measures of school achievement are useful indicators of learning competence (no matter how accurate or biased), we believe that most of the affective consequences we deal with in this chapter are influenced directly by school achievement and especially by the student's perceptions about his school achievement.

We should remind the reader that the major point emphasized in Chapters 3 to 7 is that school achievement is alterable under a number of conditions and that under favorable learning conditions achievement may be brought to a relatively high level for most students. Thus we are contending that school achievement can be greatly improved and that perception of their competence in school learning can become very positive for almost all students. Although most of the research referred to in this chapter deals with the student's perception of his competence under existing conditions, the intent of the chapter is to emphasize the liklihood that the affective consequences of school achievement under more favorable conditions can be very different from some of the negative affective consequences reported in this chapter. These, we believe, are the effects of relatively unfavorable learning conditions in the schools.

If it is true, as we believe, that the more deep-seated types of affect develop over relatively long periods in the history of the individual as a student in the schools, it is likely that most teachers may not be entirely aware of the small positive or negative changes in affect that take place in the student during the semester or academic year they are in contact with him. Also, these changes may be so small during a particular time period that even parents and peers who are in frequent contact with the student may not be aware of the changes that are taking place. For these reasons, only skilled observers who are able to record changes over a relatively long period of several years or more may be able to note the changes as well as the factors influencing such changes. Even the student may not be fully cognizant of the fact that he did not always feel the way he now does about school and about himself. Thus, we are suggesting that many of the changes in affect that can be detected only through careful longitudinal types of research and evidence gathering may seem to most observers (and even the student himself) as though the present stage of affective characteristics were always present in the individual.

It is, then, my intent in this chapter to relate the affective characteristics of the individual to his or her presumed history as a learner and to consider affect as a major consequence of the student's perception of his or her school achievement over a number of years.

MANIFEST AND LATENT CURRICULUM

For students in the United States, school attendance is a dominant feature in their lives for a 10- to 16-year period. During this period, the student devotes at least a 40-hour week to school attendance, homework, and school-related activities (for 9 months out of the year). Thus, annually, the typical student spends about 1,500 hours on school and related activities. The student who completes secondary school has devoted almost 20,000 hours to school and related activities. It is the way in which the student and the school use this tremendous amount of time that determines school achievement and the affective consequences of such achievement.

During this long period of time in some of the most impressionable stages of the individual's development, the student is being taught at least two courses of study or curricula. One is the *manifest* curriculum of the school; the other is a curriculum which is *latent* and is based on the interactions of persons within the school.

Most visible is the *manifest* curriculum the student is expected to learn. This curriculum includes the reading, mathematics, science, literature, social studies, and other school subjects that he or she is taught. This curriculum may be of great importance to the learner because of the competence he develops, the interests and attitudes he acquires, and the career opportunities which are made available to those who learn it well. Undoubtedly, it may include important as well as trivial content. It may be taught well or it may be taught poorly. It may be meaningful to some students, and it may seem meaningless and a waste of time to others. Some of it may be remembered and used repeatedly by the learners, while some of it may be forgotten quickly and discarded. The manifest curriculum is visible; it is documented in many ways; and most of the resources and personnel of the schools are dedicated to the students' learning of this curriculum.

The second curriculum is not so clearly visible. This is the *latent* curriculum which is uniquely taught to and differently learned by each student. This is the curriculum which teaches each student who he is in relation to others. It may also teach each person his or her place in the world of people, of ideas, and of activities. While the student may learn this curriculum more slowly than the other, it is likely that he will not be able to forget it as easily as he can forget the details of history, the rules of grammar, or the specifics of any subject of study in the manifest curriculum.

Although there are many ways of viewing the latent curriculum (Dreeben, 1968; Jackson, 1968; Overly, 1970), we will confine ourselves in this chapter to those aspects of this curriculum which are most clearly related to the effects of the judgmental processes in the school. It is because of the pervasive use of relative judgments about students in the school that some aspects of the latent curriculum become observable and can be studied directly. Many other aspects of the latent curriculum may be examined only through case studies of individuals or by deep-seated and complex psychological, sociological, and anthropological methods of study.

In the many hours of school attendance and schoolwork pointed up on page 141, there are few hours in which the student is not judged (relative to others) by teachers, peers, family, and others. Likewise, there are few school hours in which the student is not *judging himself* against the standards set by himself, by the teacher, by peers, and by his family. Nowhere else in his career as a worker, member of a family, citizen, or person engaging in leisure-time activities will he be judged so frequently by others and, it is possible, judged by himself. In most of these post-school activities, the individual is expected to meet some minimal standards of competence or behavior. If he does so, he is usually not judged in more detailed terms. For example, the majority of adult workers are expected to meet some minimal standard of work— usually relatively low—and are only rarely judged relative to others.

In school, the likelihood is that each student will be judged many times each day in terms of his adequacy relative to others in his class, group, or school. No matter how well he does, if others do better, he must come to know it and to place himself accordingly. No matter how poorly he does, if others do less well, he also comes to know it. Obviously, these relative judgments arise because almost all the student's school learning is as a member of a group probably of the order of twenty-five to thirty-five members. Also, these judgments are made so frequently because the schools have for so long stressed competition as a primary motivational technique. Only rarely are the judgments in school based on some criterion of adequate work or learning independent of relative performance among the students. Relative rather than absolute norms are the bases for most judgments.

Furthermore, because of the consistency of the learning tasks from one year to another, and because of the sequential nature of many of the learning tasks in a subject or field, the student who moves from one task to the next tends to remain in much the same relative position to other students (providing he remains with the same group of students or with representatives of much the same sample of students) from one year to the next. The increasing stability of school marks and test performance is well documented in the longitudinal research summarized by Bloom (1964), Bracht and Hopkins (1972), Hicklin (1962), and Payne (1963).

We believe it possible to understand some of the affective consequences of school achievement more clearly if we consider the learning task as the basic unit. As was pointed out in Chapter 2, a learning task may be thought of as requiring about one to ten hours of instruction or learning activity on the part of a student. In an academic year, a student may encounter about 150 separable learning tasks. And, over a 10-year period of school, he may encounter 1,500 separable learning tasks.

However, in the student's perception, there are really not that many separable learning tasks. Each task is not completely isolated from every other one in his view, nor is it so isolated in the teacher's view. The student comes to perceive the learning tasks in a subject or course of study as all having somewhat the same characteristics.

The curriculum and textbook makers and the teachers attempt to organize learning tasks by subjects or fields of content and then arrange the learning tasks in a sequential or logical order. Thus, in arithmetic, at the 3rd-grade level, there may be about twenty-five learning tasks arranged in a sequence that someone believes appropriate from a logical, instructional, or learning point of view. Similarly, other subjects, such as reading, language arts, science, or social studies, are also composed of learning tasks arranged in some order.

SUBJECT-RELATED AFFECT

In a subject, then, the student encounters the first learning task in a series of such tasks. He is instructed as to what to do, he is provided with instructional material, he is expected to make the appropriate efforts, and he is judged by the teacher on how well he succeeded in this learning task. Typically the student may be given some quantitative index by the teacher, such as a mark or grade, on his achievement over the learning task. Frequently he may be given some qualitative judgment or appraisal by the teacher on his work over the task. In addition, the student may judge his own success on the task by inferring whether the teacher approves or disapproves of him and his work on the task. The student may also infer how well he accomplished the task by the degree of confidence he has in the work he did, the questions he answered, or the procedures he used in responding to it. However he comes to know it, the student has a rough idea of his accomplishment of the task.

If the student secures evidence that he did the first task superbly, he is likely to approach the next task in the series with a bit more enthusiasm and confidence. If he secures evidence that he did the first task very badly, he is likely to approach the next task in the series with somewhat less enthusiasm than he approached the first task.

And so the student progresses from task to task. For each task, he secures some simple judgment about the adequacy of his performance from the teacher, himself, or both. For the most part, these judgments on each task are not made public, and a student may entertain the delusion that he is doing better or worse than he really is.

At various stages in a series of learning tasks, the grades or marks are partly made public—at least to the parents. It is here that the student may have difficulty in reconciling the report of his marks with his own more private impressions of the adequacy of his performance on each of the tasks in the subject. Especially if the mark is lower than he expected, he may believe the teacher was in error; that the test or other evidence on which the mark was based was not accurate, valid, or fair; or that the teacher was unfair and/or did not like him. Since his reported marks are more public, they are likely to have a somewhat greater effect on the student than the more private day-to-day judgments about the adequacy of performance on each of the learning tasks in the series. Marks at the end of the term or year are likely to have an even greater effect than marks given at various stages during the term. In general, the more public and official the judgments (or marks), the greater the effect they are likely to have on the student's perception of his adequacy in the subject.

Over a long series of learning tasks in a particular subject, the student comes to secure many judgments of his performance and capability with this class of learning tasks. With some variations from task to task, and with many corrections imposed on his private judgments by the more public appraisals of his performance, he comes to see his capability with this type of task as high, moderate, or low. Since he is likely to get one or more years of a particular type of task, and probably of the order of about twenty-five tasks of a particular type in a year, he is, sooner or later, forced to accept some judgment about his capability with this group of learning tasks.

If the same type of learning task (e.g., arithmetic, reading, or social studies) is used for 4 to 6 years, the student may have experiences with as many as 100 to 150 learning tasks of a particular type. Because of the similarity in the types of learning tasks, the sequential nature of many of them, and the student's gradual structuring of his aspirations and approach to and views of the tasks, there is likely to be a high relation between the adequacy-inadequacy of his performance over several years or terms. That is, the student gradually acquires a consistent performance as the tasks accumulate in larger numbers.

As these performances and the student's perceptions of them accumulate and become more consistent, his motivations for the next tasks in the series take on a stable quality. If his performance has been adequate, he approaches the next task with confidence and assurance that he can do it well. He may even develop a desire for more such tasks—they are easy to do, they can be learned, and they may even be likeable tasks because they can be mastered, solved, learned, or overcome. If his performance has been inadequate over a large number of tasks of a particular type, the student comes to believe in his inadequacy with respect to this type of learning. He approaches the next tasks in the series with marked reluctance. He expects the worst and is prepared for it. If it is painful enough, the task is avoided, approached with little enthusiasm and, if anything, marked dislike. Where the student is convinced of his inadequacy, he finds no great energy to accomplish the next task, has little patience or perseverance when he encounters difficulties, and takes little care and thoroughness in accomplishing the task (White, 1959; Atkinson & Feather, 1966).

Subject-related affect in a subject or category of learning tasks may be defined behaviorally in terms of whether or not the individual would *voluntarily* engage in additional learning tasks of this type if free to make such a choice. Subject-related affect may also be defined more subjectively in terms of the individual's liking, enthusiasm, view, preference, and desire. Here we are taking the position that the student's subjective feelings about a subject or set of learning tasks are much influenced by his *perceptions* of his adequacy or inadequacy with such tasks. In turn, his perceptions of adequacy or inadequacy are based on his previous history with such tasks and especially the previous judgments about his learning of these tasks.

Studies on the relation between achievement and measures of subject-related affect have been reported for various school subjects in Chapter 4. In general, the correlations are between +.20 and +.40, suggesting statistically, at least, that the relations are most clear for extreme students on achievement (or affect).

In Chart 6-1 we have attempted to show the longitudinal development of subject-related affect for students who were successful or unsuccessful in achievement in mathematics. It will be noted that by the end of the third year of school, the students who were in the top fifth or bottom fifth of their classes in the achievement distribution (grades) are already quite different in their affect toward mathematics. There are small changes in the subject-related affect for these extreme students after the third year of school, but it is apparent that the major developments have already taken place before the school years for which we have data in this chart.

This chart is for the extreme students only and, as such, reveals greatest differences between students. Thus, while we are suggesting

Chart 6–1. Subject Affect in Mathematics Over Years
of Schooling for Successful and Unsuccessful Students
in Mathematics Achievement

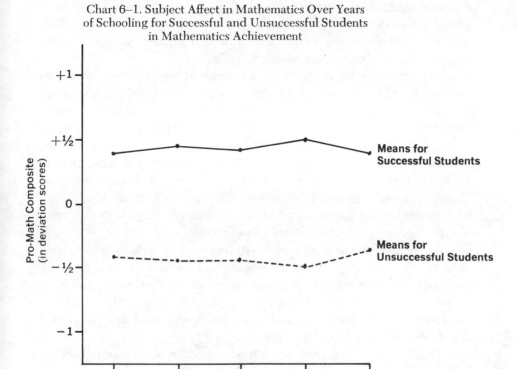

*Subject affect was measured approximately concurrent with grades at the end of the indicated year.

NOTE: Successful students were in the upper fifth on teacher's grades in mathematics, while unsuccessful students were in the lower fifth on the same criterion.

SOURCE: Adapted from Crosswhite (1972).

that there is a linear relation between evidence on achievement and the student's subject-related affect, we are also maintaining that the effect of differential achievement over a number of years in a school subject may be seen most clearly in the extreme students. A somewhat lesser effect would be anticipated (but not demonstrated here) for the students who fall between these extremes.

It should be pointed out that, although this chart appears to emphasize the effects of achievement on affect, it is likely that the phenomenon is an interactive one in which perception of achievement influences affect and affect, in turn, influences further achievement. However, our main point in this chapter is that there is an increasing differentiation of students in both achievement and affect and that over a long period or sequence of learning tasks the student develops affect related to the school subject which influences further interaction with and learning of that subject in the schools.

In summary, each of the tasks in a series of learning tasks comes to take on a special meaning for the student which is related to his sense of adequacy in accomplishing previous tasks in the series. The student's confidence in himself with respect to the type of task is enhanced or reduced by his perception of his performance over the previous tasks. Eventually, the student's prophecy for the next task in the series, based on his previous perceptions of success or failure, becomes fulfilled. Under extreme conditions, we can imagine a few individual students who resist accepting adequacy or inadequacy as their lot with this type of task, but even they cannot hold out forever.

We believe this general result will be found in each subject or type of learning experience. An accumulation of experiences with learning tasks regarded as similar or in the same category of tasks (as perceived by the student) gradually becomes stabilized for the student, and he comes to view the next task in the series (or the subject as a whole) positively, negatively, or indifferently.

This assumes that the definition of adequacy or inadequacy is based on the local situation—the school, the teachers' marking schemes, and the student's performances relative to other students in the same class. It is likely that for some few students, perceptions of adequacy or inadequacy are based on a siblinglike rivalry with a few other students in the school or class or with an actual sibling. Under these conditions, for a student to be slightly below his rival may be catastrophic, while to be slightly above may appear to him to be success. However, these are individual cases. For the most part, adequacy or inadequacy for most students is defined in terms of their standing in the upper or lower portion of the local distribution of marks.

We are thus postulating a causal relationship between clear indications of adequacy or inadequacy in learning a particular type of learning task and affect about that type of learning task. Given freedom to continue learning more tasks in the series, a high proportion of those who perceive themselves as inadequate over the previous learning tasks in the series will avoid further learning tasks of this type. In contrast, a high proportion of those who perceive themselves as very adequate will choose to learn more tasks of this type. However, with increasing age and maturity, the choices of those who perceive themselves as adequate are likely to be based on the meaningfulness of the task and its relevance to their overall desires and plans for the future. Such students have many possibilities open to them, and they will increasingly make decisions on other criteria than school-learning success alone.

Thus subject-related affect is, in our view, largely a perceptual phenomenon based on the way in which students classify learning tasks and based on the judgments they make of the adequacy of their performance relative to the other students in the school or class they attend. What we are stating here has consequences for further efforts at learning the particular subject or type of learning tasks. Indications of inadequacy over a series of learning tasks are effective in reducing further desires, interests, or motivation for this type of task. Such indications have important effects on career choice, choice of educational specialization, and even on the avocational use of a school subject or area of learning (Husén, 1967, 1969).

Success (or adequacy) in a school subject opens it up for further consideration and use. In contrast, failure (or inadequacy) in a school subject may effectively close this subject for further consideration. The system of grading and instruction operates to open doors for some students while effectively closing doors for others—and this system is independent of success or failure in any absolute sense. It is dependent on local definitions of success or failure relative to other students in the class or school.

SCHOOL-RELATED AFFECT

So far, we have been discussing a series of learning tasks which the student perceives as members of a single category. We considered the effect of a stabilizing picture of success and failure on the interests and attitudes the student develops for this type of task and his willingness to voluntarily engage in more learning tasks of the same or related type.

If we then turn to other learning tasks which the student is getting at the same time as the tasks in any particular subject, we can also ask about the effects of evidence of adequacy or inadequacy. Thus, in a single school year, the student may study as many as five or six school subjects and may encounter as many as 150 different learning tasks. As he encounters each of these tasks, he has a sense of adequacy or inadequacy about his learning of each. These impressions are corroborated or altered by marks assigned by teachers at various marking periods. As these various indices accumulate, over many learning tasks and over a number of years, the student begins to generalize about his adequacy or inadequacy with school learning tasks. If his experiences are positive (that is, the results are generally adequate), he is likely to develop a generally positive view about school and school learning. If the results are generally negative and his learning is regarded as inadequate by the student, his teachers, and his parents, he is likely to develop a negative view about school and school learning.

By school-related affect we mean a general disposition to regard the school and school learning in a positive or negative way. We are here treating school-related affect as more general than subject-related affect. If the student develops a negative (or positive) affect toward school, this affect may include the school subjects, the teachers and staff, and even the whole idea of school and school learning.

We believe that different amounts of failure (or success) may be needed for different students to develop this negative or positive affect toward school. However, we believe that this is only a matter of degree, and that all individuals who accumulate experiences of failure (or success) to some point (which varies from individual to individual) will develop negative or positive affect toward school.

Many studies have been done on the relation between school achievement and school-related affect. Some examples of such studies are those reported by Flemming (1925), Khan (1969), Khan and Weiss (1973), Kurtz and Swenson (1951), Michael, Baker, and Jones (1964), and Russell (1969). Especially for students who are extremes on school achievement, there is a relation between positive and negative school affect and indications of adequacy or inadequacy in school achievement. It is evident in some of these studies that relatively strong affect has been developed in many students by the end of the elementary period of schooling.

In Chart 6-2 we have summarized the development of affect toward school (and reading) over the 3rd to the 12th year of school for students who were in the top and bottom fifth on a national test of reading achievement. Ideally, we should have had an overall index of school achievement, but could not find an appropriate longitudinal study for this purpose. We are using reading achievement as an approximation of general school achievement (Bloom, 1974a). It will be noted that students in the top and bottom fifths of the achievement distribution are already quite different in their affect toward the school by the end of the 3rd year of school. While there is further differentiation in affect up to the 9th year of school, the changes after the primary school period are relatively small. We believe the early stabilization of school-related affect is likely to be the effect of the large number of learning tasks and

Chart 6–2. Affect Toward School Over Years of Schooling
for Successful and Unsuccessful Students in Reading Achievement

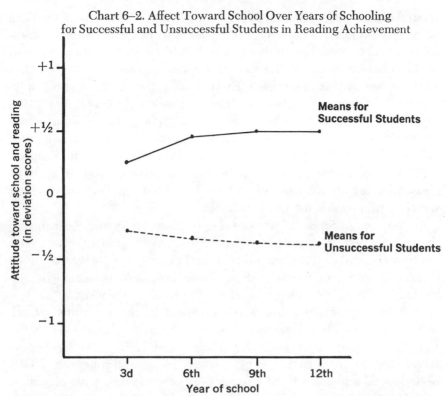

NOTE: Successful students were in the upper fifth on reading test scores, while unsuccessful students were in the lower fifth on the same criterion. This chart is based on the total white population in Coleman's study of students at different grade levels.

SOURCE: Adapted from Coleman (1966b).

the many experiences of success or failure the student has had. Thus, in our view, the student by the end of the 6th grade has encountered as many as 800 to 900 learning tasks which he views as school tasks.

We believe that the degree of certainty of school-related affect is likely to be somewhat greater for the negative attitudes and views than it is for the positive attitudes and views. While indications of success in school are likely to result in positive affect toward it, other variables may enter in to determine whether the school and school learning is viewed as positive and favorable (e.g., values of parents, peer-group attitudes, and meaningfulness of schooling for the individual's career aspirations).

However, the negative attitudes and views about school and school learning are much more generalized than the negative attitudes and interests toward a specific subject or type of learning task. Subject-related affect is specific, and while it generalizes to a class of learning tasks, it need not extend beyond the members of the category. School-related affect generalizes to the whole institution of the school, to most of the school subjects, to the staff of the school, and even to the other students who attend the school. Emphasizing the negative affect only, repeated evidence of inadequacy in school makes the entire institution the source of the individual's sense of inadequacy, and he must avoid the institution or find some way of reducing the amount of pain it gives to him. This he does by retreating, attacking, or minimizing its effect on him. Such negative attitudes, if developed fully enough, may have consequences for all later efforts to do school learning or learning which is in any way related to schools.

The consequence of school-related affect for further learning in the schools is relatively clear. If much of school-related affect is developed by the end of the elementary school period, it is likely that much of later learning in the school has been largely determined by the student's view of the school developed in these early years.

But even more important is the effect of the student's school-related affect on his willingness to learn in his post-school years. In the UNESCO report *Learning to Be* (Faure et al., 1972), the position is taken that in modern societies further learning throughout life is regarded as a major adaptive mechanism for dealing with change—whether the change be in the area of work or in the larger developments in the society. If negative attitudes toward school and school learning have been developed, these have serious consequences for the individual's use of further learning as an adaptive method of dealing with his own problems as an adult as well as in part determining the life-style and response to the many changes likely to take place in the society in which he lives.

ACADEMIC SELF-CONCEPT

In both subject-related affect and school-related affect, the object of the affect is *outside* the individual. The student develops positive affect toward a school subject, or he develops negative affect toward a school subject (or something in between). He develops positive affect toward school and school learning or he develops negative affect toward school and school learning (or something in between). While there is a difference in generality between these two types of affect as we have defined them, in both, the *object* of the affect is external to the individual.

If this process of adequate or inadequate appraisals with regard to learning tasks is generalized over a large number of tasks over a number of years, eventually the object of appraisal for the student becomes partially shifted from the school subjects or the school to the *self*.

For the individual to work and study in an environment in which the majority of learning tasks over a period of years is accompanied by self-appraisals and external appraisals as adequate, is to develop in the individual a general sense of adequacy—at least in connection with school activities. Similarly, if most of the encounters with learning tasks are accompanied by appraisals of inadequacy, the individual is likely to develop a deep sense of inadequacy in connection with school activities.

While we recognize that some individuals may need more successful-unsuccessful learning experiences before they come to accept a particular view of themselves, we believe this is only a matter of degree. Given a sufficient number of unsuccessful learning experiences, almost everyone must eventually succumb to an acceptance of a self view about learning which is negative or inadequate. Similarly for the successful encounters with learning experiences, given enough of them, one must eventually come to a positive view of oneself as a learner.

We do not believe that a few successful or unsuccessful experiences have a major effect on the academic self-concept. In fact, it is possible that occasional unsuccessful experiences which can be turned by the individual into successful experiences may be of special significance in strengthening the individual's self image. However, it is the frequency and consistency of adequacy or inadequacy over a period of years which has its major effects on the academic self-concept.

We do not know what level of objective success or failure will be interpreted by the individual as success or failure. But, in general, we believe that to be in the top third or top fifth of his class group (grades of A and B) over a number of years in a variety of school subjects is likely to be interpreted by the student as adequate or as success. Also, to be in the bottom third or fifth of his class group (grades of D and F) over a number of years must leave the individual with a negative self-view—at least in the academic area.

One study which attempted to test this hypothesis about the continued effect of success or lack of success on academic self-concept was done by Kifer (1973). He selected students who were in the upper fifth as well as students who were in the lowest fifth of their classes in grades 1 to 2, grades 1 to 4, grades 1 to 6, and grades 1 to 8. He gave these students an adaptation of the Brookover Test of Self-Concept of Ability (academic self-concept). The students were in three schools in a middle-class suburb of Chicago. Kifer was attempting to study the development of academic self-concept by a quasi-longitudinal method.

The results of the study are summarized in Chart 6-3. Here it may be seen that the students in grades 1 to 2 are almost the same in their average self-concept of ability, even though one group received the top fifth of teachers' marks for two years while the other group was at the bottom fifth of teachers' marks over these two years. The two achievement groups become more distinct in their self-concept of ability by grade 4, even more by grade 6, and by grade 8 they are very different in their average self-concept of ability. Although similar research is needed in which the *same* students are followed in a true longitudinal design over eight years, the evidence provided by Kifer leaves the strong inference that self-concept of ability is in large part dependent

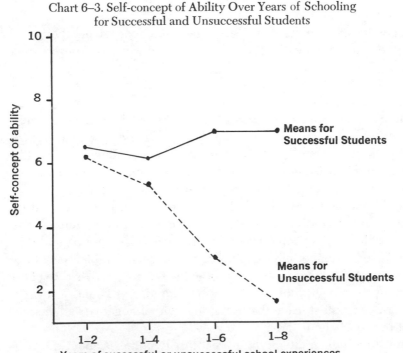

Chart 6–3. Self-concept of Ability Over Years of Schooling for Successful and Unsuccessful Students

NOTE: Successful students were in the upper fifth on teacher's grades, while unsuccessful students were in the lower fifth on the same criterion.

SOURCE: Adapted from Kifer (1973).

on the students' perception of their relative achievement (teachers' marks) over these critical years in the elementary–junior high school period.

Torshen (1969) in summarizing a number of studies found that the average relation between academic self-concept and school achievement (teachers' marks) measured at different grade levels is about +.50. In Chapter 4 of this book a similar set of results have been reported. In Torshen's own study she found a correlation of +.46 between students' marks at the grade 5 level and their academic self-concept. Kifer (1973) also related self-concept of ability (similar to Torshen's academic self-concept) to teachers' marks for samples of students at the 5th and 7th grade. He found a correlation of +.23 for his 5th grade sample and a correlation of +.50 for his 7th grade sample. While the results for the 5th grade are lower than usually found, the tendency for higher correlations to be found with increased number of years of school is present here.

It is evident in these studies that the academic self-concept is relatively clearly defined by the end of the primary school period. The magnitude of these correlations indicate that, for the extreme students (upper and lower fifth) on academic achievement, the relations between academic self-concept and school achievement are very strong, with little overlap in academic self-concept between these extreme groups. These estimates are supported by Kifer's results as summarized in Chart 6-3.

It is probable that occasional individuals who are in the lower third or fifth of their class may take some comfort in the fact that a few members of their class are in even worse academic shape, but this is probably of little comfort over a long period of time. So too, some individuals may be depressed that a few members of their class are slightly higher than they are, but again we believe that to be in the top third or fifth of their class will eventually be interpreted in a positive way by most students in this group.

It is the middle group of students who may be least affected by their school achievement insofar as academic self-concept may be concerned. They are given enough positive evidence of their adequacy to balance the negative evidence, or at least they can take some comfort that they are more adequate than a sizable proportion of their peers. Undoubtedly, they must turn to other areas of activity and to other aspects of themselves to find more positive signs of their personal worth and adequacy.

In taking these views, we are assuming that each individual seeks desperately for some positive signs of his own adequacy and worth. If these indications are denied in one area, the individual must seek other areas in which he can find such indications.

In the work of Sears (1963) in measuring self concept, there are a number of areas in which an individual may appraise himself. Some of these may be clearly classified as *academic* self-concept, such as learning, school subjects, work habits, and relations with the teacher. Others which may be classified as *nonacademic* self-concept have to do with self-appraisals with regard to athletics, relations with boys and girls, relations with others, and appearance (Torshen, 1969).

There is a low but positive relation between these two large categories of self-concept. Torshen found a correlation of +.35 at grade 5, while Kifer, using somewhat different measures of general self-esteem and academic self-concept, found correlations of +.31 and +.35 at grades 5 and 7. Kifer also observed in his quasi-longitudinal study of successful and unsuccessful students (as judged by teachers' marks) that the general self-esteem of the successful students remained relatively high over the 8 years of school, while the general self-esteem of the unsuccessful students dropped markedly from grade 4 to grade 6 and was still low by the end of grade 8.

The evidence suggests that individuals who are low in *academic self-concept* may be high, average, or low in *nonacademic self-concept*. It is likely that individuals who are low in both are in great difficulty, and we estimate from the correlations that this may be true for up to one-half of the students who are low in academic self-concept.

It is possible for some individuals who are low in academic self-concept to get considerable comfort from a positive nonacademic self-concept. However, the academic self-concept is important in its own right as determining whether or not the individual will voluntarily engage in school-related learning when he is free to do so. Also, a low academic self-concept increases the probability that an individual will have a negative general self-concept.

We believe that the individual who is denied positive reassurance of his worth in school is impelled to seek positive reassurance of his worth wherever he can find it. If society offers him opportunities for work which are satisfying and rewarding financially as well as otherwise, the individual can find positive indications of self-worth here. However, in a highly developed society like the United States, negative indications of school achievement (including school dropouts) are likely to provide serious barriers against securing skilled or higher occupational employment. Some individuals must turn to less socially approved areas (e.g., gangs, illicit activities) to find the rewards and self-approval denied them in school and school-related activities.

In summary, successful experiences in school are likely to result in a positive academic self-concept and increase the probabilities of a positive general self-concept. Unsuccessful experiences in school are likely to result in a negative academic self-concept and increase the probabilities that the individual will develop a negative general self-concept. But the individual strives desperately to secure some assurance of his self worth, and if he is denied it in one area, he will search for it elsewhere. The likelihood of his finding it is considerably decreased by consistent lack of success in the school.

MENTAL HEALTH

An individual develops a positive self regard and a strong ego by continual evidence of his adequacy—especially in early childhood and in the periods of latency (age 6 to 11) and adolescence. Since the school period (ages 6 to 18) occupies these latter two periods, we regard continual evidence of success or failure in the school as likely to have major effects on the individual's mental health.

While mental health and self concept cannot be sharply distinguished, we may think of mental health as concerned more directly with ego development, with reduction in general anxiety, and with the ability to take stress and frustration with a minimum of debilitating affect.

There is considerable empirical support for relating the individual's perception of his adequacy in school learning to the development of related interests, attitudes, and academic self-concept. When we turn to mental health, we must be more *speculative* because of the difficulties in defining and measuring it. Moreover, there is only limited research which directly relates adequacy in school learning to mental health. Some support for these speculations may be drawn from a longitudinal study by Stringer and Glidewell (1967) which related the academic progress of elementary school pupils to indications of mental illness. A more recent study by Torshen (1969) of the relation between teachers' grades, self-concepts, and indications of mental health gives some further support to these ideas. However, the crucial empirical test of these hypotheses has not been done (at least to this writer's satisfaction).

If the school environment provides the individual with evidence of his adequacy over a number of years, especially in the first few years of school supported by consistent success over the next four or five years, we believe that this is likely to provide a type of *immunization* against mental illness for an indefinite period of time. Such an individual should be able to surmount crises and periods of great stress without suffering too much. His own sense of adequacy and his personal and technical skills (some learned in school) should enable him to use realistic methods in surmounting these crisis situations.

It is not likely that all students in the upper third of their classes in school achievement would secure this ego strengthening from adequacy in school learning. However, we believe this may be true for up to two-thirds of students in the upper third of their classes (i.e., over 20 percent of students). We are not quite sure why the other one-third should lack this immunization. Probably some of these are compulsive students who achieve school success at great personal cost. Perhaps, also, some of these are highly competitive students who make school grades and competition with others more central than the learning represented by these grades. Perhaps, also, some of these are overly docile students who lose independence by conforming overly much to the demands of adults (parents, teachers) without developing their own personal goals.

At the other extreme are the bottom third of the students who have been given consistent evidence of their inadequacy in the school learning environment over a period of 5 to 10 years. Such students rarely secure any positive reinforcement in the classroom and are unlikely to secure positive rewards from teachers or parents. We would expect such students to be infected with emotional difficulties arising from the rarity with which they can secure any sense of adequacy in the school environment and especially in the classroom. There must be an increasing spiral in which some difficulty in learning at one point becomes exaggerated at a later point with gradually a sense that there is nothing one can do right in such a situation.

From this, we would expect that up to two-thirds of the students in the bottom third of their classes (about 20 percent of students) over a period of years should exhibit symptoms of acute distress and alienation from the world of school and adults. Again, we can only speculate about how and why some students can escape from the infection likely to result from a deep sense of inadequacy in school. Some students must be able to secure a strong and positive sense of adequacy in their work, with their peers, and from their parents to compensate for the effects of the school. Others may find it possible to reject the school experiences as irrelevant to their own goals, or they may regard the judgments of the school as unfair and thus escape from the effect of what would otherwise be negative experiences and judgments.

For students in both the upper and lower extremes, we would expect the effects to be most pronounced when the parents are most interested and concerned about the educational achievement of their children. When the parents' educational aspirations for their children are high, they will reward achievement and punish lack of achievement. Under such conditions, the reward and punishment system of the school is paralleled by the reward and punishment system of the home. For such children the affective consequences of school achievement should be far greater than when the home has a different basis for reward and punishment than does the school.

We would also expect that the effects of failure in the cognitive learnings in the school would be minimized when the school includes many types of learning and activity which have relatively low relations to the more academic cognitive types of learning (i.e., athletics, social activity, art, music, vocational instruction). Under such conditions, it is likely that a high proportion of students can experience some degree of success in some school-related activities and thus escape from a complete sense of failure in connection with the school.

The speculations and hypotheses on the preceding pages may be derived from such work as White (1959) on competence motivation, Erikson (1963) on stages in development, and Bower (1962) in his review of research on mental health in education. In spite of the speculative nature of this section of the chapter, the suggestive research already done, the theoretical work of child development specialists, and the experiences of psychiatric and psychological workers give indications in the direction spelled out here. The extreme importance of this area for the individual and the society makes it necessary that these speculations and hypotheses be the subject of more definitive research.

SUMMARY

In this chapter we have attempted to point up some of the affective consequences of school achievement and the student's perception of his adequacy in school learning. Although we recognize that the student's affect about school learning influences his school achievement and in turn that his school achievement influences his affect about school learning, we have chosen to emphasize what we believe to be the causal effect of school achievement on the affective consequences for the student.

The relation between the student's perception of his adequacy in a particular subject and his affect toward that subject after a number of years is relatively clear. Success or lack of success in a school subject eventually is a major force in determining how the student feels about the subject and his desire to learn more about that subject.

The relation between the student's perception of his adequacy in school over a number of years and his affect toward the school and school learning is also relatively clear. Success or lack of success in school learning eventually is a major force in determining how the student feels about school and school learning and his desire for further learning in school, college, or out-of-school in the adult years.

We also considered the effect of the student's perception of his adequacy in school learning on his view of himself as a learner (academic self-concept) as well as on his general view of himself (general self-concept). The evidence is quite clear that, with time, the student tends to develop an academic self-concept which reflects his perception of his adequacy in the school learning tasks. Successful and unsuccessful students develop very different academic self-concepts.

While the evidence is not equally strong, there are indications that the two kinds of self-concept (academic self-concept and general self-concept) are related and that a low academic self-concept will, under some conditions, be accompanied by a relatively low general self-concept. The first is clearly influenced by the adequacy of the school learning, while the second is, we believe, influenced by the school learning as well as many other factors in the individual's life experiences.

Finally, we have speculated about the ways in which the adequacy of school learning may influence the individual's mental health. While we have put forth our speculations in relatively strong form, we believe that much further research will be needed before the possible causal relations between adequacy in school learning and mental health will be understood.

7

SUMMARY OF THE PARTS OF THE THEORY AND THEIR INTERRELATIONS IN SELECTED STUDIES

INTRODUCTION

In Chapters 3, 4, and 5 we have attempted to study the separate effects of Cognitive Entry Behaviors, Affective Entry Characteristics, and Quality of Instruction on student learning.

The separate analysis of these three variables is of value in searching for some of the causes of learning difficulties in school situations—and especially in group learning situations. If the Quality of Instruction is low, then much can be done to improve the situation, and when this has been done, the differential results between the improved and the previous learning situation should approach the levels we have suggested in Chapter 5. The achievement of students under ideal or optimal instructional conditions should be higher and the variability of the group should be less than a comparable group of students under less favorable conditions of instruction. Similarly, if the necessary Cognitive Entry Behaviors are provided to the students before a learning task or course, then again under the improved situation the learning should be higher and the variability of the group should be less than that a group of students who lack the essential cognitive entry behaviors (see Chapter 3). Finally, if the students can come to regard the new learning in a more positive way (positive Affective Entry Characteristics), then their achievement should be higher and their variation in learning under these improved conditions should be less than that of a group of students who have negative affective entry characteristics (see Chapter 4).

All of this is to state that when each of these variables is treated *separately*, the theory gives an approximation of the effects on learning that can be expected *if* the treatment is effective. But educators, except for research purposes, are not interested in isolating one variable from another. Education deals with the child as a whole and ideally attempts to provide effective conditions for the learning in the school or elsewhere. The educators are interested in doing everything they can to improve, by whatever means are available to them, the learning of all the students in their care.

If these variables are *alterable* as we have maintained in Chapters 3, 4, and 5, then the educator wishes to alter *all* the variables under his control, rather than one at a time. If he cannot alter all three simultaneously, then he would like to determine what is likely to occur if he could alter two of them or, in the final case, only one of them. It should be recognized at the outset that these three variables interact with each other and that when they do, the final achievement results will not reflect the simple addition of the effects of Cognitive Entry plus Affective Entry plus Quality of Instruction. Thus, if Quality of Instruction (Q of I) is effective, it should alter Cognitive Entry Behaviors (CEB) as well as Affective Entry Characteristics (AEC) over time, and this should be reflected in the final achievement means and variances. Similarly, if CEB is altered, it should simultaneously alter AEC as well as improve the student's ability to learn *in spite* of relatively poor quality of instruction. The interactive effect of these three variables should increase the student's level of learning and reduce the final variability of the student's achievement, but it will be quite rare for them to reduce the variability to zero as might be expected if these were truly separable variables.

The task of this chapter is to determine some of the combined effects of two or more of the variables in this theory of school learning and to contrast the empirical results with some theoretical values we believe to be possible. The evidence will largely be drawn from the micro-studies we have reported on in the previous chapters. However, in addition we will refer to a few selected macro-studies which yield approximations to our theoretical values.

In this chapter, we will also attempt to describe some of the underlying learning processes as influenced by the variables in this theory of school learning and then analyze the results of the micro-studies in terms of these learning processes.

THE MODEL AND THEORETICAL ESTIMATES

Achievement Variation in School Settings

In Chart 7-1, we have indicated three possible sets of distributions of school achievement in the elementary grades. The first set (A) is what we typically observe in a subject like reading or arithmetic. At the end of the second grade there is considerable variation in the distribution of achievement. This variation increases each year until by the end of grade 6, it may be approximately doubled. While some of this increased variation may be ascribed to the nature of the measurements and to the increased precision of achievement measurement in the higher grades, few would doubt that increased variation in student achievement is a real phenomenon that will not go away merely by improving our measurements.

Chart 7–1.

Some Possible Distributions of School Achievement

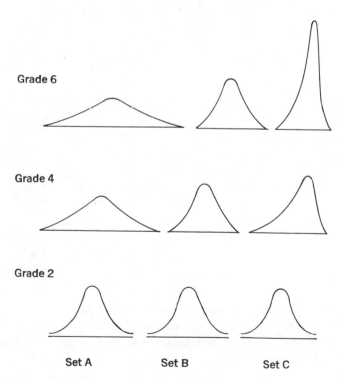

Grade 6

Grade 4

Grade 2

Set A   Set B   Set C

Quite in contrast to the first set is a theoretical set of curves (B) in which the variation in achievement remains constant from grade to grade. It is possible that a few schools or classes may be found with results like this, but these are likely to be rare instances. Such curves might be expected if there is considerable stability of general intelligence and other relevant aptitudes during the ages 6 to 12, and if the school or homes do a very good job of helping individual learners whenever they encounter special difficulties in the learning. Such curves should not be too difficult to produce if a school staff deliberately sought to achieve the student learning suggested by them.

But the third set (C), in which the variation decreases each year until by the 6th grade it is only a fraction of the variation in the 2nd grade, is something that is rarely encountered. And yet, this is precisely the change in distributions that we believe is possible both theoretically and practically. Although we have not found or produced curves like these over a six-year school period, studies of both mastery learning and control classes in particular courses or subjects yield curves over a semester or year like sets C and A (that is, for decreasing variation in achievement over time in the mastery learning classes and, in contrast, increasing variation over time in the control classes).

How is this accomplished in a single course and what are the underlying variables that account for such vastly different pictures of student achievement?

In Chart 7-2, we have sketched a sequence of ten learning units. Think of these as the chapters or units in a course, such as arithmetic, algebra, physics, chemistry, or even a second language. Think of these as a highly sequential set of units such that unit 5 could not be learned before unit 2 or 3, while a high level of competence in unit 1 is required if unit 2 is to be learned adequately, and so on throughout the sequence. Assume also that if a student does not learn a unit adequately at the time it is taught, he cannot learn (or relearn) it at a later time.

Now, under condition A, let us assume that 90 percent of the students learn unit 1 adequately, while 10 percent do not. Under the assumptions indicated in the foregoing paragraph, these 10 percent will not learn any of the later units (2 to 10) adequately because unit 1 is basic to all that follows. Let us assume that while 90 percent of students learned unit 1 adequately, some of these will not learn unit 2 adequately. Similarly, for each additional unit, it is assumed that additional students fall by the wayside until by unit 10 only 10 percent learn it adequately, while 90 percent do not. If these students are then given a

Chart 7–2.

Student Achievement under Two Conditions

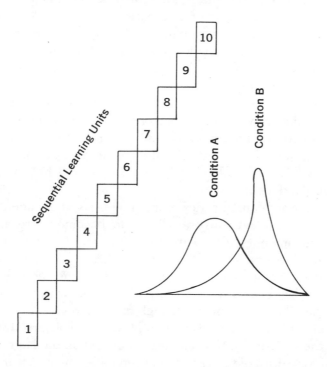

summative test in which all ten units are equally represented, the curve of achievement is likely to approximate a normal distribution with considerable individual variation.

Under condition B, let us also assume that 90 percent of the students learn unit 1 adequately while 10 percent do not. But, under condition B, these 10 percent are then helped (outside of regular class time) until at least 5 percent or more have achieved adequate learning of unit 1. The proportion of students with adequate learning of unit 1 will now reach 95 percent (the original 90 percent plus the additional 5 percent) before they enter unit 2. Assume that this process is repeated on each unit and the goal is always to have 95 percent of the students achieve adequate learning of a unit before embarking on the next unit in the sequence. Using the same summative examination as in condition A, we should find that over 90 percent of the students under condition B reach about the same level of achievement as the top 10 percent of the students under condition A. The two distributions will be roughly as indicated in Chart 7-2. Under these assumed situations, the distribution of achievement for condition A resembles curve A for grade 6 in Chart 7-1, while the distribution of achievement for condition B resembles curve C at grade 6 in the same chart.

There is no doubt that students under condition B (the mastery learning condition) are provided with more time and help than is available to the students under condition A. What has been especially exciting in the actual research on mastery learning is the shift in amount of time and help required at each of the units in a course as depicted in Chart 7-2. In the early units there may be great variation in the amount of time and help required to bring various students to adequate learning over each unit. If all goes well, the amount of extra time required decreases, while the student variation in time and help required is considerably reduced.

Thus, in a sequential series of learning tasks, the students (under mastery learning conditions) are likely to become more and more similar in the amounts of time and help they require to reach a given criterion of achievement. In these studies a given criterion of achievement has been maintained, while the amount of time and help needed to achieve it has been varied. In turn, the variation in time and help required gradually decreases. Although the variation in time and help required never reaches a vanishing point, we have observed situations in which the variation in time and help required on the later units was only about one-third of the variation observed on the first learning task (or unit) in the sequential series. We recommend further research on this type of teaching-learning situation and hope that other workers also find situations in which the *crutch* of additional time and help is gradually discarded until most of the students learn easily without the need of such additional learning aids. It is, however, more common to find situations in which mastery learning approaches succeed in bringing the students to a given criterion level of achievement, even if one cannot eliminate most of the variation in time and help required.

But we must return to the idealized situation of mastery learning with less and less variation in time and help required. Why should (or does) it work? What are the underlying variables which account for both achievement and time differences in sequential learning situations? We believe there are three types of variables which account for the major difference between conditions A and B in Chart 7-2. These variables should be useful in understanding the conditions under which individual differences in school achievement are likely to be maximized, and they can help us create conditions under which individual differences in achievement and learning can be minimized.

Cognitive Entry Behaviors (CEB)

Education and learning in the schools are built on sets of prior learnings largely cognitive in nature. For each learning task there are some prerequisite learnings that are required if the student is to attain mastery of the task. We have chosen to call these prerequisite learnings *Cognitive Entry Behaviors* (Glaser, 1970). It is possible to construct test instruments to determine the extent to which students possess these prerequisite behaviors, and there are psychometric techniques available to establish the extent to which hypothesized entry behaviors are necessary (or unnecessary) for the learning of a specific task.

In Chart 7-2, condition A, one reason for inadequate learning of each task was the lack of the prerequisite cognitive entry behaviors (largely developed in the prior learning tasks). The reasons for students becoming both successful and more efficient in their learning over units 2 to 10 under condition B was that they were acquiring the prerequisite entry behaviors before entering each of the subsequent learning tasks. Note that the determination of the entry behaviors required is a much more complex problem for unit 1 than for the subsequent units, since unit 1 becomes (by definition) the prerequisite for unit 2, and unit 2 for unit 3, and so on. In other words, the problem of defining and evaluating cognitive entry behaviors is more difficult for the beginning of a sequential series of learning tasks than it is for learning tasks within the series.

On the basis of both macro- and micro-studies (in Chapter 3) we have come to the conclusion that cognitive entry behaviors can account for up to one-half of the variance of achievement on courses or individual learning tasks. That is, if all the students possess the necessary cognitive entry behaviors required for a particular learning task or course, the level of achievement can be expected to be very high, and the variation in the achievement should be only 50 percent of the variation of a group of learners who differ greatly in their cognitive entry behaviors. In terms of this theory, cognitive entry behaviors— the prerequisite learning required for the new learning task(s)—is a key variable in accounting for the learning of students. We view cognitive entry behaviors as a part of the relevant learning history of the student which must be taken into consideration in instruction and curriculum development if students are to be really given an opportunity to learn effectively in the schools.

In Chart 7-3, we have suggested that if all the learners in a learning task possess the necessary cognitive entry behaviors, the achievement of the group should show only about 50 percent of the variation of a group that varies widely in the possession of the necessary cognitive entry behaviors. One can demonstrate this in learning studies by *selecting* students who possess the necessary entry behaviors, by using statistical control procedures, or by actually *teaching* the students the necessary *prerequisite entry behaviors* before they proceed to the particular learning task.

Affective Entry Characteristics (AEC)

Motivation to attempt a new learning task is in part determined by the individual's perception of his success or failure with previous learning tasks which he believes to be similar or related. Such motivation is largely predicated on the student's belief that the new learning task is in some way related to previous learning tasks he has encountered. It is the student's perception of his history with presumably related learning tasks which is of importance—even though the new task may be in no way directly related to previous learning tasks he has experienced. Over a period of time, the learner acquires relatively fixed notions about his competence with such learning tasks, and these determine the efforts he will make, the degree of confidence he has in the effectiveness of his efforts, and what he will do when he encounters difficulties or obstacles in the learning.

We regard the *Affective Entry Characteristics* as a compound of interests and attitudes toward the subject matter of the learning task and the school and schooling; they also include more deep-seated self-concepts and personality characteristics. Some of these components may be highly changeable, while others may be relatively stable. This is, in part, a function of age and previous experiences. While it is *not* impossible for learners to achieve mastery on a learning task if they have negative affective entry characteristics, it is very difficult. We believe that it is sometimes possible to present a learning task so that the students will regard it as independent of previous learning tasks and may approach it with positive or even neutral affect. Operationally, what is sought is an openness to the new learning task, a willingness to

Chart 7–3. Estimated Effect of Selected Variables on Variation in School Achievement

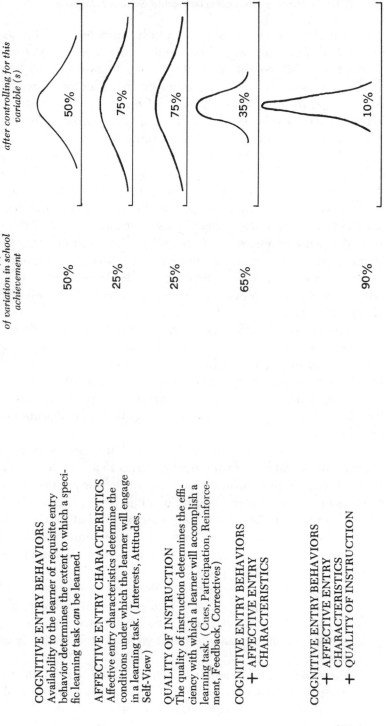

	Probable limit of percent of variation in school achievement	Probable residual variation after controlling for this variable (s)
COGNITIVE ENTRY BEHAVIORS Availability to the learner of requisite entry behavior determines the extent to which a specific learning task *can* be learned.	50%	50%
AFFECTIVE ENTRY CHARACTERISTICS Affective entry characteristics determine the conditions under which the learner will engage in a learning task. (Interests, Attitudes, Self-View)	25%	75%
QUALITY OF INSTRUCTION The quality of instruction determines the efficiency with which a learner will accomplish a learning task. (Cues, Participation, Reinforcement, Feedback, Correctives)	25%	75%
COGNITIVE ENTRY BEHAVIORS **+ AFFECTIVE ENTRY CHARACTERISTICS**	65%	35%
COGNITIVE ENTRY BEHAVIORS **+ AFFECTIVE ENTRY CHARACTERISTICS** **+ QUALITY OF INSTRUCTION**	90%	10%

make the effort required, and, hopefully, sufficient confidence in the self to strive to overcome real or imagined obstacles in the learning.

In Chart 7-2, condition A, the reason for inadequate learning of each task was partly the creation of negative affective entry characteristics by failure or at least the lack of clear success on the previous learning tasks. Under condition B, students were acquiring positive affect before entering subsequent learning tasks.

In Chapter 4 we came to the conclusion that the learners' affective entry characteristics could account for up to one-fourth of the variance of achievement on courses or learning tasks. We view affective entry characteristics as an important part of the individual's learning history which has consequences for each new learning situation in the school. If all the learners are comparable and positive in their affective entry characteristics, the learning achievement should be higher and the variation in achievement reduced by up to 25 percent in comparison with a group of learners who differ greatly in their affective entry characteristics.

The effect of affective entry characteristics on subsequent achievement can be demonstrated in learning studies by comparing the achievement of students who differ in affective entry characteristics, by using affective entry measures as a statistical control for later achievement measures, or by attempts to improve affect and observing the effect of these changes on both subsequent affective measures and later learning.

In Chapter 4, we expressed the view that under certain conditions it would be possible to bring most students to a high level of affective entry characteristics during a new set of learning tasks even though this was not the case at the beginning of the set. Again, we believe that affective entry characteristics are so important that much of the attention of teachers should be addressed to encouraging the development of positive affective characteristics toward school learning and self at every stage in the school process.

In Chart 7-3, we have suggested that if all the learners in a learning task are similar in their possession of positive affective entry characteristics, then the achievement of the group would show about 75 percent of the variation of a group that varies widely with regard to such characteristics.

One striking phenomenon we have noted about affective entry characteristics is that they are primarily within-school variables. That is, the student typically gains his perceptions about how well he is doing from his position within a group of his peers. He also gets most of the feedback on his success from the teacher and local evaluations rather than from national standardized achievement tests. It is thus possible to find two schools with minimal overlap on standardized achievement test distributions such that the top students in the lower school have highly positive affective entry characteristics, while the bottom students in the higher school have very negative affective entry characteristics—even though the two subgroups may be very similar in their scores on the standardized achievement test. The main point to note is that affective entry characteristics are largely perceptual phenomena arising from the student's perception of how well he is learning and that this is usually based on the evidence and judgments he receives from the teachers, parents, and his peers in the school or class.

Since affective entry characteristics are usually found to be related to cognitive entry behaviors, our best general estimate of the combined effect of *both cognitive and affective entry characteristics* is represented by a multiple correlation of about +.80 (see Chart 7-3). That is, up to two-thirds of the variance on achievement measures can be accounted for by the combined effects of these entry characteristics. Some support for this estimate comes from longitudinal studies of grades and other achievement measures within a school, where previous achievement indices correlate about +.80 with achievement in the same subject over several semesters or years. We regard such previous achievement indices as combinations of cognitive and affective entry characteristics.

Quality of Instruction (Q of I)

In spite of the many pessimistic notes about the lack of measurable effects of the teacher or school on learning (largely derived from large-scale survey and evaluation projects), we are of the view that the *Quality of Instruction* students receive has a demonstrable effect on their achievement and learning processes over one or more learning tasks.

Our problem has been to make more explicit just what it is that constitutes poor or good quality of instruction. We have found it difficult to get much on this process by observing a teacher instructing a group of thirty or more learners since the teacher appears to spend so much of his effort in managing the students rather than in managing the learning.

One approach to determining the specific aspects of quality of instruction may be derived from observing a very good tutor attempting to teach something to one student. What is the interaction that appears to promote the learning of this one student?

Perhaps the clearest subvariable in quality of instruction has to do with the *cues* that the tutor uses to make clear what is to be learned, what the student is to do, and how he is to do it. One may observe that the tutor uses a variety of ways of explaining, illustrating, demonstrating, etc., what is to be learned. The good tutor appears to adapt or alter the cues to present those which work best for the particular learner. For some students, the cues can be derived from written materials; for others it may be oral explanations; and for still others it may be combinations of demonstrations or models with explanations, etc. This aspect of quality of instruction is similar to Carroll's (1963) model in which he defines quality of instruction as the degree to which the presentation, explanation, and ordering of the elements of the task to be learned approach the optimum for a given learner.

A second aspect of quality of instruction is the extent to which it gets the learner in active *participation* or practice of the responses to be learned. While some of this participation may be overt and observable by the tutor, it is also likely that covert participation may be as effective in some situations as the more overt or observable participation. The good tutor has little trouble in observing the active participation of the learner in the process. Furthermore, he recognizes that there may be individual differences in the amount of practice or participation needed, and he can easily secure enough evidence to determine when the individual student has practiced sufficiently.

Finally, the good tutor uses *reinforcement* (positive or negative) at various stages in the learning process. The tutor adapts his reinforcers to the learner since what is an excellent reward for one student may not operate in the same way for another. The tutor uses a variety of reinforcers (both extrinsic and intrinsic); he adapts them to the needs of the learner; and he provides them to the learner as frequently as they are needed and at the points in the learning process where they are likely to be most effective.

These three aspects of quality of instruction (cues, participation, reinforcement) may be observed with little difficulty in an effective tutor-student interaction. These three may be derived from such theories of learning as Dollard and Miller (1950), and although the terms may differ, they can be found in some respect in almost every theory of learning as summarized by Hilgard and Bower (1966).

But so far we have been approaching the problem of quality of instruction as though we had an ideal tutor with one learner. This is a far cry from the teaching under group conditions with thirty or more learners in the typical school classroom. While cues, participation, and reinforcement are necessary in both individual and group learning situations, there are quantitative as well as qualitative differences in the two situations. We note in the tutor-learner situation that the tutor constantly adapts to the individual learner on the basis of a great deal of immediate evidence he is receiving from the learner in the learning process. In the group situation, the very skillful teacher must develop a variety of techniques for managing the instruction and for adapting to the varying needs and requirements of the different learners in the situation.

What is needed by all teachers in group learning situations is *feedback* evidence on the effectiveness of the learning process for individual students. Teachers also need to make relatively rapid use of *corrective* procedures when and where they are needed. Where mastery learning has been effective, it has made use of relatively explicit formative evaluation procedures as feedback devices to determine what the student has learned as well as what he still needs to learn before proceeding to the next learning task in the sequence. Furthermore, through the use of a variety of instructional materials, students helping each other, or tutors and aides, mastery learning procedures have made it possible to quickly apply correctives with regard to cues, participation, and reinforcement where the learners have specific difficulties in the learning process.

Under condition A in Chart 7-2, the main reason for students having increasing difficulty as they proceed from unit 1 to unit 10 is that nothing was done to correct inadequacies in the learning as they were encountered by the different students. In contrast, in condition B, formative evaluations accompanied by correctives for each learning task were used before the students proceeded to the next learning unit.

In Chapter 5, we came to the very tentative conclusion that the quality of instruction (cues, reinforcement, participation, and feedback-correctives) provided to the learners could account for about one-fourth of the variation in achievement over a learning task or course. We regard this as a minimal estimate because we could find very few studies in which the quality of instruction approached the optimal level we believe possible. This is the one aspect of our theory where the school has the greatest opportunity to make a real difference in the learning of students since the quality of instruction is under the direct control of teachers and the schools. However, the most effective methods of instruction we could find—in contrast with the more conventional methods—typically accounted for no more than about one-fourth of the variation in learning. In Chart 7-3, we have suggested that if the quality of instruction approaches the ideal in effectiveness, student level of achievement should be increased, and variation in achievement should be only about 75 percent of the variance found in learning situations where the qualities of instruction approach those more customarily found in the schools.

It is possible to demonstrate the effectiveness of differential quality of instruction by comparing the learning of students under tutoring conditions with comparable students under group instruction, by the use of mastery learning methods in contrast with control conditions of group instruction for comparable student groups, and by observational studies where very skillful teachers are contrasted with less skillful teachers both in terms of instructional procedures used as well as learning results for their students.

Because the quality of instruction cannot be predicted from the teacher's experience, education, or other characteristics, it is difficult for administrators or student advisors to assign students to teachers who will provide high or low quality of instruction. If these conditions are true, the quality of instruction will be relatively independent of the student's characteristics. When cognitive entry behaviors, affective entry characteristics, and quality of instruction are combined, they should account for something *more* than 80 percent of the variation in *level of achievement* or in the *rate of achievement*. In Chart 7-3, we have suggested that, under ideal conditions, the combination of all three variables could account for as much as 90 percent of the variation or that a group of learners under the most favorable conditions should show only 10 percent of the variation of a group under less favorable school conditions.

Undoubtedly, these three major variables do not account for all the sources of variation in achievement, but they do indicate that when properly taken into consideration, the variation in achievement still to be accounted for may be only a fraction of the original variation in student achievement. Thus, while variation in achievement does not reach a vanishing point, under these theoretical and practical considerations, they do account for sufficient variation in the learning of a task or a series of learning tasks to enable us to hope that the proper utilization of these major variables in the school learning processes will enable educators to improve the effectiveness of the schools by a significant degree.

PROCESSES INVOLVED IN THE MICRO-LEVEL STUDIES

The micro-level studies we have already reported on in Chapters 3, 4, and 5 may be used to explore the processes involved in the development of *Cognitive Entry Behaviors* and *Affective Entry Characteristics* in relation to different *Qualities of Instruction*. These microstudies used mastery and control methods of instruction with comparable groups of students over a series of learning tasks. Although each study made use of what was believed to be a sequential series of learning tasks, the studies involved such different subjects as a second language, statistical probability, matrix arithmetic, and a science course.

In each of these studies, students were placed into a mastery learning section and a control section of the course so that the two groups of students were roughly equivalent on measures of previous achievement and aptitude. Where possible, the same teacher taught both sections. The subject matter was the same, the learning materials used were identical, and the instructor(s) attempted to use similar instructional procedures.

For the control group, instruction was given on the first learning task followed by a criterion-referenced test over the task. However, the results of this test were not communicated to the students. At a later time, using the same instructional schedule as the mastery group, the students were instructed over the second learning task and tested again but not given feedback on the results. This process was repeated for each learning task in the series. Finally, the students were given an overall summative test at the end of the series of learning tasks.

For the mastery group, the same original instruction and testing was done, but immediately following the tests (formative tests) the detailed results were reported to each student. This report indicated whether the student had attained the mastery criterion or not. If *not*, the items on which the student was incorrect were identified, and each student was provided with *additional time and help* until he reached the mastery criterion over the selected ideas or items he had missed. Usually a parallel formative test was used to determine when the student had attained the mastery criterion. All students proceeded to the instruction over the second learning task as a group (on the same schedule as the control group), were tested, and, if necessary, were given additional time and help until each one had attained the mastery criterion. This was repeated for each learning task. Finally, the mastery students were given the same summative test as the control group at the end of the entire series of learning tasks.

Thus, the main difference between the two groups was that the mastery students were given *feedback* on what they had learned and what they still needed to learn to achieve the mastery criterion plus additional time and help to reach the criterion, while the control students were not provided with feedback or additional time and help. In terms of Quality of Instruction, both groups were provided with about the same original group instruction on each learning task. However, the mastery groups were then given *feedback and corrective instruction* in which the cues, amount of practice, and reinforcement were adapted to the needs and characteristics of the individual. Thus, group instruction was all that the control students received, while the mastery students received both group instruction *and* individualized instruction—instruction adapted to the needs of each individual.

In terms of Cognitive Entry Behaviors, both groups began with approximately equal CEB for the first learning task in the series. However, the feedback and correctives were intended to bring each student in the mastery group to high cognitive entry behaviors for each subsequent learning task. In contrast, the control group was likely to be highly varied and somewhat lower in cognitive entry behaviors than the mastery group for each of the learning tasks after the initial one.

In terms of Affective Entry Characteristics, both groups were approximately equal in AEC for the first learning task, while it was anticipated that the mastery group would tend to become more positive in interests and attitudes toward the learning than the control group. This anticipation is based on the general observations cited in Chapter 4 that affective entry tends to be more positive with high achievement than with low achievement. Also, we are assuming a causal relation between level of achievement on a learning task, the student's perception of his adequacy and inadequacy with such learning tasks, and his affective characteristics toward the learning task.

In Chart 7-4, we have shown an *idealized* summary of the ways in which cognitive entry behaviors and affective entry characteristics change for mastery and control students when the quality of instruc-

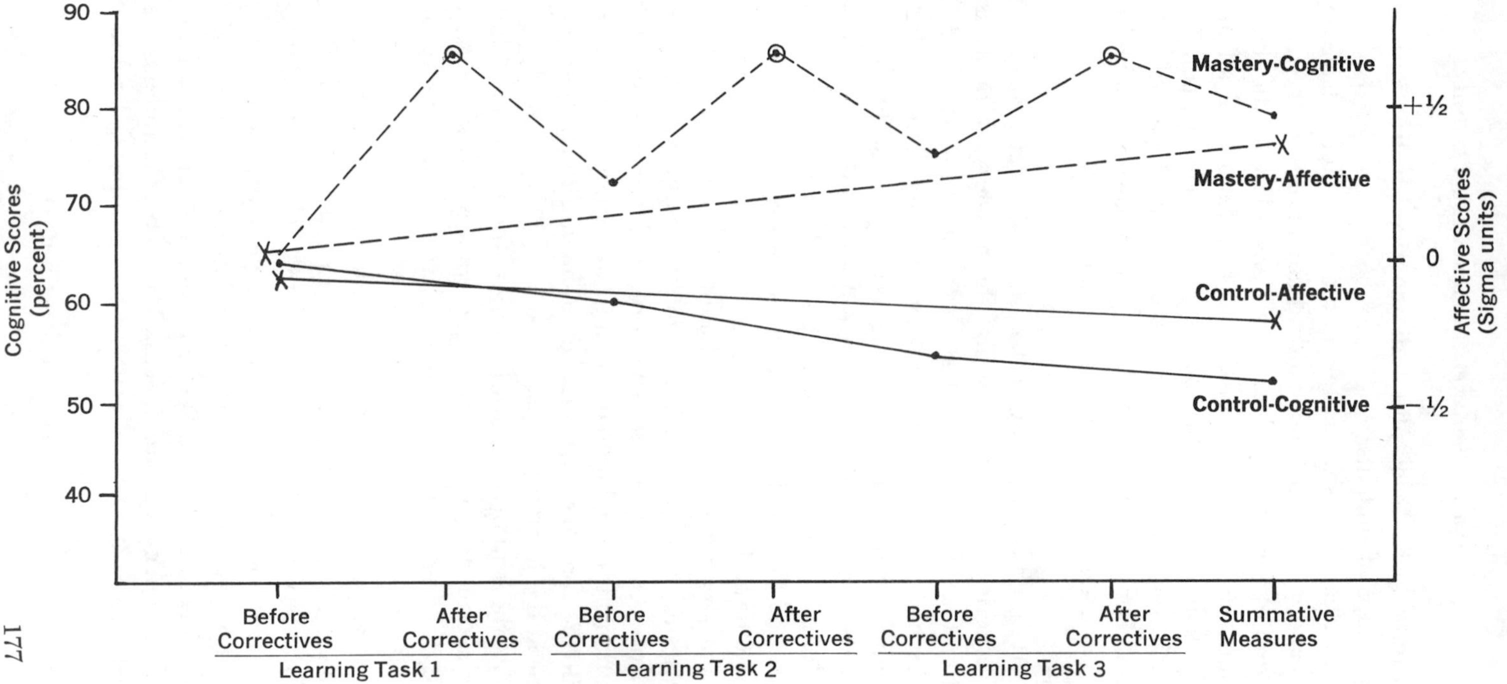

Chart 7-4. Idealized Differences between Mastery and Control Students over a Series of Learning Tasks

tion (largely feedback plus individualized instruction) differs for the two groups of students.

In Chart 7-4, both mastery and control groups have approximately the same mean score (and standard deviation)[1] on the first test given at the end of Learning Task 1. However, following the test, the mastery students are given additional time and help until all (or almost all) students have attained the mastery criterion on the parallel form of the test. (In the chart, the criterion was set at 85 percent of the possible score.) For the mastery students, the mean score after correctives is approximately 85 percent and the standard deviation is approximately zero.

At the end of Learning Task 2 (before correctives), the mean score on the criterion-referenced test for the mastery students is somewhat higher than for the control students, and the standard deviation is somewhat smaller for the mastery students than it is for the control students. Again the mastery students are given additional time and help until they have attained the mastery criterion on a parallel test. After this help the mean score on the test is about 85 percent of the possible score, and the standard deviation is approximately zero.

At the end of Learning Task 3 (before correctives), the mean score for the mastery students is considerably higher than for the control students, and the variation is less for the mastery students than for the controls. Once again, the mastery students who need it are given additional time and help until they have attained the mastery criterion, while the control students are given *no additional time and help* at any point in the learning series.

At the end of the learning series, the two groups differ greatly in their summative test results, with the mastery students having a significantly higher mean score and a relatively smaller standard deviation than the control students.

If we concern ourselves only with the test results immediately after each learning task, we can note the increasing differentiation between the mastery and the control students. That is, two groups that had almost identical means and standard deviations at the end of Learning Task 1 are very different in both means and standard deviations by the end of Learning Task 3. We can also note that in comparison with the achievement over Learning Task 1, the control students are decreasing in achievement over each successive learning task while the mastery

[1]Standard deviations are not depicted in Chart 7-4.

students are increasing in achievement over each successive learning task.

It is not difficult to explain why the two groups differ so much on each learning task after the corrective instruction has been given to the one group (mastery) and not given to the other group (control). Individualized instruction can, if properly used, provide each of the mastery learning students with the time, help, and special cues, reinforcement, and practice he needs. Since this was not given to the control students, their scores remain the same as they were at the end of group instruction.

What is more difficult to explain is why the two groups increasingly differ at the *end of group instruction*. While we can only speculate about this, we believe two processes are at work here. In terms of our theory, it is clear that the mastery students—after feedback and corrective instruction—have higher cognitive entry behaviors (with almost no variation) for subsequent learning tasks (after the first learning task) than do the control students. They should then find it easier to learn the next learning task under group instruction. In contrast, the control students tend to enter the subsequent learning tasks with decreasing cognitive entry behaviors (and much variation). Thus, the presence of higher and lower *cognitive entry behaviors* is one explanation for the increasing achievement of the mastery learning students and the decreasing achievement of the control students. Similarly, the increasing homogeneity of the mastery learning students and the increasing heterogeneity of the control students may be explained on the same basis.

An alternative explanation is that the mastery learning students quickly learn that they are not finished with a learning task until they have attained the criterion level of achievement on that task. The control students learn that as soon as they have taken the criterion-referenced test—no matter how well or poorly they have performed— they are expected to do nothing further with that task. While we can only speculate about this, we believe that mastery learning students tend to recognize that if they do not reach mastery at the end of group instruction, they must learn further under individualized instruction until they have reached the criterion. In these micro-studies they could avoid the subsequent additional work and individualized instruction only if they reached a mastery criterion at the end of group instruction. This leads them, we speculate, to devote themselves during group instruction to more active learning and higher involvement in the learning process. We will return to this idea on pages 185–188 of this chapter.

A third partial explanation for the increasing level of achievement of the mastery learning versus the control students is in terms of their *affective entry characteristics.* As students reach higher levels of achievement, they view themselves and the subject more positively, while as they reach lower levels of achievement, they view themselves and the subject more negatively. This is well demonstrated in the interest and attitude measures used in these studies and the increasing divergence of the two groups in terms of average scores on the affective measures as shown in Chart 7-4.

Finally, on the final or summative measure of achievement, the mastery learning and the control groups are very different in terms of both mean levels of performance as well as in terms of variability of achievement. Thus, two groups of students who were approximately equal in cognitive entry behaviors as well as affective entry characteristics *before* instruction and at the end of group instruction on the first learning task are quite different at the end of a series of learning tasks. The differences may be explained in terms of one group being given a higher quality of instruction than the other—largely in terms of group instruction plus feedback and individualized instruction for the mastery learning group while only group instruction was provided the control students. But, in addition to quality of instruction differences, we can note increasing differences between the two groups in cognitive entry behaviors and affective entry characteristics. Thus, the two groups differ on all three variables in our theory—Q of I, CEB, and AEC. The process involved is a combination of all three variables with Q of I in part explaining the differences in CEB and AEC.

EVIDENCE IN SUPPORT OF PROCESS CHANGES

Changes in Cognitive Learning
In Chart 7-4 we have shown the *idealized* process changes in mastery and control groups of students in terms of cognitive as well as affective changes. In both types of measures it was anticipated that the two groups would be similar at the end of Learning Task 1 (before correctives) but would increasingly diverge in their cognitive as well as affective development on each new learning task.

In Table 7-1 we have shown for each micro-study the changing *cognitive* means and standard deviations of the mastery and control-groups on successive learning tasks as well as on the summative tests. In each case, the results are shown for the original learning (before feedback and corrective instruction were given to the mastery group) as well as after corrective instruction for the mastery group. The results, in general, are similar to those shown in Chart 7-4. That is, increasing relative means for the mastery groups and decreasing means for the control groups or increasing differences in achievement means between the two groups. In addition, the relative variation of the mastery groups tends to decline, while it tends to become larger for the control groups. Although it is rare that the two groups had identical performances on the original learning over the first learning task, it is clear in each of the micro-studies that the ratio of the variances of the two groups is highest on the first learning task and tends to decline on each successive learning task. Thus, the median of the ratios of variance on the first learning task is approximately 75 percent (mastery/control), while the median on the original learning over Learning Task 3 is approximately 60 percent. On the summative test, the median variance ratio is approximately 20 percent. That is, the mastery group variation on the final summative achievement measure is only one-fifth that of the control students.

Changes in Affective Characteristics

Throughout the book we have indicated theoretical or estimated values only for the cognitive learning outcomes. We have not made similar estimates of the effect of changing quality of instruction and cognitive entry behaviors on affective learning outcomes. However, we would expect similar relative improvements in affective changes for the mastery groups and stable or declining affective characteristics for the control groups. Also, we would expect changing ratios of variances for the two groups, with decreasing variances for the mastery groups and increasing variances for the control groups.

It should be remembered that in the micro-studies we have used affective measures which tap only the student's interest in a subject or his attitude toward it. It was not anticipated that a brief micro-study of several weeks of learning would be likely to have profound consequences on the student's basic view of himself as a learner.

In four of the micro-studies we have evidence on changes in affect. In each of these studies there are relatively small differences between the mastery and control students on the initial measures of affective characteristics. However, the differences between the two groups on

TABLE 7-1. COGNITIVE AND AFFECTIVE CHANGES OVER LEARNING TASKS FOR MASTERY AND NON-MASTERY STUDENTS

| Study | Learning Task 1 | | | | Learning Task 2 | | | | Learning Task 3 | | | | Summative Measure | |
| | Original Instruction | | Corrective Instruction | | Original Instruction | | Corrective Instruction | | Original Instruction | | Corrective Instruction | | | |
	M	σ	M	σ	M	σ	M	σ	M	σ	M	σ	M	σ
MATRIX ALGEBRA (Anderson, 1973)														
Cognitive:														
Mastery	64.8	11.9	85.0	0.0	65.7	14.5	85.2	0.9	75.5	13.8	86.4	4.3	79.8	8.4
Non-mastery	65.3	13.6			51.0	19.6			49.1	18.3			59.3	19.5
ML/NM	99%				130%				154%				135%	
σ^2 ML / σ^2 NM	76%				55%				57%				19%	
Affective:														
Mastery	2.5	.8			3.0	.6			2.9	.7			3.1	.7
Non-mastery	2.4	1.0			2.5	.9			2.3	.9			2.4	1.0
MATRIX ALGEBRA (Block, 1970)														
Cognitive:														
Mastery	60.0	22.3	88.0	6.5	57.5	20.0	89.0	5.5	73.5	14.5	89.0	4.8	61.5	11.0
Non-mastery	51.0	23.0			47.5	23.0			57.0	24.5			48.0	21.5
ML/NM	118%				121%				129%				130%	
σ^2 ML / σ^2 NM	94%				76%				35%				26%	
Affective:														
Mastery	18.3	2.4			19.6	1.2			24.6	2.7			24.9	2.0
Non-mastery	17.4	2.5			17.6	2.8			21.8	4.5			21.0	5.4

IMAGINARY SCIENCE (Arlin, 1973)

Cognitive:

	Task 1	Task 2	Task 3	Task 4
Mastery	78.2*	75.4	75.8	17.0
Non-mastery	71.2	55.0	49.8	37.2
ML/NM	110%	137%	152%	219%
σ^2 ML	16.9	24.2	18.5	
σ^2 NM	19.5	21.0	18.3	22.9
	76%	111%	102%	18%
	94.6	93.3	92.6	
	13.9	18.4	11.1	9.6†

Affective:

	Task 1	Task 2	Task 3	Task 4
Mastery	3.1	2.9	2.7	
Non-mastery	2.8	2.4	2.2	
	1.0	1.2	1.2	
	1.0	1.2	1.2	

ELEMENTARY PROBABILITY (Levin, 1975)

Cognitive:

	Task 1	Task 2	Task 3	Task 4
Mastery	60.5	75.5	59.4	74.0
Non-mastery	63.5	66.0	49.5	52.3
ML/NM	95%	114%	120%	143%
σ^2 ML	21.0	17.5	18.0	13.7
σ^2 NM	21.5	21.5	17.5	15.3
	95%	67%	106%	80%
	90.5	92.5	88.5	
	8.0	6.0	8.5	

Affective:

	Task 1	Task 2	Task 3	Task 4
Mastery	25.6			34.2
Non-mastery	26.5			27.9
	5.7			8.4
	6.2			7.0

*This is not the initial learning task.

†This is the time required for each group to reach the criterion of mastery on Learning Task 4.

183

TABLE 7-1 (continued)

	Learning Task 1				Learning Task 2				Learning Task 3				Summative Measure	
	Original Instruction		Corrective Instruction		Original Instruction		Corrective Instruction		Original Instruction		Corrective Instruction			
	M	σ	M	σ	M	σ	M	σ	M	σ	M	σ	M	σ
SECOND LANGUAGE (Binor, 1974)														
Cognitive:														
Mastery	55.0	8.8	66.0	9.2	64.2	5.4	73.2	4.8	73.3	6.7	79.2	3.4	86.4	3.3
Non-mastery	49.6	12.5			55.4	11.3			60.8	11.7			66.8	16.7
ML/NM	111%				116%				120%				130%	
$\dfrac{\sigma^2 \text{ ML}}{\sigma^2 \text{ NM}}$		50%				23%				33%				4%

the last measure of affective characteristics tend to be larger. In other words, the two groups which were approximately similar in initial affective characteristics tend to be increasingly divergent (where we have measures at each learning task); at the last measure of affect the two groups are very dissimilar.

In spite of the clear trend toward divergent means in the affective measures, the relative variance of the two groups does not clearly follow the trends reported for the cognitive measures. In two of the studies, the mastery group has the same or greater variance on the final measures than the control group, while in the other two studies, the mastery groups have less variance on the final affective measure than the control groups.

Whether improved measures of affect under longer-term experimental studies would more nearly approximate the results for the cognitive changes is a subject for future research. We can conclude with the limited evidence available in the micro-studies that the effect of improved cognitive behaviors and more favorable qualities of instruction for the mastery students is to increase the differences between mastery and control students with regard to measures of interest or attitude toward the school subjects being studied.

Process Changes in Learning Effectiveness

We have already pointed out in our idealized picture of the change process that it is anticipated that with higher cognitive entry behaviors, higher affective entry characteristics, and good quality of instruction students would use their time for learning more effectively than would students who are relatively low in entry behaviors and have poor quality of instruction. In the micro-studies, the cognitive performance of the students at the end of the original instruction on each learning task gives us an opportunity to test this since the group instruction for each new learning task represented similar instructional conditions, time conditions, and test procedures.

It will be recalled that after the original instruction on each new learning task, the mastery students were given feedback and additional time and help until almost all the students reached the mastery criterion on a formative test, while no feedback or additional time and help was provided for the control students. Thus, while the two groups were given comparable conditions on each new learning task, the mastery students were provided with a higher quality of instruction and higher cognitive entry behaviors *prior* to the new learning task, while the control students were not.

In the five studies summarized in Table 7-1 it will be noted that there were some differences in the original achievement on Learning Task 1. The mastery students learned an average of about 10 percent more in the same time as did the control students. These differences are attributable to less than perfect matching of the two groups. If we view the two groups as differing in the quality of instruction, we can regard the original achievement over Learning Task 2 as the criterion of the effectiveness of the differential treatment over Learning Task 1. In the micro-studies reported in Table 7-1 the average mastery group learned about 20 percent more than the average control group under the *same conditions* in Learning Task 2. A second comparison is to view the two groups as having differential learning conditions over Learning Task 1 plus 2 and regard the original learning over Learning Task 3 as the criterion of the effectiveness of this differential treatment. In Table 7-1 it will be noted that the average mastery group learned about 30 percent more under the same original learning conditions in Learning Task 3 than did the average control group.

What these figures indicate is that the effect of positive entry characteristics (cognitive plus affective) and improved quality of instruction is to increase the relative learning effectiveness of the mastery students, while the less positive entry characteristics and less favorable quality of instruction decrease the relative learning effectiveness of the control students when they encounter successive new learning tasks in a sequential series.

We have only a few studies which attempt to measure the actual degree of student involvement in the original learning situation. From the fact of increased achievement of the mastery students relative to the control students on successive learning tasks, we would anticipate that they were using the learning time available more effectively and that they would display a higher proportion of time-on-task.

In the Anderson (1973) study, the students' use of time was directly studied by determining the amount of overt attention they displayed at selected time intervals as well as the amount of covert relevant thinking they reported at selected points in the original learning situation for each learning task. Anderson converted these observations into estimates of the percent of the time that each student was on the task— *time-on-task*.

On the first learning task, the mastery students were on task 74 percent of the time, while the control students were on task 76 percent of the time. Their achievement on Learning Task 1 was approximately equal. On the second learning task, the mastery students were on task 79 percent of the time, while the control students were on task only 65 percent of the time. Their achievement on Learning Task 2 shows a sizable differential in favor of the mastery group (30 percent more under similar learning conditions). On the third learning task, the mastery students were on task 83 percent of the time, while the control students' time-on-task had dropped to 63 percent. The difference in achievement on Learning Task 3 (about 50 percent more under similar learning conditions) reflects this differential in use of time. Thus, in this study there is little mystery as to why the two groups show increasing differences in achievement—they are increasingly different in their involvement (time-on-task) on successive learning tasks. Anderson reports a correlation of +.66 (.75 corrected) between time-on-task and final achievement.

Özcelik (1974) also attempted to measure the relation between the degree of overt and covert involvement and final achievement in two college courses. Although he does not report differentials between mastery and non-mastery students, he found correlations between degree of involvement and final achievement of +.60 (.76) for the college biology course and +.50 (.56) for a college algebra course. In Chapter 5 we have reported an average correlation of +.58 between various indices of overt and covert attention or involvement and learning gains as measured by achievement tests.

Such evidence suggests the rather obvious point that learning is likely to be greater if the students give more time and attention to the learning tasks. Furthermore, the degree of involvement (as well as the learning achievement) is affected by the quality of instruction and the extent to which students enter learning tasks with appropriate entry characteristics. In the Anderson study the multiple correlation between *time-on-task* and quality of instruction plus cognitive entry behaviors plus affective entry characteristics was +.57 (.66); for the Özcelik study it was +.51 (.61) in the biology course and +.46 (.58) in the algebra course.

Another approach to time use under differential conditions of instruction was to use learning rate as an indicator. In two of the micro-studies, the learning rate was estimated by dividing the amount learned (number of questions answered correctly) into the amount of time used. In the Block study he used the original learning on Learning Task 3 as the critical task. In his 95 percent mastery group (held to 95 percent as the criterion of mastery) he found that the mastery group learned almost 40 percent more per unit of time than did the control group.

In his study, Arlin required both mastery and control students to reach the same criterion level (85 percent mastery) on his final task. The non-mastery students needed more than twice as long (2.2) to reach the criterion as did the mastery students. That is, the mastery students learned 200 percent more per unit of time than did the control students on this critical learning task.

What these studies demonstrate is that student learning effectiveness can be increased or decreased by positive or negative changes in entry characteristics (CEB and AEC) and that the quality of instruction (Q of I) is a major causal factor in producing these changes. Degree of involvement, time-on-task, rate of learning, and level of achievement on critical learning tasks are all symptoms of these changes in learning effectiveness.

Variation in Time Use

It has been pointed out that under mastery learning some students need more time and help to reach the mastery criterion than do others. Carroll (1963), Glaser (1968), and Atkinson (1968) have estimated that to reach a criterion of mastery some students may need five times as much time as do other students. In making these crude estimates, they were using the total amount of elapsed time from the beginning to the end of the task. That is, the amount of clock time consumed by students from the beginning of the task until they reached the criterion of mastery.

In three of the micro-studies (see Table 7-2) the investigators attempted to keep accurate records of the total amount of elapsed time used by the students in the mastery group to reach the criterion of mastery on each learning task. In the three studies it is evident that the variation in amount of time used is greatest on Learning Task 1 while it is considerably smaller for the later learning tasks. Thus, in the Arlin (1973) study, the variation on the final task (Learning Task 4) is less than one-half of what it was on the first learning task. In the Block (1970) study, the variation in elapsed time on Learning Task 3 is less than 40 percent of what it was on Learning Task 1, while in the Anderson (1973) study, the variation in time for Learning Task 3 is about two-thirds of the elapsed time variation on Learning Task 1. Thus, in these three studies

TABLE 7-2. *VARIATIONS IN ELAPSED TIME AND TIME-ON-TASK FOR MASTERY STUDIES OVER LEARNING TASKS*

| | Elapsed Time (Variance)* | | | Time-on-Task (Variance)* |
	Arlin (1973)	Block (1970)	Anderson (1973)	Anderson (1973)
Learning Task 1	192.2	252.8	23.3	6.3
Learning Task 2	123.2	77.4		4.0
Learning Task 3	102.0	88.4	14.4	2.3
Learning Task 4	92.2			
σ^2 Final Learning Task / σ^2 First Learning Task	48%	35%	66%	36%

*Standard deviation squared (σ^2).

189

the students became more and more similar in the amount of elapsed time they needed to reach the mastery criterion.

Anderson (1973), in reviewing these studies, attempted to determine the range of elapsed time used to achieve the criterion score by these students. His results are summarized in Chart 7-5. It will be seen that on Learning Task 1, the highest ratio of *elapsed times* for the slowest to the fastest student is 7½ to 1, while the lowest ratio is about 3½ to 1. By the end of Learning Task 3 it is as high as 4 to 1 and as low as 2 to 1. Thus, there is evidence in these three studies of not only decreasing variation in the amount of elapsed time required, but there are also indications that the extreme students become more and more similar in the amount of time required to attain the mastery criterion in these studies.

Anderson also investigated the amount of *time-on-task* used by the mastery students to reach the mastery criterion. This is an attempt to measure the active working time used by these students instead of the elapsed or clock time used by them. In Table 7-2, the Anderson study shows the declining variability of the mastery students in time-on-task required to attain mastery. The variability (standard deviation squared) for his third learning task is only 36 percent of the variability of these students on the first learning task. In terms of slowest to fastest student,

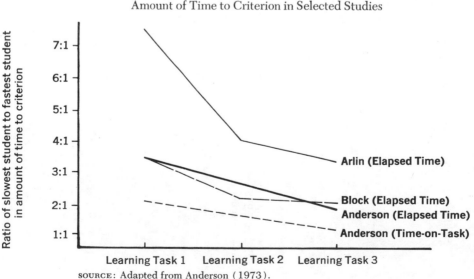

Chart 7–5. Ratio of Slowest Student to Fastest Student in Amount of Time to Criterion in Selected Studies

SOURCE: Adapted from Anderson (1973).

Anderson found that on Learning Task 1 the slowest student needed more than twice as much on-task time as did the fastest student. In contrast, on Learning Task 3, the slowest student needed only 1⅓ as much on-task time as the fastest student (see Chart 7-5).

Perhaps the main conclusion to be drawn from these limited studies of time—whether elapsed time or time-on-task—is that rate of learning or amount of time needed to learn to some criterion of achievement is an *alterable characteristic*. That is, when students are provided with the time and help they need to learn and when this produces positive entry characteristics (cognitive and affective), students not only become better able to learn, they also become able to learn with less and less time. Finally, the evidence in these limited studies suggests that the differentiation between good and poor learners, or fast and slow learners, tends to be reduced to a point where it is difficult to measure in hours or minutes. In other words, the terms fast learner and slow learner, under the favorable learning conditions indicated in these studies, have little to recommend them as practicable distinctions. Who is fast and who is slow changes from learning task to learning task, and the final differences between fast and slow are exceedingly small and can only be measured if the units of time measurement are exceedingly fine.

EVIDENCE IN SUPPORT OF THE MODEL

Micro-studies

In Chapters 3, 4, and 5 we have attempted to estimate the upper limits of the effect on achievement variation separately of Cognitive Entry Behaviors, Affective Entry Characteristics, and Quality of Instruction, respectively. The micro-studies enable us to determine whether *correlational* and *experimental* results based on two or more of these three variables yield values consistent with the estimates cited in Chart 7-3.

In Table 7-3, we have presented the results for five of the micro-studies. For each study, we have shown the results for the control students who did not have feedback and corrective instruction. Since the control students had only one type of instruction, we cannot estimate the effect of quality of instruction for this group. We have also shown the results for the total group of students in each study, and since these combine the mastery learning (who did have feedback and corrective instruction for each learning task) with the control students (who did not), it is possible to determine the effect of the differential

TABLE 7-3. THEORETICAL AND OBSERVED RELATIONS BETWEEN ACHIEVEMENT AND COMPONENTS OF THE MODEL
(BASED ON MICRO-STUDIES)

Summative Measures vs.	Estimated Theoretical Values	Anderson (1973)		Block (1970)		Levin (1975)		Binor (1974)		Arlin (1973)	
		Control	Total	Control	Total	Control	Total	Control	Total	Control	Total
CORRELATIONS											
Cognitive Entry	.70	.68	.48	.74	.64	.72	.49	.96	.77	.49	.46
Affective Entry	.50	.17	.21	.22	.16	.16	.01			.39	.36
Cognitive + Affective Entry	.80	.69	.51	.74	.64	.72	.49			.50	.50
Quality of Instruction	.50		.52		.32		.55		.65		.58
Cognitive Entry + Quality of Instruction			.71		.67		.75		.91		.69
Cognitive Entry + Affective Entry + Quality of Instruction	.95		.71		.67		.75				.69
ACHIEVEMENT VARIANCE											
σ^2 Mastery / σ^2 Control	10%		19%		26%		76%		4%		18%*

*Variance on Learning Task 4—time to mastery criterion.

192

instruction or quality of instruction combined with the other variables—the entry characteristics. In each study the correlations are with
the final summative achievement test at the end of each experiment.

It will be seen in these five studies that the correlations for cognitive entry behaviors and affective entry characteristics with the summative achievement measures are somewhat higher for the control
group than they are for the total group—probably because the variation
on the final achievement measures for the mastery students is much
smaller than for the control students (even though both groups are
comparable in entry behaviors), and this is partly due to the effect of the
differential quality of instruction provided for the two groups.

For Cognitive Entry Behaviors, the correlations for the control
group approach the estimated upper-limit values cited in Chapter 3,
while for the total group they are much smaller than this, with the Binor
(1974) study as the one exception.

For the Affective Entry Characteristics, the correlations are much
lower than the estimated upper limits. However, this may be largely
due to the very limited measures of affect used in these brief studies. As
was stated in Chapter 4, we would expect the upper limits of affective
entry to involve self-concept measures and especially self-concept of
academic achievement over a number of years of school experience.
Interest and attitude toward the subject rarely yield values approaching
the upper limit cited as the theoretical value in Table 7-3.

The correlations for the cognitive plus affective entry characteristics are not much higher than those for the cognitive measures only. For
the control groups these average about +.70. If these are corrected for
the unreliability of the summative measures, these values would be
about .10 higher. Thus, they are close to the theoretical value, but this is
largely attributable to the cognitive entry characteristics which account
for somewhat greater variance than is to be expected in terms of our
estimated upper limits.

For the total groups, the combination of cognitive entry behaviors
and affective entry characteristics correlates about +.50 (about +.60
when corrected for unreliability) which is considerably below the
estimated correlation value of +.80. Again, the limited measures of
affective entry and the reduced variance of the mastery group help to
explain this.

As was pointed out, the effect of Quality of Instruction could be
determined only for the total group (mastery plus control students). The
correlation between quality of instruction and summative achievement

in the studies is somewhat higher than we would expect on the basis of the values reported in Chapter 5. However, it should be remembered that these are experimental studies in which feedback and correctives were given to one group and denied to the other. The differences between the mastery and control groups have been reported on pages 175 to 185 to show the intricate interrelations between the quality of instruction, the cognitive entry behaviors, and the affective entry characteristics and the ways in which their combined relations develop with the final achievement measures. It is likely that the unique effects of quality of instruction cannot, especially in these studies, be clearly separated from the effects of the other variables. These correlations which are already above those to be expected from the estimated values would be even higher if corrected for the unreliability of the achievement measures.

In these studies, the combined effect of cognitive entry behaviors plus quality of instruction in determining final achievement is very high. The correlations for the total group average about +.70 (about +.10 higher if corrected for unreliability of the achievement measures only). Although we have not estimated the combined effect of CEB plus Q of I, we would speculate that it should be at least as high as the effect of CEB plus AEC—and this is approximately what is evident in these studies. Thus, for the control group (where quality of instruction cannot be separately determined in these studies) the correlation between cognitive entry behaviors plus affective entry characteristics with summative achievement is of the same order of magnitude as the correlation between cognitive entry behaviors plus quality of instruction for the total group.

We have difficulty in these studies in combining all three variables since the affective entry characteristics contribute relatively little over what has already been contributed by cognitive entry behaviors and/or quality of instruction. We may conclude that combining CEB plus AEC or combining CEB plus Q of I typically yields correlations of about +.70 (about +.80 when corrected for unreliability). This is far from the correlation of +.95 expected as the upper limit for the effect of these three variables on achievement.

Whether or not research over longer periods of time than is represented in these micro-studies will yield higher values more closely approximating the upper limits we have estimated is a task for further investigation.

We had estimated that when these three variables are working to the limits we believe possible, the variation of students' achievement should be reduced to about 10 percent of what might otherwise be expected. In the micro-studies, the investigators began with groups of students who were roughly comparable in entry characteristics and who were quite comparable at the end of the first learning task (before feedback and correctives). The combined effect of Q of I, CEB, AEC, and time use has already been described in the section on process changes in the micro-studies.[2] Of special interest here is the reduced variance of the mastery versus the control students on the final summative measures in these studies. This is shown in the last line of Table 7-3. Typically, with one exception (the Levin study), these values approximate about 20 percent. That is, the mastery group provided with favorable learning conditions has only about 20 percent of the variation in achievement of the control group which was provided with less favorable learning conditions.

We would infer from this that the experimental conditions *reduced* the variability of the mastery students by 80 percent in contrast to that obtained by a comparable group of students with less favorable learning conditions. This value found in the experimental studies suggests that the intricate combination of CEB plus AEC plus Q of I produces an effect greater than could be determined by our correlation studies which should have a combined R of about $+.90$ (in order to reduce the variance to this level). Whether the lower correlation value is due to the unreliability of our measures and the lack of appropriate corrections, we do not know. In general, we believe that the reduced variance is one useful index of what the theory of school learning promises—if the full weight of it can be implemented in a practicable way in the schools.

Macro-studies

We have made extensive use of the literature on educational research to determine the *separate* effects of each of our major variables on school learning. We could find very few studies in the literature which dealt directly with two or more of the major variables. And, for the most part, we have had to resort to a small number of selected micro-studies to find evidence on the interrelations of the major variables and their combined effects on student learning.

In Table 7-3, we have reported the relative achievement variance of the mastery learning and control classes as one indication of the

[2]See pp. 180–191.

combined effect of the variables in this theory of school learning. There we indicated that under the special conditions in these micro-studies, the final variance in achievement of the mastery learning class was as low as 20 percent of that of the control class.

Similar types of evidence may be sought from selected macro-studies where there is some indication that different qualities of instruction, cognitive entry behaviors, and affective entry character-istics are involved.

Mastery Learning Studies   Since the theory developed here has been much influenced by our mastery learning studies, it is most likely that macro- as well as micro-studies of mastery learning are likely to involve at least differential quality of instruction as well as differential cognitive entry behaviors for mastery and control classes. If mastery methods are effective, they should also have some effect on the affec-tive characteristics of the students.

Although mastery methods are utilized widely in the schools and colleges, it is difficult to find many research reports on the studies in which mastery and control groups are compared with similar measures of achievement time, etc. Teachers are more interested in their teach-ing and their effects on learners than in research studies about teaching or learning. Careful reports on mastery learning and control classes in the schools are a rarity. While James Block (1974), in his book *School, Society, and Mastery Learning*, has summarized the results of about fifty mastery learning studies, not all of these are useful for our purpose.

In Table 7-4, we have summarized the results of twelve care-fully selected studies. These are studies in which a mastery learn-ing class and a control class were provided with similar conditions of group instruction, but the mastery students were given additional time and help following the formative tests given at the end of each learning task. These are studies where both groups of students were given a common criterion-referenced summative achievement test. Usually, the report on these studies gives some attention to the procedures which make it likely that the students were provided with feedback and that they made some use of the corrective procedures which were available. Finally, these are studies in which the difference between the achievement means of the mastery and control classes are at least a half of a standard deviation—that is, they are studies which were effective in producing distinctly different distributions of achieve-ment—although they were far from achieving differences as great as those reported in the micro-studies. Our primary interest in these

TABLE 7-4. COMPARISON OF EXPERIMENTAL AND CONTROL CLASSES ON SUMMATIVE TEST RESULTS—MASTERY LEARNING STUDIES

Study	Level	Subject	Experimental			Control			Test	$\dfrac{M_E - M_C}{\sigma\ \text{control}}$	$\dfrac{\sigma^2 E}{\sigma^2 C}$
			N	Mean	S.D.	N	Mean	S.D.			
Lee et al. (1971)	5th	Arithmetic	1,895	71.4	21.4	1,410	52.8	21.1	Summative	0.9 σ	103%
		Science	1,723	69.3	17.3	1,310	49.5	22.3	Summative	0.9 σ	60%
	6th	Arithmetic	1,806	73.5	19.0	1,104	54.3	22.3	Summative	0.9 σ	73%
		Science	1,985	74.0	18.4	1,271	55.3	19.1	Summative	1.0 σ	93%
Pillet (1975)	9th	French	24	3.46	0.59	22	3.07	0.79	Grades based on final test	0.5 σ	56%
Mayo & Longo (1966)	Coll.	Electronics	113	78.2	4.5	113	72.4	6.7	Summative	0.9 σ	46%
Kersh (1971) (Class 222)	5th	Mathematics	30	30.3	3.8	21	26.1	4.7	Summative	0.9 σ	65%
Jones et al. (1975)	Jr. Coll.	Business	26	68.5	13.9	33	56.9	16.0	Final examination	0.7 σ	75%
		Economics	19	64.4	16.3	24	52.8	13.2	Final examination	0.9 σ	153%
		Biology	33	74.6	12.4	20	64.4	12.6	Final examination	0.8 σ	97%
		Biology	15	60.7	10.1	93	46.5	15.0	Final examination	0.9 σ	45%
Jones et al. (1975)*	Jr. Coll.	Summary of 4 courses	98	3.52	0.5	75	2.51	1.4	Grades based on final tests	0.7 σ	13%

*ML students met minimal requirements in terms of mastery learning procedures.

197

studies is the extent to which the achievement variance of the experiment group is sharply reduced in contrast to the control group. This may be seen in the last column of Table 7-4.

In the twelve studies reported here, there are four studies where the variation of the experimental class is approximately equal to or greater than that of the control class—in spite of sizable differences in achievement in favor of the experimental class.

In the remaining eight studies, the median variation of the experimental group in contrast with the control group is about 60 percent. This is a considerable difference from the 20 percent reported for the selected micro-studies. Evidently, under regular school conditions, mastery learning can produce sizable achievement differences even though it does not provide the most favorable conditions for learning and reduction of individual differences that we believe to be possible.

However, a word must be added about two of the studies. The Lee (1971) study was done in South Korea and involved large samples of students in the 5th and 6th years of school. It should be noted that in this study the typical class had seventy or more students, and the teachers had only a few hours of orientation to the mastery learning procedures which they were to use. This is a far cry from the micro-studies with smaller classes and careful attention to *each* student's feedback and corrective procedures.

The last entry in Table 7-4 is a special study by Jones and his colleagues (1975) in a junior college. While in this college they found sizable achievement differences between the mastery and control classes taught by the same instructor, the faculty were certain that some of the students were not actually making use of the feedback information or the corrective procedures. Each teacher identified the students who missed a large number of classes, rarely made use of the corrective procedures, and rarely gave evidence on the repeated formative tests that they had done anything to correct their difficulties on particular learning tasks. When these students were eliminated from the analysis, the students who had met the minimal conditions for *participating* in the mastery procedures had only 13 percent of the variation that was found in the control classes. The point is that mastery learning procedures work well only if the students actually make use of the procedures.

A more comprehensive summary of the effects of mastery learning school studies as well as Keller Personalized Instruction studies (largely

at the   ''--~ level) is being published by Block and Burns (1976). In
this s┌   ┐ the experimental and control classes on
level   relative variability of achievement
score   to those reported in Table 7-4 and
Tabl

                                 tion Studies   By far the most widely
use   is the Keller system of instruction. In
this   expected to master each learning task
bel   Each student goes at his own pace, and
his   y determined by the number of learning
ta   astered. Much of the learning is through
ir   aterials of instruction with some help by
t   . While students differ in their rate of
1   clear that those who complete the course
                                 ach unit before moving to the next unit—
                                 ve the necessary cognitive entry behaviors
                                 ore they enter it.
                                 at over a million college students make use
                                 ar, only a few studies have been reported in
which   ontrol groups of students are compared on a
common, final criterion-referenced examination.[3] In Table 7-5, we have
reported on a few of these studies where the difference in means was .4
of a standard deviation or greater. In these studies the median experimental group has about two-thirds of the variance of the control classes.
This is about the same as that found for the mastery learning classes
reported in Table 7-4.

We may conclude from these macro-studies that we have a long
way to go before the typical study in the schools produces the variance
reduction we believe to be possible when the theory of school learning
is applied under highly favorable conditions.

Other Approaches   We do not believe that some variant of mastery learning strategies is the only way in which this theory of school
learning can be implemented or studied. There are other ways in which
this theory can be investigated and tested. Thus, studies of students
learning under favorable tutoring situations versus comparable students learning under regular group instruction should yield approximations of some of the limits of learning with respect to achievement

---

[3]See Block and Burns (1976) for studies on this point.

TABLE 7-5. COMPARISON OF EXPERIMENTAL AND CONTROL CLASSES ON SUMMATIVE TEST RESULTS—
KELLER "PERSONALIZED SYSTEM OF INSTRUCTION"

Study	Level	Subject	Experimental			Control			Test	$\dfrac{M_E - M_C}{\sigma \text{ control}}$	$\dfrac{\sigma^2 E}{\sigma^2 C}$
			N	Mean	S.D.	N	Mean	S.D.			
Moore et al. (1969)	College	Biology	31	59.0	14.8	30	67.4	17.0	Error scores	.5 σ	76%
		Psychology	34	13.5	4.5	37	15.9	5.6	Final examination	.4 σ	65%
Sheppard & MacDermot (1970)	College	Psychology	168	73.1	12.1	92	66.8	11.9	Common final examination	.5 σ	103%
Moore et al. (1973)	College	Physics	17	120.3	23.9	17	99.0	35.4	Common final examination	.6 σ	46%
Bostow & O'Connor (1973)	College	Educational psychology	20	90.3	5.2	21	85.9	10.1	Common final examination	.4 σ	26%
Condo (1974)	College	Calculus	20	77.1	12.0	17	71.4	14.7	Common final examination	.4 σ	67%
Smith (1968)	College	Spanish	9	61.3	8.1	9	56.1	14.1	Common final examination	.4 σ	33%

differentials, time differentials, and affective outcomes. We have searched for such tutoring situations but have been able to find almost none which yield evidence such as reported in Tables 7-4 and 7-5.

We explored (with little success) the possibility of collecting data like those reported in Tables 7-4 and 7-5 on systematic instructional approaches, such as programmed instruction, computer-assisted instruction, or systematic instruction in small groups (with frequent feedback and correctives) such as the Distar reading program, subgroup instruction in arithmetic, etc. We believe such programs will eventually yield considerable basic data which may be used to test the ideas in this theory and its practicable implementation under school conditions.

Similarly, the developmental research being done by curriculum centers throughout the world should eventually bear very directly on the limits of this theory—especially when they study the effects of the new curriculum and instructional approaches under conditions which approximate the ideal for the new curriculum.

All of this is to state that the interrelation of the variables in this theory is a problem that has been touched only at the surface. The separate contributions of the variables is relatively clear. However, the ways in which the variables in combination alter both the teaching and learning processes as well as the cognitive and affective outcomes of the learning is largely a problem of the future. New ways of gathering data under a variety of teaching-learning conditions will be necessary if we are to more fully understand human limits to learning and the extent to which favorable learning conditions alter both the learning characteristics of students and the instructional characteristics of teachers and the schools.

8
CONCLUSIONS
AND IMPLICATIONS

NATURE OF THE THEORY

A *Causal System*

In the previous chapters of this book we have attempted to describe and document a theory of school learning which accounts for variation in school learning under a great variety of conditions. Implicit in the entire work is the attempt to regard school learning as a *causal* system in which a few variables may be used to predict, explain, and determine different levels and rates of learning. This causal system makes explicit the notion that the *present* learning is an outgrowth of *previous learning and learning conditions* and that, in turn, the present learning will have consequences for *future* learning.

It is the history of the individual learner which in large part determines his present learning, and it is this accumulated history (past and present) which will have major consequences for his future learning. The central focus of much of this book is the search for ways in which this historical determinism can be altered when it is in the best interests of the learner and the society. Our own effort on mastery learning strategies was to search for learning conditions which would reduce historical determinism and provide a fresh start for the majority of learners who needed it. Nevertheless, we do not underestimate the power of the history of the learner to determine much of his future learning, and our emphasis throughout the book is on the role of the schools in providing the most favorable conditions for learning throughout the individual's school career, whether it be to correct for the learner's previous conditions (in the interest of the present learning) or to assure the learner's future learning.

The theory attempts to make explicit the ways in which the learners' previous characteristics and the quality of instruction determine the outcomes of the learning process whether the outcomes be different

202

levels of learning, different rates of learning, or such affective outcomes of learning as attitudes toward the learning or attitudes about the self. The causal system described by these variables is amenable to modification at a number of points with consequent changes in the outcomes of learning.

If we have been successful in developing the appropriate causal links in a theoretical view of the school learning process, it should be subject to further testing in a variety of ways. The simplest test is whether it is of *predictive* value. Here, the theory attempts to indicate the general predictive values of the quality of instruction and particular student characteristics for the prediction of selected learning outcomes. Although the general values have been derived from particular groups of students, subjects of study, and levels of education, the claim is that these values are more general than the specific instances on which they have been based. It is to be hoped that other educational researchers will test the generalizability of these claims in a great variety of new instances in order to determine the limits of the applicability of such claims, the special conditions under which they are upheld, and some of the sources of error in the prediction of school learning.

As a causal system, the theory makes claims for its *explanatory* value in a great variety of school learning situations. That is, it attempts to account for particular learning phenomena in terms of the selected variables in the theory. Here it represents a kind of special pleading and particular style of explanation which may not be as widely accepted as the author might desire. Each of us prefers to explain observable phenomena in our own way and style, and it is difficult to accept the type of explanations others may find satisfactory. We would expect many challenges to the explanatory system represented by this theory in spite of a great deal of evidence as to its predictive or experimental value. In many ways this set of circumstances is a healthy one if each different explanatory system is subjected to empirical verification. This work would be of great benefit to education if it resulted in alternative explanatory systems being made more explicit and if the competing explanatory systems would then be subjected to a variety of empirical and theoretical validations.

However, for this writer, the critical test of a causal system in education should be the extent to which it can be used to produce changes in the learning of students. Throughout this book there is an attempt to provide evidence on the effect of a change in particular variables on the learning outcomes of students. These studies determine the effect of alterations of particular characteristics of students and the quality of instruction on changes in the levels of learning, the rate of learning, and the learners' interests and attitudes. These studies of changes were done under school conditions as well as under experimental-laboratory conditions. Here it is to be hoped that educational researchers and teachers can be induced to make changes of a similar nature in students and in the learning conditions in order to determine the extent to which they secure the results which are consistent with (or different from) theoretical expectation.

While a causal system of school learning can be tested under limited school conditions or under special learning laboratory conditions, the ultimate test of such a system is whether or not it applies to entire schools and school systems. We are quite optimistic about the results of testing this system over a term or year in particular courses taught by highly motivated teachers. However, we are pessimistic about the likelihood that an entire school or school system can or will exert the effort to test this theory in practice over the entire curriculum and the different levels of learning represented in the school.

A Value-neutral System

Since we have presented this theory as a causal system of the relations between selected variables and selected learning outcomes, it constitutes a value-neutral system. That is, it can be used to *predict* what will happen under particular conditions, it offers *explanations* for why things happen the way they do, and it states what *will occur* if particular student characteristics and instructional conditions are altered in specific ways. In effect, the theory states that if educators want student learning outcomes of a particular type, then they must produce certain changes in the student and/or the instructional conditions. The theory further states that if educators do not provide these conditions and changes, then the learning outcomes they will produce in students will be very different. To this extent, the theory is neutral about the desirability of each type of outcome or its opposite. All it does is indicate the consequences of doing certain things or of not doing them.

The theory is concerned with processes of learning in school situations rather than with particular educational objectives, subject matter, or parts of the curriculum. In this sense it takes no position about what learning is desirable for particular students, schools, or societies. While this work refers to particular school subjects and objectives of education (and especially to the research literature on these subjects and objectives), these are used to illustrate the generalizability of the variables used in the theory rather than to advocate particular types of learning in the schools.

In describing and documenting the theory we have attempted to reduce (and, whenever possible, eliminate) our own advocacy of particular learning outcomes. Thus, the same variables may be used to increase individual differences in learning or to reduce these individual differences. Different qualities of instruction may be used (and even advocated by different educators)—the theory should enable the teacher or the educational researcher to anticipate particular outcomes without special advocacy of one approach versus another.

In spite of our attempt to be neutral about learning outcomes and the variables that we believe are causally linked to them, the perceptive reader must by this time have become aware that while the theory may be presented as value neutral, the author is not. Most of this writer's professional career has been in the field of education, and it is impossible at this stage of my career to remain truly neutral about learning outcomes. I believe that most educators who have a deep commitment to education and the educational process must value some outcomes of the educational process in preference to others. So it is with me!

Behind the theory and its development are some values which must be evident to every careful reader of this book. These values are implicit in our long search for a theory of school learning, and no apologies at this late stage can truly remove them from the theory itself. While these values may sound like platitudes, there is some point in stating them.

1. Better learning (higher achievement) is an improvement over poor learning (lower achievement) for the individual student, the individual teacher, the school, and even the larger society.

2. A sense of competence and mastery over aspects of the environment (including what is taught in the schools as they are now or as they may come to be) is preferable to a sense of failure, incompetence, or frustration for learners as well as for teachers.

3. The distribution of school achievement is a direct consequence of student involvement in the learning process and of instructional processes used by teachers and others in the school situation. Each distribution is causally related to the variables we have described, and ignorance about them does not free the teacher or the school from responsibility for them. We prefer distributions which are indicative that most students have mastered what the school has to teach.

In spite of our awareness of the underlying values that gave meaning and energy to our search for the major variables in school learning, we can only claim at this time that we have attempted to describe them with a minimum of special pleading or justification. Our readers, however, must have their own value positions and views about what is good or desirable in education and what is not. Undoubtedly, some of our readers will have difficulties in reconciling our views of the causal variables in school learning with the value positions they have developed in their long experience with school learning—their own and the students and classes they have been involved with. None of us in education is truly value free.

In spite of this, the claim of this book is that a few major variables will explain much of individual differences in school learning, that the control and alteration of these variables will reduce or increase individual differences in school learning, and that this will, in turn, have consequences for many aspects of the school, the curriculum, teaching, individual characteristics, and other related aspects of the community and the larger society.

If this claim is supported by further research and effort in both the school and the educational laboratory, then this theory cannot remain value neutral. The prediction and control of individual differences in school achievement has *consequences* which affect all of us whether we be parents, students, teachers, school administrators, taxpayers, or government officials. In every society which places great emphasis on education and schooling, the consequences of success or failure in the schools are far-reaching and must have effects on every part of the society including our very concept of the nature of man and the human condition.

Each of our readers will see positive and negative implications of this theory for his or her own involvement with education and the schools. Each will see implications which go far beyond the schools and which vitally affect each individual in a society and the major values and myths on which a society is based. We would be remiss if we did not point to some of the implications of a theory like this and to some of the values that we see being affected by this theory.

Minimum Assumptions about Human Nature

In the work on mastery learning (Bloom, 1971; Block, 1971, 1974) and in the work on this theory we have restricted ourselves to very few assumptions about human nature. We began the work on mastery learning with the view that most individuals could learn what the schools had to teach *if* they were provided with the time and help they needed. This was an assumption that led us to the search for the means of helping most students to reach the mastery learning criteria set for different subjects. In some ways this was more an assumption about the educational process than it was about the nature of man.

While we hoped that we could demonstrate equality of learning under favorable conditions, this did not require *assumptions* about the equality of man—it required *evidence* about the equality of learning. That is, we had implicit assumptions which guided our research, but the theory in its present form does not require the user of the theory to accept our original assumptions. What the user must be prepared to accept is strong evidence for or against particular learning outcomes. Equality of learning is one of these outcomes.

We began the work on the theory with the assumption that different learners needed different amounts of time to learn a particular learning task. As we come to this final chapter we question our original assumption. When learners are approximately equal in their cognitive and affective characteristics and when they are given optimal qualities of instruction, we *find* little difference in the amount of time they require to mastery a particular learning task. Thus we have come to recognize that our original assumption about variability in time to mastery is likely to be true *only* when the characteristics of the learners and the quality of instruction are less than favorable.

We have made no major assumptions about hereditary characteristics and their possible influence on school learning. We leave the search for these to others—as far as this theory is concerned. As educators we are searching for the most favorable conditions we can find or develop in both the learners and the instruction. The consequences of these favorable conditions for the learning outcomes is what the entire book is about.

Thus, while we have been guided in our research by a number of assumptions—most of them implicit in our work rather than in our statements—few of these assumptions are required by the theory in its present form. On the other hand, it is to be hoped that the evidence produced by the research on the theory and the relevant literature referred to in this book will lead the reader to accept certain assumptions about education, the potential effectiveness of the schools, and the nature of man insofar as school learning is concerned.

HUMAN NATURE AND SCHOOL LEARNING

The Nature of Man and Woman

We have developed elaborate myths about human variability. We take great pride in noting our personal uniqueness and delight in the possibility that we are the one person in the entire world with a particular combination of characteristics. There must be some very fundamental psychological and philosophical reasons for our great concern about personal distinctiveness.

However, coupled with this quest for uniqueness is our equally great interest in belonging to a group and sharing in the values, life-styles, and other characteristics that make for membership in a group. We do not pride ourselves that our prayers to God are different from all other persons in the religious sect to which we belong. Nor do we create a life-style (e.g., clothes, food, art, and music) which we believe to be absolutely unique. We prefer to be like other members of a group that we identify with. Again, we suspect that there are profound psychological and philosophical reasons for our need to identify with one or more well-defined groups.

It is in the school, however, where these two views come into conflict. Although much of the curriculum of the school or higher education is prescribed and common to all students in a particular group, stream, or program, we as teachers and educators all too frequently take the view that the learning of students will vary greatly and the learning characteristics of each student will be unique.

The major finding resulting from the application of this theory is that only minor differences *need* be present in the learning of different students in a particular course or subject. To put it more strongly, each student may be helped to learn a particular subject to the same degree, level of competence, and even in approximately the same amount of time if the major variables in this theory are appropriately taken into consideration in the learning process.

Equality of learning outcomes and virtual equality in the learning process (time, help, means) are very hard to accept in societies which have long accepted the concept of widespread individual differences in school learning. Common observation has supported this concept, and societies have built their entire educational system on this concept—although leaders in different societies would explain these differences in different ways—heredity, environment, religion, ethnic qualities, and even God and chance.

If humans are born equal or can become equal with regard to learning, then the home and the school have responsibilities far greater than they have assumed in the past. If equality of learning is possible, then the selective function of schools must be largely abandoned in favor of the developmental functions which schools must increasingly serve.

If equality of learning is achievable through the application of this theory more widely than we have been able to do in the past, then societies must look elsewhere for grounds on which people are treated other than equally. That is, notions about learning inequality would no longer be a basis for the sorting of persons into more favored and less favored categories. (However, this would not preclude sorting mechanisms on the *amount* of education finally achieved or the *type* of education finally completed satisfactorily.) We are not so naïve as to assume that societies would not continue to seek other methods of sorting people—appearance, personal qualities, strength, family origin, religion, race, and other factors. However, modern technologically oriented societies which use education and schooling as the basis for developing the various types of competence needed by the society must (if this theory is supported) now begin with the premise that most members of the society are *capable* of acquiring each type of competence needed and that personal qualities and environmental factors (including the schools) determine which individuals will finally acquire each type of competence.

While this may be difficult for societies and the educational systems to accept, it may be even more difficult for the individual and his family to accept. Superiority and inferiority between siblings within a family with regard to learning have been widely accepted. Even more has this been accepted as true between individuals from different families. This has become a powerful rationalization in accounting for learning variation within and between families, and, in turn, this rationalization has been effective in determining the effort and motivation individuals put into school learning and aspirations for school-related careers.

Nature of Talents

At any point in time in a particular society there exists a variety of talents or aptitudes for a large number of special areas of study—music, art, literature, science, mathematics, human relations, athletics, etc. Such talents were believed to come into existence by complex interactions of heredity and environment. Given such a belief, the evidence on the existence of such talents, and great variability in the measured or observed degrees of each talent (or complex of talents), it became the responsibility of schools—aided by testing and other procedures—to identify such talents and to do whatever was possible to enhance them and guide the possessors of them to appropriate specialized training programs and career opportunities. This was regarded as a very efficient process of securing for the society the specific talents it needed at any particular time. There is no doubt that the selection of talents is a much simpler and more efficient process than the creation or development of talents.

One implication of this theory is that talent *can be developed.* That is, if most students can be brought to a high level in the learning of a particular set of subject matters, skills, and abilities, then for most purposes this constitutes the development of talent whether it be in science, mathematics, the arts, or any other field of human interest.

Many characteristics or abilities that we have regarded as talents require long periods of development to bring to a high level. Some require very early development followed by long periods of specialized learning and encouragement. Great musical skill may require early encouragement and learning opportunities followed by systematic training over long periods of time. Similarly, mathematical ability, complex psychomotor abilities, great verbal facility, and many other complex and highly developed types of competence may require some combination of early learning opportunities (before age 6) followed by highly skilled teaching or tutoring, followed by systematic development and practice over a number of years.

The point of this is that a large proportion of the great "talents" we have come to recognize in most fields of human endeavor did not just happen, did not come about purely by chance, or were "discovered" by someone at maturity. Most of these great talents were the products of systematic development over relatively extended periods of time. "Instant genius" is largely a fiction of the mass media. Many of the great talents identified by psychological tests and other techniques are discovered after many years of prior development.

A society which needs a large number of people with particular talents cannot depend purely on selection methods for finding such talents. It must take the necessary steps to develop them relatively early and to train or educate for such talents in a systematic way over relatively long periods of time.

Thus, a society which needs a large proportion of its citizenry who can solve complex problems, adapt to rapidly changing circumstances, develop verbal communication to a high level, and learn complex new ideas relatively quickly must take steps to encourage these qualities in the early years of childhood and then provide systematic educational methods to develop these qualities to a high degree during the school years. This is not any easy set of tasks, but if these are the talents that are vital for the society in the future, they can be developed and encouraged so that a high proportion of the population will possess them whether the means for developing them are in the home, the school, or other educative aspects of the larger society.

Similarly, if each member of the society is to develop some special talent in the arts—writing, painting, sculpture, music, dance or drama—these can be encouraged early and developed systematically over a number of years.

This is not to take the view that everyone will be interested in developing each talent. What is contended is that almost everyone is capable of developing most of the commonly recognized talents or abilities if the motivation is available (or can become developed) in the individual, if the individual is provided with sensitive learning opportunities (sensitive to his or her needs and state of development), and if the appropriate learning provisions are available over the relatively lengthy sequence of learning steps needed to bring the talents to the necessary level of development.

The theory expounded in this work thus specifies some of the conditions or variables needed in the history of the learner to bring him to the high development of any particular talent. What it does not specify is the precise content, objectives, and subject matter of the specific talent at any stage in its development. It holds the promise that under appropriate conditions a sizable proportion of a population can be brought to a high level of development in almost any major talent, ability, or quality desired in a society.

THE THEORY AND THE SCHOOLS

Errors and Education

The system of schooling which occupies 10 or more years of education for the majority of children and youth in each society does great good for some and may be very damaging for others. It offers all an opportunity to learn the fundamental cognitive and affective characteristics required in complex societies, and it makes available to all the history and major ideas developed within the society as well as those which transcend the particular society. But, it does so on its own terms.

The students are taught in groups of twenty to forty in such a way that some students learn well while others learn less well. Each group of students is largely at the mercy of a particular teacher, and the interactions which are favorable for some students may be far from favorable for others.

Typically, the students are passed from one teacher to another at the end of the particular academic term, and the errors developed in the student's learning in one term are compounded with the errors made in subsequent academic terms. The errors in this system are eventually built into the student, and only rarely is he able to fully recover from them.

Some students may have these errors reduced at various times by the home environment which corrects difficulties in learning as they occur and helps the students to overcome them before it is too late. Other students may be helped by tutors—especially when the home has the resources to select and support a tutor at points when the student is most in need of this type of help.

One set of major flaws in the educational system is converted into the student's feelings of inadequacy as a learner and his lowered aspirations for further learning. The second set of flaws is evident when the student does not adequately develop the cognitive learning and other prerequisites he will need for subsequent learning.

The major thesis of this book is that a system of feedback to the teacher and students can reveal the errors in learning shortly after they occur, and if appropriate corrections are introduced as they are needed, the educational system can be a *self-correcting* system so that errors made at one time can be corrected before they are compounded with later errors.

In effect, a self-correcting system of schooling can become a minimal-error system of education (insofar as learning errors may be reduced as they occur) with consequent positive effects on students' affective and cognitive characteristics. Elsewhere, we have made the point that much of individual differences in learners are the effects of a system of schooling which is full of errors. A minimal-error (or error-correcting) system of schooling may approach the effectiveness for learning of a system of tutoring in which a highly gifted and sensitive tutor interacts with one student at a time.

Whether or not an error-correcting system of schooling can reach this level of learning outcomes, there is little doubt that such a system of schooling is far more attractive than one that constantly makes errors which are compounded over time.

Strength of the Educational Process

In recent years it has become popular to view schools and the educational process as relatively weak in contrast with heredity, the home, and sociological and economic forces in the society. The implications of this theory are that the school and the learning process are capable of being very strong—so strong that individual learners can be made either *equal* or very *unequal* with regard to particular learning outcomes. No institution (other than the family) in a society has the potential power over individuals and their well-being that the schools have. In large part this great potential is due to the number of years (and the ages) during which students attend school.

While this potential may be very great, it is clear that the reality of school effects has been far from this potential. This has been especially apparent in the large national and international school surveys such as Coleman (1966a), Plowden (1967), Husén (1967), Comber and Keeves (1973), Purves (1973), and Thorndike (1973). Part of this relative weakness may be ascribed to the fact that schooling is largely a group process—twenty to forty students form a class in which the welfare and development of the individual may be neglected because of preoccupation with the entire group of students. Some of the apparent weakness of the schools may be due to lack of clear-cut objectives for education and their implementation by carefully developed instructional materials and procedures. Responsible also is the fact that the schools rarely enlist the full motivation and energies of students in the learning process.

What is maintained is that the schools are *potentially* able to make very great differences in the careers and lives of their students. More favorable and systematic efforts can increase the capabilities of students to learn what the schools have to teach. Theoretically, almost all the students can learn to a relatively high level anything the schools have to teach.

Mastery learning research and practice has already amply demonstrated that the large majority of students in a class can learn selected subjects up to as high a level as the most able students in the group. Usually, there has been some extra expenditure of time and help in achieving such results. The present theory holds out the possibility of such achievement being accomplished with an actual saving of student time over the entire course or program.

But, the issue in the long run is not a cost-benefit analysis of school learning and the conditions under which a particular set of results may be obtained. The central issue is what is worth learning in the schools and the means by which the student's motivation and capabilities are fully engaged in the learning process. Related to this is the important question of what is a significant set of objectives for school learning and the curricular decisions to fully implement the educational objectives that are important for a particular learner, school, or society.

In the past, the schools tended to be very wasteful of human and material resources. Only a small percent of students were expected to learn well what the schools had to teach. As a result, the schools frequently taught a particular subject, such as mathematics, physics, or history, to millions of students with the hope that a small percent of such students would turn out to be especially "gifted" and could be encouraged to go on to some advanced work in the field. In effect, the schools taught millions of students in the hope that a few thousand would be selected for more advanced specialization in the particular subject field.

If the schools can bring a large majority of students to the level of learning that was hitherto expected of only the most gifted and able students, it can no longer be with expectation that such students will go on to do advanced work in the subject. No field could possibly use so many "gifted" students. More and more it will be necessary to ask whether the time and effort required to learn a subject to a high level can be justified for the particular students, the school, and the society. Thus, the increased ability to control and determine the school learning of our students places upon educators increased responsibility for providing a curriculum which is in the best interests of the students and the society.

The Task of the Schools

Traditionally, the schools have been charged with giving each student an equal opportunity to learn what the schools have had to offer. While no one was ever able to demonstrate that each student had exactly the same opportunity to learn, there have been many demonstrations that particular groups of students have had less opportunity to learn in the schools than other groups by virtue of social and economic position, race, religion, ethnic background, geographical location, and so on.

In spite of the evidence for or against equality of opportunity, many teachers and school leaders have tried their best to be as fair as possible to all students and to provide each student with some measure of equality of opportunity. Few teachers or school administrators who have professional commitments to education could live with themselves if they viewed themselves as giving opportunities to some children while denying them to others. What is at issue is not whether teachers "believe" they are fair or not, rather it is what children are *able to do* at given points in their educational careers.

One implication of the theory is that *equality of learning outcomes* can be a goal of education rather than *equality of opportunity.* Such a goal suggests that teachers must find ways of giving each child the help and encouragement he needs when he needs it rather than ensuring identical treatment of all children. *Inequality of treatment* may be needed, at least at certain stages of the learning process, if children are to attain equality of learning outcomes. It means that the teachers and the instructional material and procedures should emphasize acceptable levels of learning for all children rather than be satisfied that each has been "treated" fairly and equally.

But, even if *equality of outcomes* is a goal, there must be some limitations on this if the schools are to be realistic and not set goals which are completely unattainable.

There will always be some learners who because of background characteristics—including heredity and home environmental characteristics—will learn at a rate and at a level of complexity which far exceeds that of the average student. We believe this constitutes no more than 1 or 2 percent of the students in a typical class of students. We suspect that such students will pose complex problems of classroom management, but that no effort should be made to retard their drive and incentives to learning in order to keep them in step with other students.

In addition, we believe there will always be some learners who because of background characteristics—including heredity, home environmental characteristics, and organic or functional disturbances—will learn at a slower rate or at a lower level of complexity than the average student. We believe this probably constitutes no more than 1 to 3 percent of the students in a typical class. We believe such students can make effective learning progress but will need more time, attention, and resources to make this possible. This also poses difficult problems of classroom management, but much can be done for these students by the large majority of teachers.

It is the middle 95 percent of students where *equality of outcomes* is a realistic possibility for most teachers who carefully and systematically apply appropriate instructional means to student differences.

A second qualification has to do with when and where inequality of treatment is to be preferred to equality of opportunity.

The research cited in this book stresses the importance of help and support in the early phases of the learning rather than in the later phases. In a new course or subject, the application of differential support and correctives at the beginning of the course (the first quarter or third of the course) is likely to be accompanied by less need for this at later stages or parts of the course. On the other hand, it is not likely that the same effort and help in the last part of the course (the last third or quarter) will have as great an effect as it will at the beginning. Remediation too late in the course is not likely to have as much effect as feedback and correctives at earlier stages.

Similarly, it is likely that the greatest benefits of unequal treatment would be at the beginning of a new school stage rather than in later years. Thus, unequal treatment in the first two or three years of school should yield greater long-term benefits than such treatment in the last year or two of primary education. Similarly, unequal treatment in the first year or two of secondary education should yield greater benefits than such treatment in the last year or two of secondary school.

Another way of viewing the problem is to think of learning sequences over 2 or more years—arithmetic, language development and reading, science, second language, or other subjects. Here, the implication is that unequal treatment in the first terms or courses in a long sequence has greater benefits than the same amount of effort at later points in the subject sequence.

A third qualification has to do with which parts of the curriculum are most vital for equality of outcomes.

Here we would take the position that some types of learning are likely to be more important for the general welfare of students than are others. For example, verbal ability and reading competence are important because they affect the students' learning of most subjects in the curriculum. Since most instructional material and instruction in the schools is largely verbal in nature, students who lack adequate verbal ability and reading competence are unlikely to be able to succeed in other parts of the school curriculum (Bloom, 1974a; Thorndike, 1973).

There are some arithmetical and mathematical types of competence that are necessary as a basis for the rest of the arithmetic-mathematics sequence in the schools. Much of this competence is also needed for the science courses and to a lesser degree the social science parts of the school curriculum.

One might also stress certain types of reasoning and problem-solving abilities, skills in using libraries and other information sources, and some of the skills of organizing and presenting arguments, reports, and other expositions in the school setting.

In all of these, the attempt is to locate the particular kinds of learning which are both important in their own right as well as important for other parts of the school learning process. These are likely to represent the "survival" skills required to reach a satisfactory level of learning anywhere in the schools and, perhaps, necessary also for solving the many problems encountered in the larger society. We doubt that this brief listing includes the entire range of basic learning which is of great importance for all students. However, the identification of such learning is of the utmost importance in determining where equality of outcomes or at least a minimal level of competence is desirable for all students.

Finally, it is quite possible that there are parts of the school program where equality of opportunity may be preferred to equality of outcomes.

We believe that some parts of the school program may be of interest to students for exploratory and recreational purposes rather than necessarily for serious academic interests. These might include many of the elective courses as well as those courses and experiences which the students want to "try" but do not have a strong and serious interest in, at least in the beginning.

Some students wish to learn some of the sports and other physical activities of the schools without committing themselves to such activities. Similarly, there are many humanistic subjects, such as the arts, music, or poetry, which students may wish to explore.

The student should increasingly—with age and experience—be able to make decisions about where his or her learning is to be purposive and systematic and where the learning is to be exploratory and even for "fun."

REFERENCES

Airasian, P. W. *Formative Evaluation Instruments: A Construction and Validation of Tests to Evaluate Learning over Short Time Periods.* Unpublished doctoral dissertation, University of Chicago, 1969.

Airasian, P. W. The Use of Hierarchies in the Analysis and Planning of Chemistry Instruction. *Science Education,* 1970, *54,* 91–95.

Airasian, P. W. The Use of Hierarchies in Curriculum Analysis and Instructional Planning. *California Journal of Educational Research,* 1971, *22,* 34–41.

Airasian, P. W., & Bart, W. M. Ordering Theory: A New and Useful Measurement Model. *Educational Technology,* 1973, *13,* 56–60.

Anderson, L. W. *Time and School Learning.* Unpublished doctoral dissertation, University of Chicago, 1973.

Anthony, Bobbie C. M. *The Identification and Measurement of Classroom Environmental Process Variables Related to Academic Achievement.* Unpublished doctoral dissertation, University of Chicago, 1967.

Arlin, M. N. *Learning Rate and Learning Rate Variance under Mastery Learning Conditions.* Unpublished doctoral dissertation, University of Chicago, 1973.

Atkinson, J. W., & Feather, N. T. (Eds.). *A Theory of Achievement Motivation.* New York: John Wiley & Sons, Inc., 1966.

Atkinson, R. C. Computer-based Instruction in Initial Reading. In *Proceedings of the 1967 Invitational Conference on Testing Problems.* Princeton: Educational Testing Service, 1968.

Barr, A. S. The Measurement and Prediction of Teaching Efficiency: A Summary of Investigations. *Journal of Experimental Education,* 1948, *16,* 203–283.

Bellack, A. A., et al. *The Language of the Classroom.* New York: Teachers College Press, 1966.

Binor, S. *The Relative Effectiveness of Mastery Learning Strategies in Second Language Acquisition.* Unpublished master's dissertation, University of Chicago, 1974.

Block, J. H. *The Effects of Various Levels of Performance on Selected Cognitive, Affective, and Time Variables.* Unpublished doctoral dissertation, University of Chicago, 1970.

Block, J. H. (Ed.). *Mastery Learning: Theory and Practice.* New York: Holt, Rinehart and Winston, 1971.

Block, J. H. (Ed.). *Schools, Society, and Mastery Learning.* New York: Holt, Rinehart and Winston, 1974.

Block, J., & Burns, R. B. Mastery Learning. In L. S. Shulman (Ed.), *Review of Research in Education,* 4. Itasca, Ill.: F. E. Peacock, Publishers, 1976.

Bloom, B. S. Thought Processes of Students in Discussion Classes. In S. J. French (Ed.), *Accent on Teaching.* New York: Harper & Brothers, 1954.

219

Bloom, B. S. *Stability and Change in Human Characteristics.* New York: John Wiley & Sons, Inc., 1964.

Bloom, B. S. Learning for Mastery, Chapter 3 in B. S. Bloom, J. T. Hasting, & G. F. Madaus, *Handbook on Formative and Summative Evaluation of Student Learning.* New York: McGraw-Hill Book Company, 1971.

Bloom, B. S. Implications of the IEA studies for Curriculum and Instruction. *School Review,* 1974a, 82, 413–435.

Bloom, B. S. Time and Learning. *American Psychologist,* 1974b, 29, 682–688.

Bloom, B. S., Hastings, J. T., & Madaus, G. *Handbook on Formative and Summative Evaluation of Student Learning.* New York: McGraw-Hill Book Company, 1971.

Bloom, S. *Peer and Cross-Age Tutoring in the Schools.* Washington, D.C.: National Institute of Education, 1976.

Bostow, D. E., & O'Connor, R. J. A Comparison of Two College Classroom Testing Procedures. *Journal of Applied Behavior Analysis,* 1973, 6, 599–607.

Boswell, James. *Life of Johnson* (Vol. I). London: Oxford University Press, 1924, p. 652.

Bower, E. M. Mental Health in Education. *Review of Educational Research,* 1962, 32, 441–454.

Bracht, G. H., & Hopkins, K. D. Stability of Educational Achievement. In G. H. Bracht, K. D. Hopkins, & J. C. Stanley (Eds.), *Perspectives in Educational and Psychological Measurement.* Englewood Cliffs, N.J.: Prentice-Hall, 1972.

Brookover, W. B., Shailer, T., & Paterson, A. Self-concept of Ability and School Achievement. *Sociology of Education,* 1964, 37, 271–278.

Brophy, J. E., & Good, T. L. Teachers' Communication of Differential Expectations for Children's Class Room Performance: Some Behavioral Data. *Journal of Educational Psychology,* 1970, 61, 365–374.

Carroll, J. B. A Model of School Learning. *Teachers College Record,* 1963, 64, 723–733.

Carroll, J. B. *The Teaching of French as a Foreign Language in Seven Countries: International Studies in Evaluation,* V. New York: John Wiley & Sons, Inc., 1975.

Coleman, J. S., et al. *Equality of Educational Opportunity.* Washington, D.C.: U.S. Government Printing Office, 1966a.

Coleman, J. S., et al. *Supplemental Appendix to the Survey on Equality of Educational Opportunity.* Washington, D.C.: U.S. Government Printing Office, 1966b.

Comber, L. C., & Keeves, J. P. *Science Education in Nineteen Countries: International Studies in Evaluation,* I. New York: John Wiley & Sons, 1974.

Condo, P. *The Analysis and Evaluation of a Self-paced Course in Calculus.* Paper presented at First Annual National Conference on Personalized Instruction in Higher Education, Washington, D.C., 1974.

Crawford, J., et al. *Evaluation of the Impact of Educational Research and Development Products.* Final Report, Palo Alto, Calif.: American Institutes for Research, 1972.

Cronbach, L. J., & Snow, R. E. *Aptitudes and Instructional Methods.* New York: Irvington, 1976.

Crosswhite, F. J. Correlates of Attitudes toward Mathematics. In *National Longitudinal Study in Mathematics Achievement.* Report 5, No. 20, edited by Wilson, J. W. and Begle, E. G. Palo Alto, Calif.: School Mathematics Study Group, 1972.

Dahlöff, U. *Ability Grouping, Content Validity, and Curriculum Process Analysis.* New York: Teachers College Press, 1971.

Dave, R. H. *The Identification and Measurement of Environmental Process Variables that are Related to Educational Achievement.* Unpublished doctoral dissertation, University of Chicago, 1963.

Dolan, L. *Affect and School Achievement: Some Theoretical and Empirical Issues.* Unpublished manuscript, University of Chicago, 1974.

Dollard, J., & Miller, N. E. *Personality and Psychotherapy.* New York: McGraw-Hill Book Company, 1950.

Domas, S. J., & Tiedeman, D. Teacher Competence: An Annotated Bibliography. *Journal of Experimental Education,* 1950, *19,* 101–218.

Dreeben, R. *On What Is Learned in School.* Reading, Mass.: Addison-Wesley Publishing Co., 1968.

Dunkin, M. J., & Biddle, B. J. *The Study of Teaching.* New York: Holt, Rinehart and Winston, 1974.

Erikson, E. H. *Childhood and Society.* New York: W. W. Norton, 1963.

Farquhar, W. W., & Christensen, E. W. *Academic Achievements of Eleventh Grade Puerto Rican High School Students.* East Lansing, Mich.: Educational Publication Series No. 43. College of Education, Michigan State University, 1967.

Faure, E., et al. *Learning to Be.* Paris: UNESCO; London: Harrap, 1972.

Feather, N. T. Performance at a Difficult Task in Relation to Initial Expectation of Success, Test Anxiety, and Need Achievement. *Journal of Personality,* 1965, *33,* 200.

Flanders, N. A. *Analyzing Teacher Behavior.* Reading, Mass.: Addison-Wesley Publishing Co., 1970.

Flemming, C. W. A Detailed Analysis of Achievement in High School. *Teachers College Contributions to Education* (No. 196). New York: Bureau of Publications, Teachers College, Columbia University, 1925, 35–47.

Gagné, R. M. Learning Hierarchies. *Educational Psychologist,* 1968, *6,* 1–9.

Gagné, R. M., & Paradise, N. E. Abilities and Learning Sets in Knowledge Acquisition. *Psychological Monographs,* 1961, 75 (14, Whole No. 218).

Glaser, R. Adapting the Elementary School Curriculum to Individual Performance. In *Proceedings of the 1967 Invitational Conference on Testing Problems.* Princeton: Educational Testing Service, 1968.

Glaser, R. Evaluation of Instruction and Changing Education Models, in Wittrock, M. C., and Wiley, D. E. (Eds.), *The Evaluation of Instruction.* New York: Holt, Rinehart and Winston, 1970.

Haggerty, L. H. An Empirical Evaluation of the Accomplishment Quotient: A Four Year Study at the Junior High School Level. *Journal of Experimental Education,* 1941, *10,* 78–90.

Hanson, R. A. *The Development of Verbal Intelligence: A Longitudinal Study.* Unpublished doctoral dissertation, University of Chicago, 1972.

Havighurst, R. J. Minority Subcultures and the Law of Effect. *American Psychologist,* 1970, *25,* 313–322.

Hess, R. L., & Shipman, V. Early Experience and the Socialization of Cognitive Modes in Children. *Child Development,* 1965, *36,* 869.

Hicklin, W. J. *A Study of Long-range Techniques for Predicting Patterns of Scholastic Behavior.* Unpublished doctoral dissertation, University of Chicago, 1962.

Hilgard, E. R., & Bower, G. H. *Theories of Learning* (3rd ed.). New York: Appleton-Century-Crofts, 1966.

Husén, T. (Ed.). *International Study of Achievement in Mathematics: A Comparison of Twelve Countries* (Vols. I and II). New York: John Wiley & Sons, 1967.

Husén, T. *Talent, Opportunity and Career*. Stockholm: Almqvist and Wiksell, 1969.

Jackson, P. W. *Life in Classrooms*. New York: Holt, Rinehart and Winston, 1968.

Jamison, D., Suppes, P., & Wells, S. The Effectiveness of Alternative Instructional Media: A Survey. *Review of Educational Research*, 1974, *44*, 1–67.

Jones, E. L., Gordon, H. A., & Schechtman, G. L. *Mastery Learning: A Strategy for Academic Success in a Community College*. Los Angeles: ERIC Clearinghouse for Junior Colleges, 1975.

Kersh, M. E. *A Strategy for Mastery Learning in Fifth-Grade Arithmetic*. Unpublished doctoral dissertation, University of Chicago, 1971.

Khan, S. B. Affective Correlates of Academic Achievement. *Journal of Educational Psychology*, 1969, *60*, 216–221.

Khan, S. B., & Weiss, J. The Teaching of Affective Responses. In R. M. W. Travers (Ed.), *Second Handbook of Research on Teaching*. Chicago: Rand McNally & Co., 1973.

Kifer, E. *The Effects of School Achievement on the Affective Traits of the Learner*. Unpublished doctoral dissertation, University of Chicago, 1973.

Kim, H. *Learning Rates, Aptitudes, and Achievements*. Unpublished doctoral dissertation, University of Chicago, 1968.

Kurtz, J. J., & Swenson, E. J. Student, Parent, and Teacher Attitude toward Student Achievement in School. *School Review*, 1951, *59*, 273–279.

Lavin, D. E. *The Prediction of Academic Performance*. New York: Russell Sage Foundation, 1965.

Lee, Y. D., et al. Interaction Improvement Studies on the Mastery Learning Project. *Final Report on Mastery Learning Program*. Educational Research Center, Seoul National University, November 1971.

Levin, T. *The Effect of Content Prerequisite and Process-oriented Experiences on Application Ability in the Learning of Probability*. Unpublished doctoral dissertation, University of Chicago, 1975.

Lewis, E. G., & Massad, C. F. *English as a Foreign Language in Ten Countries: International Studies in Evaluation*, IV. New York: John Wiley & Sons, 1975.

Malpass, L. F. Some Relationships between Students' Perceptions of School and Their Achievement. *Journal of Educational Psychology*, 1953, *44*, 475–482.

Marjoribanks, K. (Ed.). *Environments for Learning*. London: National Foundation for Educational Research Publishing Company, Ltd., 1974.

Mayo, G. D., & Longo, A. A. Training Time and Programmed Instruction. *Journal of Applied Psychology*, 1966, *50*, 1–4.

McClelland, D. Toward a Theory of Motive Acquisition. *American Psychologist*, 1965, *20*, 321–333.

Michael, W. B., Baker, D., & Jones, R. A. A Note Concerning the Predictive Validities of Selected Cognitive and Non-Cognitive Measures for Freshmen Students in a Liberal Arts College. *Educational and Psychological Measurement*, 1964, *24*, 373–375.

Moore, J. W., Mahan, J. M., & Ritts, C. A. Continuous Progress Concept of Instruction with University Students. *Psychological Reports*, 1969, 25, 887–892.

Moore, J. W., Hauck, W. E., & Gagné, E. D. Acquisition, Retention, and Transfer in an Individualized College Physics Course. *Journal of Educational Psychology*, 1973, 64, 335–340.

Morrison, H. C. *The Practice of Teaching in the Secondary School*. Chicago: University of Chicago Press, 1926.

Morsh, J. E., & Wilder, E. W. Identifying the Effective Instructor: A Review of the Quantitative Studies, 1900–1952. Research Bulletin No. AFPTRC-TR-54-44. San Antonio, Tex.: USAF Personnel Training Research Center, 1954.

Overly, N. V. (Ed.). *The Unstudied Curriculum*. Washington, D.C.: Association for Supervision and Curriculum Development, National Education Association, 1970.

Özcelik, D. A. *Student Involvement in the Learning Process*. Unpublished doctoral dissertation, University of Chicago, 1974.

Payne, M. A. *The Use of Data in Curricular Decisions*. Unpublished doctoral dissertation, University of Chicago, 1963.

Pearson, W. *An Attempt to Design Instructional Techniques to Accommodate Individual Differences in Learning Rate*. Unpublished doctoral dissertation, University of Chicago, 1973.

Peterson, P. *A Review of the Research on Mastery Learning Strategies*. Unpublished manuscript, International Association for the Evaluation of Educational Achievement, 1972. (Also Stanford Center for Research and Development in Teaching, Stanford, Calif.)

Pillet, E. E. A Study of Affective and Cognitive Development in an Introductory French Course. Personal communication, 1975.

Plowden Report. *Children and Their Primary Schools*. A report of the Central Advisory Council for Education (England). London: Her Majesty's Stationery Office, 1967.

Purves, A. C. *Literature Education in Ten Countries: International Studies in Evaluation*, II. New York: John Wiley & Sons, 1973.

Resnick, L. B., Wang, M. C. & Kaplan, J. D. *Behavior Analysis in Curriculum Design: A Hierarchically Sequenced Introductory Mathematics Curriculum*. Pittsburgh: Learning Research and Development Center, 1970.

Rosenshine, B. *Teaching Behaviours and Student Achievement*. London: National Foundation for Educational Research, 1971.

Russell, I. L. Motivation for School Achievement: Measurement and Validation. *Journal of Educational Research*, 1969, 62, 263–266.

Scannell, D. P. Differential Prediction of Academic Success from Achievement Test Scores. Unpublished doctoral dissertation, State University of Iowa, 1958.

Sears, P. S. *The Effect of Classroom Conditions on the Strength of Achievement Motive and Work Output of Elementary School Children*. Final Report. U.S. Cooperative Research Project, 1963, No. 873.

Sheppard, W. C., & MacDermot, H. G. Design and Evaluation of a Programmed Course in Introductory Psychology. *Journal of Applied Behavior Analysis*, 1970, 3, 5–11.

Smith, B. O., Meux, M. O., et al. *A Study of the Logic of Teaching*. Urbana: Bureau of Educational Research, University of Illinois, 1962.

Smith, M. I. Teaching to Specific Objectives. *Second Progress Report for the Development of a County-wide Articulation in Foreign Language Instruction through Common Measurement Procedures.* Stanislaus County (California) School's Office, 1968.

Stephens, J. M. *The Process of Schooling: A Psychological Examination.* New York: Holt, Rinehart and Winston, 1967.

Stringer, L. A., & Glidewell, J. C. *Early Detection of Emotional Illnesses in School Children: Final Report.* Missouri: St. Louis County Health Department, 1967.

Thorndike, R. L. *Reading Comprehension Education in Fifteen Countries: International Studies in Evaluation,* III. New York: John Wiley & Sons, Inc., 1973.

Torshen, K. *The Relation of Classroom Evaluation to Students' Self-concepts and Mental Health.* Unpublished doctoral dissertation, University of Chicago, 1969.

Tyler, R. W. *Basic Principles of Curriculum and Instruction.* Chicago: The University of Chicago Press, 1950.

Walberg, H. J. Social Environment as a Mediator of Classroom Learning. *Journal of Educational Psychology,* 1969, *60,* 443–448.

Washburne, C. W. Educational Measurements as a Key to Individualizing Instruction and Promotions. *Journal of Educational Research,* 1922, *5,* 195–206.

White, M. A., & Duker, J. Models of Schooling and Models of Evaluation. *Teachers College Record,* 1973, *74,* 293–307.

White, R. W. Motivation Reconsidered: The Concept of Competence. *Psychological Review,* 1959, *66,* 297–333.

Williams, T. H. *Competence Dimensions of Family Environments.* Paper presented at American Educational Research Association Annual Meeting, Chicago, 1974.

Wolf, R. The Measurement of Environments. In A. Anastasi (Ed.), *Testing Problems in Perspective.* Washington, D.C.: American Council on Education, 1966.

APPENDIXES

Appendix to Chapter 3

Table 3-A. Relation between Prior Achievement Measures and Subsequent Achievement Measures with a Time Difference between Measures of One Year   228

Table 3-B. Relation between Prior Achievement Measures and Subsequent Achievement Measures with a Time Difference between Measures of Two or More Years   230

Table 3-C. Relation between Composite Aptitude Measures and Subsequent Achievement Measures   232

Table 3-D. Relation between Selected Aptitude Subtest Measures and Subsequent Achievement Measures   235

Table 3-E. Relation between Reading Comprehension and Achievement in Various Subjects   237

Appendix to Chapter 4

Table 4-A. Relation between Affect toward Subject and Student Achievement   244

Table 4-B. Relation between Affect toward School and Student Achievement   249

Table 4-C. Relation between Academic Self-Concept and Student Achievement   252

Appendix to Chapter 5

Table 5-A. Relation between Use of Cues and Student Achievement (Group Measures)   258

Table 5-B. Relation between Use of Reinforcement and Student Achievement (Group Measures)   260

Table 5-C. Relation between Use of Participation and Student Achievement (Group Measures)   262

Table 5-D. Relation between Use of Participation and Student Achievement (Individual Measures)   263

Appendix References   267

APPENDIX TO CHAPTER 3

APPENDIX TABLE 3-A. *RELATION BETWEEN PRIOR ACHIEVEMENT MEASURES AND SUBSEQUENT ACHIEVEMENT MEASURES WITH A TIME DIFFERENCE BETWEEN MEASURES OF ONE YEAR*

STUDY	SAMPLE CHARACTERISTICS		PRIOR ACHIEVEMENT MEASURE	SUBSEQUENT ACHIEVEMENT MEASURE	OBSERVED r	CORRECTED r*
	GRADE LEVEL	SIZE				
READING AND ENGLISH						
Payne (1963)	2–3	74	Metropolitan Reading	Metropolitan Reading	.86	.91
	2–3	106	Metropolitan Reading	Metropolitan Reading	.84	.88
Townsend (1950)	4–5	123	Metropolitan Reading Comprehension	Metropolitan Reading Comprehension	.78	.83
Townsend (1950)	5–6	56	Stanford Reading	Stanford Reading	.88	.97
	6–7	56	Stanford Reading	Stanford Reading	.90	.99
Jacobs and Spaulding (1954)	5–6	97	Stanford Paragraph Meaning (Form D)	Stanford Paragraph Meaning (Form J)	.74	.81
			Stanford Paragraph Meaning (Form G)	Stanford Paragraph Meaning (Form Y)	.82	.89
Gnauck and Kaczkowski (1961)	7–8	90	Iowa Test of Basic Skills Reading	Iowa Test of Basic Skills Reading	.74 M† .84 F	.80 .91
			Language	Language	.77 M .78 F	.80 .81
			Vocabulary	Vocabulary	.84 M .87 F	.91 .95
Townsend (1950)	7–8	129	Metropolitan Reading Comprehension	Metropolitan Reading Comprehension	.70	.75
Traxler (1949a)	8–9	150	Coop Reading Test	Coop Reading Test	.82	.90
	9–10	160	Coop Reading Test	Coop Reading Test	.85	.93
Traxler (1949b)	7–8	36	Coop Reading Test	Coop Reading Test	.85	.93
	8–9	36	Coop Reading Test	Coop Reading Test	.87	.96
	9–10	36	Coop Reading Test	Coop Reading Test	.87	.96
	10–11	36	Coop Reading Test	Coop Reading Test	.87	.96
	11–12	36	Coop Reading Test	Coop Reading Test	.79	.87

MATHEMATICS

Study	Grade	N	Test	Test		
Payne (1963)	1–2	74	Metropolitan Arithmetic	Metropolitan Arithmetic	.75	.79
	1–2	106	Metropolitan Arithmetic	Metropolitan Arithmetic	.77	.81
	2–3	74	Metropolitan Arithmetic	Metropolitan Arithmetic	.81	.90
	2–3	106	Metropolitan Arithmetic	Metropolitan Arithmetic	.64	.71
	5–6	74	Metropolitan Arithmetic	Metropolitan Arithmetic	.72	.80
	5–6	106	Metropolitan Arithmetic	Metropolitan Arithmetic	.76	.87
Jacobs and Spaulding (1954)	5–6	97	Stanford Arithmetic Reasoning (Form D)	Stanford Arithmetic Reasoning (Form J)	.72	.82
	5–6	97	Stanford Arithmetic Reasoning (Form G)	Stanford Arithmetic Reasoning (Form Y)	.76	.84
	5–6	97	Stanford Arithmetic Computation (Form D)	Stanford Arithmetic Computation (Form J)	.74	.86
	5–6	97	Stanford Arithmetic Computation (Form G)	Stanford Arithmetic Computation (Form Y)	.79	.88
Townsend (1948)	4–5	129	Metropolitan Arithmetic Fundamentals	Metropolitan Arithmetic Fundamentals	.53	.58
	4–5	129	Metropolitan Arithmetic Problems	Metropolitan Arithmetic Problems	.71	.79
Townsend (1950)	5–6	56	Stanford Arithmetic	Stanford Arithmetic	.47	.57
	6–7	56	Stanford Arithmetic	Stanford Arithmetic	.80	.89
Gnauck and Kaczkowski (1961)	7–8	90	Iowa Tests of Basic Skills—Arithmetic	Iowa Tests of Basic Skills—Arithmetic	.72 M .80 F	.80 .89
Townsend (1948)	7–8	129	Metropolitan Arithmetic Fundamentals	Metropolitan Arithmetic Fundamentals	.65	.72
	7–8	129	Metropolitan Arithmetic Fundamentals	Metropolitan Arithmetic Fundamentals	.73	.81

*These values are corrected for the unreliability of the instruments.   †The letter "M" or "F" indicates "male" or "female."

229

APPENDIX TABLE 3-B. RELATION BETWEEN PRIOR ACHIEVEMENT MEASURES AND SUBSEQUENT ACHIEVEMENT MEASURES WITH A TIME DIFFERENCE BETWEEN MEASURES OF TWO OR MORE YEARS

STUDY	SAMPLE CHARACTERISTICS		PRIOR ACHIEVEMENT MEASURE	SUBSEQUENT ACHIEVEMENT MEASURE	OBSERVED r	CORRECTED r
	GRADE LEVEL	SIZE				
READING AND ENGLISH						
Payne (1963)	1–3	74	Metropolitan Reading Test	Metropolitan Reading Test	.59	.64
		106			.70	.76
	2–5	74	Metropolitan Reading Test	Metropolitan Reading Test	.78	.84
		106			.73	.79
	3–5	74	Metropolitan Reading Test	Metropolitan Reading Test	.81	.88
		106			.82	.89
Kraus (1973)	3–6	80	Metropolitan Reading Test	Metropolitan Reading Test	.80	.87
		85			.80	.87
	6–9	80	Metropolitan Reading Test	Metropolitan Reading Test	.81	.88
		85			.84	.91
Kvaraceus and Lanigan (1948)	6.9–8.9	27	Iowa Tests of Basic Skills Reading Language Vocabulary	Iowa Tests of Basic Skills Reading Language Vocabulary	.75 .61 .74	.91 .74 .91
Alexander (1961)	6–8		Chicago Reading Tests	Chicago Reading Tests		
School A		58			.77	.86
School B		53			.91	.99
School C		43			.86	.96
Traxler (1949b)	9–12	36	Coop Reading Test	Coop Reading Test	.82	.87
	10–12	36	Coop Reading Test	Coop Reading Test	.82	.88
Aaron (1946)	8–10	885	Coop English Composite	Coop English Composite	.82	.86
Adam (1940)	9–12	241	Coop English Composite	Coop English Composite	.77	.81
Hicklin (1962)	10–12	92	Teachers' Marks	Teachers' Marks	.79	.93
Flanagan (1964)	9–12	2,014 M 2,044 F	Reading Comprehension	Reading Comprehension	.71 .77	.77 .84
Flanagan (1964)	9–12	1,977 M 2,119 F	Literature	Literature	.72 .72	.90 .95

ARITHMETIC AND MATHEMATICS

	N	Test		
Payne (1963)				
1–3	74	Metropolitan Arithmetic Test	.71	.76
	106	Metropolitan Arithmetic Test	.71	.76
2–5	74	Metropolitan Arithmetic Test	.69	.77
	106	Metropolitan Arithmetic Test	.61	.68
3–5	74	Metropolitan Arithmetic Test	.74	.82
	106	Metropolitan Arithmetic Test	.71	.79
3–6	74	Metropolitan Arithmetic Test	.78	.87
	106	Metropolitan Arithmetic Test	.64	.71
Flanagan (1964)				
9–12	1,977 M	Mathematics Information	.72	.87
	2,119 F	Mathematics Information	.69	.86
	1,883 M	Arithmetic Reasoning	.65	.86
	2,006 F	Arithmetic Reasoning	.68	.94
	1,799 M	High School Mathematics	.69	.82
	1,919 F	High School Mathematics	.67	.84

SCIENCE

	N	Test		
Flanagan (1964)				
	1,977 M	Biological Science	.64	
	2,119 F	Biological Science	.62	
	1,977 M	Physical Science	.75	.92
	2,119 F	Physical Science	.72	.96

APPENDIX TABLE 3-C.   RELATION BETWEEN COMPOSITE APTITUDE MEASURES AND SUBSEQUENT ACHIEVEMENT MEASURES

STUDY	SAMPLE CHARACTERISTICS		COMPOSITE APTITUDE MEASURE	ACHIEVEMENT CRITERION	OBSERVED r	CORRECTED r
	GRADE LEVEL	SIZE				
READING						
Weiner and Feldmann (1963)	K	126	Reading Prognosis Test	Gates Primary Reading Sentence Reading	.78	.88
				Paragraph Reading	.81	.91
		72	Reading Prognosis Test	Gates Primary Reading Sentence Reading	.68	.76
				Paragraph Reading	.72	.81
		54	Reading Prognosis Test	Gates Primary Reading Sentence Reading	.74	.83
				Paragraph Reading	.77	.87
University School District, Missouri (1970)	K–1	78 M	Metropolitan Readiness	Stanford Achievement Tests Reading	.62	.71
				Paragraph Meaning	.63	.71
Kottmeyer (1947)	1	3,115	Metropolitan Readiness	Gates Word Recognition and Sentence Reading	.46	.51
Craig (1937)	1	63	Self-Constructed Readiness	Self-Constructed Achievement	.57	
Wilmore (1939)	1	82	Self-Constructed Readiness	Self-Constructed Achievement	.49	
Lee, Clark, and Lee (1934)	1	164	Lee-Clark Reading Readiness	Lee-Clark Reading Achievement	.49	.52
Dean (1939)	1	116	Metropolitan Readiness	Metropolitan Reading Achievement	.59	.65
Edminston and Hollahan (1946)	1	115	Alice and Jerry Readiness	Metropolitan Reading Achievement	.59	
Spaulding (1956)	1	63	Harrison-Stroud Readiness	Gates Primary Reading Test	.46	
Traxler (1947)	1	34	Metropolitan Readiness	Metropolitan Reading Achievement	.79	.88
Huggett (1938)	K.5–1.5	19	Van Wagenen Readiness	Detroit Reading Test	.63	.70
	1	19	Van Wagenen Readiness	Detroit Reading Test	.71	.77
Hopkins and Sitkei (1969)	1	157	Lee-Clark Readiness	Lee-Clark Reading Test	.61	.65
Gates (1939)	1.0–1.5	182	Van Wagenen Readiness	Reading Achievement	.68 (est.)	.71
Gates et al. (1939)	1	97	Van Wagenen Readiness	Reading Achievement	.52	.54
		97	Stone-Grove Readiness	Reading Achievement	.62	.64
Gates (1940)	1.0–1.5	173	Gates Reading Readiness	Reading Achievement	.71	.73

Study (year)	Grade	N	Predictor Test	Criterion		
Mitchell (1962)	1	919	Metropolitan Readiness Test	Metropolitan Reading Achievement Reading	.51	.57
Calfee and Venezky (1968)	1	96	Metropolitan Readiness Test	Stanford Primary Achievement Test Paragraph Meaning	.58	.65
Powell and Parsley (1961)	1–2	703	Lee-Clark Reading Readiness	California Reading Test Total	.82	.88
				Comprehension	.43	.49
Lee, Clark, and Lee (1934)	1	164	Lee-Clark Reading Readiness	Reading Grades	.49	.57
Gates (1940)	1	173	Seven Reading Readiness Tests	Midterm Reading Grade	.71	
Harrison (1938)	1	120	Metropolitan Readiness	Reading Grades	.49	.58
Wilson and Burke (1937)	1	25	Metropolitan Readiness	Reading Grades	.57	.68
Dean (1939)	1	116	Monroe Reading Aptitude	Reading Grades	.41	.49
Deputy (1930)	1	103	Self-Constructed Readiness	Reading Grades	.66	
Gates (1939) *(five different qualities of instruction)*	1	A 32	Gates Reading Readiness	Midterm Reading Grade	.70	.79
		A 37	Gates Reading Readiness	Midterm Reading Grade	.72	.82
		B 23	Gates Reading Readiness	Midterm Reading Grade	.56	.64
		B 12	Gates Reading Readiness	Midterm Reading Grade	.61	.69
		C 18	Gates Reading Readiness	Midterm Reading Grade	.71	.81
		D 14	Gates Reading Readiness	Midterm Reading Grade	.77	.87
		E 20	Gates Reading Readiness	Midterm Reading Grade	.22	.25
ARITHMETIC						
Calfee and Venezky (1968)	1	Six groups (191 to 246)	Metropolitan Readiness Tests	Metropolitan Achievement Tests Arithmetic Concepts and Skills	.64	.69
				Stanford Achievement Test	.65	.70
				Arithmetic Reasoning	.63	.68
ALGEBRA						
Hanna, Bligh, Lenke, and Orleans (1969)	8	1,105	Orleans-Hanna Algebra Prognosis Test	Lankton First Year Algebra Test	.78	.88
				Mid-Year Grade	.68	.78
				Final Grade	.66	.75
Lenke, Bligh, and Kane (1971)	8	335	Orleans-Hanna Algebra Prognosis Test	Mid-Year Algebra Test	.73	.79
				Mid-Year Grade	.72	.83
				Final Test	.77	.83
				Final Grade	.70	.80
Shaw (1956)	8.8–9.9	275	Iowa Algebra Aptitude Test	Lankton Algebra Test	.54	.63
Dicker (1933)	8.9–9.5	83	Rogers Math Ability Test	Breslich Algebra Test	.64	
Layton (1941)	9	141	Lee Test of Algebra Ability	Cooperative Algebra Test	.66	.71

APPENDIX TABLE 3-C (continued)

STUDY	SAMPLE CHARACTERISTICS		COMPOSITE APTITUDE MEASURE	ACHIEVEMENT CRITERION	OBSERVED r	CORRECTED r
	GRADE LEVEL	SIZE				
ALGEBRA (continued)						
Lee and Hughes (1934)	9	213	Lee Test of Algebra Ability	Columbia Research Bureau Algebra Test	.62	
Osburn and Melton (1963)	9	155	Orleans Algebra Prognosis Test	Cooperative Algebra Test	.66	.72
	9	155	Orleans Prognosis Test	Self-Constructed Final Exam	.61	
	9	155	Iowa Algebra Aptitude Test	Cooperative Algebra Test	.64	.72
	9	155	Iowa Algebra Aptitude Test	Self-Constructed Final Exam	.66	
Sabers and Feldt (1968)	9 Modern	555	Iowa Algebra Aptitude Test	Self-Constructed Achievement Test	.78	
	Traditional	375	Iowa Algebra Aptitude Test	Self-Constructed Achievement Test	.75	.83
	Modern	555	Iowa Algebra Aptitude Test	Teacher's Mark	.71	
	Traditional	375	Iowa Algebra Aptitude Test	Teacher's Mark	.64	.74
FIRST COURSE IN SECOND LANGUAGE						
Carroll (1959)	10–11		Modern Language Aptitude Test	Teachers Grades		
		42		Spanish–German	.71	.82
		75		Latin	.53	.61
		113		Spanish	.60	.70
		104		French	.56	.65
		40		German	.60	.70

APPENDIX TABLE 3-D. RELATION BETWEEN SELECTED APTITUDE SUBTEST MEASURES AND SUBSEQUENT ACHIEVEMENT MEASURES

STUDY	SAMPLE CHARACTERISTICS		SPECIFIC APTITUDE MEASURE	ACHIEVEMENT CRITERION	OBSERVED r	CORRECTED r
	GRADE LEVEL	SIZE				
FIRST GRADE READING						
Weiner and Feldman (1963)	K	126	Reading Prognosis Test Meaning Vocabulary	Gates Primary Reading Test Reading	.60	.67
				Paragraph Reading	.67	.78
Calfee and Venezky (1968)	1	191–246	Metropolitan Readiness Test Word Meaning	Metropolitan Achievement Test Word Knowledge	.53	.68
				Word Discrimination	.45	.58
				Reading	.48	.62
University School District, Missouri (1970)	K–1	78 M	Metropolitan Readiness Test Word Meaning	Stanford Achievement Reading	.30	.40
				Paragraph Meaning	.24	.32
Metropolitan Achievement Tests: Manual (1965)	1	Six groups 191–246	Metropolitan Readiness Test Word Meaning	Metropolitan Achievement Test Word Discrimination	.42	.54
				Word Knowledge	.35	.45
				Reading	.38	.49
FIRST GRADE ARITHMETIC						
Traxler (1947	1	38	Metropolitan Readiness Test Numbers	Metropolitan Achievement Test, Arithmetic	.64	.72
University City School District Missouri (1970)	1	78 M	Metropolitan Readiness Test Numbers	Stanford Achievement Test, Arithmetic	.63	.72
Metropolitan Achievement Tests: Manual (1965)	1	Six groups 191–246	Metropolitan Readiness Test Numbers	Metropolitan Achievement Test, Arithmetic	.61	.70

APPENDIX TABLE 3-D (continued)

STUDY	SAMPLE CHARACTERISTICS		SPECIFIC APTITUDE MEASURE	ACHIEVEMENT CRITERION	OBSERVED r	CORRECTED r
	GRADE LEVEL	SIZE				
SECOND LANGUAGE						
Carroll (1959)	10–11		Modern Language Aptitude	Teacher's Mark		
		42	Words in Sentences	German/Spanish	.70	.84
		113		Spanish	.53	.64
		40		German	.58	.70
		75		Latin	.46	.55
		104		French	.48	.58
Gardner and Lambert (1965)	High school	96	Modern Language Aptitude Words in Sentence	French Grade	.51	.62
ALGEBRA						
Wilson and Begle (1972)	9	1,295	Number	Algebra Achievement Test	.53	.73

| STUDY | SAMPLE CHARACTERISTICS | | READING COMPREHENSION MEASURE | ACHIEVEMENT MEASURE | OBSERVED r | CORRECTED r |
	GRADE LEVEL	SIZE				
LITERATURE AND LANGUAGE ARTS						
Iowa Tests of Basic Skills (I.T.B.S.), Manual (1956)	5	437	I.T.B.S. Reading	I.T.B.S. Language Total	.77	.81
Thorndike (1973)	7	464	I.T.B.S. Reading	I.T.B.S. Language Total	.74	.78
	8 (approx.)	(National samples)	IEA Reading Achievement Tests	IEA Literature Achievement Tests		
				Belgium (Flemish)	.66	.83
				Belgium (French)	.64	.80
				England	.77	.92
				Finland	.69	.85
				Italy	.60	.76
				New Zealand	.75	.90
				Sweden	.72	.87
				USA	.70	.83
SRA High School Placement Test Manual (1968)	9	275	SRA Reading Comprehension	SRA Language Arts		
Flanagan (1964)	9	3,915 M	Reading Comprehension	Literature Achievement	.75	.87
		3,864 F			.69	.81
	10	3,846 M	Reading Comprehension	Literature Achievement	.70	.83
		3,727 F				
	11	3,619 M	Reading Comprehension	Literature Achievement	.69	.81
		3,557 F				
	12	3,027 M	Reading Comprehension	Literature Achievement	.70	.83
		3,061 F				
Davis Reading Test, Manual—Psych. Corp. (1958)	High school 11–12	A. 372	Davis Reading Test	English course grade	.58	.74
		325	Davis Reading Test	English course grade	.64	.82
		B. 130			.54	.69
		74			.61	.78
		C. 59	Davis Reading Test	English course grade	.60	.77
		D. 125	Davis Reading Test	English course grade	.46	.59
		106			.44	.56
		E. 113	Davis Reading Test	English course grade	.53	.68
		89			.37	.47
		F. 58	Davis Reading Test	English course grade	.15	.19
		245			.58	.74

APPENDIX TABLE 3-E (continued)

STUDY	GRADE LEVEL	SIZE	READING COMPREHENSION MEASURE	ACHIEVEMENT MEASURE	OBSERVED r	CORRECTED r
LITERATURE AND LANGUAGE ARTS (continued)						
	High schools	G. 70	Davis Reading Test	English course grade	.46	.59
		61			.40	.51
		I. 114	Davis Reading Test	English course grade	.43	.55
		117			.36	.46
		J. 111	Davis Reading Achievement	English course grades	.40	.51
		110			.29	.37
		K. 109	Davis Reading Achievement	English course grades	.44	.56
		L. 106	Davis Reading Achievement	English course grades	.43	.55
		71			.41	.53
		M. 159	Davis Reading Achievement	English course grades	.46	.59
		176			.35	.45
Thorndike (1973)	12 (approx.)	(National samples)	IEA Reading Achievement Tests	IEA Literature Achievement Tests		
				Belgium (Flemish)	.59	.79
				Belgium (French)	.55	.72
				England	.52	.68
				Finland	.46	.63
				Italy	.57	.73
				New Zealand	.53	.74
				Sweden	.56	.72
				USA	.69	.84
MATHEMATICS						
California Achievement Tests, Manual (1963)			California Achievement Test	California Achievement Test		
	1		Reading Comprehension	Arithmetic Reasoning	.56	.75
				Arithmetic Fundamentals	.44	.51
	2		Reading Comprehension	Arithmetic Reasoning	.77	.92
				Arithmetic Fundamentals	.57	.64
	3		Reading Comprehension	Arithmetic Reasoning	.65	.75
				Arithmetic Fundamentals	.35	.38
	4		Reading Comprehension	Arithmetic Reasoning	.60	.73
				Arithmetic Fundamentals	.34	.39
	5		Reading Comprehension	Arithmetic Reasoning	.75	.89
				Arithmetic Fundamentals	.68	.79
Cottrell (1968)	3	18	Stanford Achievement Test Reading	Stanford Achievement Test Arithmetic	.86	.99

Study	Grade	N	Reading Test	Arithmetic/Math Test	r	r
Payne (1963)	1	74	Metropolitan Reading Test	Metropolitan Arithmetic Test	.51	.54
		106	Metropolitan Reading Test	Metropolitan Arithmetic Test	.60	.63
	2	74	Metropolitan Reading Test	Metropolitan Arithmetic Test	.72	.76
		106	Metropolitan Reading Test	Metropolitan Arithmetic Test	.73	.70
	3	74	Metropolitan Reading Test	Metropolitan Arithmetic Test	.58	.79
		106	Metropolitan Reading Test	Metropolitan Arithmetic Test	.71	.63
	5	74	Metropolitan Reading Test	Metropolitan Arithmetic Test	.67	.77
		106	Metropolitan Reading Test	Metropolitan Arithmetic Test	.47	.72
	1–2	74	Metropolitan Reading Test	Metropolitan Arithmetic Test	.54	.49
		106	Metropolitan Reading Test	Metropolitan Arithmetic Test	.72	.57
	2–3	74	Metropolitan Reading Test	Metropolitan Arithmetic Test	.58	.79
		106	Metropolitan Reading Test	Metropolitan Arithmetic Test	.66	.63
	3–5	74	Metropolitan Reading Test	Metropolitan Arithmetic Test	.65	.71
		106	Metropolitan Reading Test	Metropolitan Arithmetic Test	.71	.70
	5–6	74	Metropolitan Reading Test	Metropolitan Arithmetic Test	.79	.77
		106	Metropolitan Reading Test	Metropolitan Arithmetic Test		.85
Iowa Test of Basic Skills (I.T.B.S.), Manual (1956)	4	437	I.T.B.S. Reading	I.T.B.S. Arithmetic Concepts	.68	.75
				Problem Solving	.66	.75
				Total Arithmetic	.72	.77
	7	464	I.T.B.S. Reading	I.T.B.S. Arithmetic Concepts	.70	.80
				Problem Solving	.61	.74
				Total Arithmetic	.72	.79
Kraus (1973)	3–6	80	Metropolitan Reading Test	Metropolitan Arithmetic Test	.69	.77
		85	Metropolitan Reading Test	Metropolitan Arithmetic Test	.78	.87
	6	80	Metropolitan Reading Test	Metropolitan Arithmetic Test	.73	.81
		85	Metropolitan Reading Test	Metropolitan Arithmetic Test	.80	.89
Balow (1964)	6	368	Stanford Achievement Test Reading	Stanford Achievement Test Arithmetic	.46	.53
Chase (1960)	6	119	Gates Reading to Note Details	Iowa Every Pupil Test Arithmetic	.40	.55
Cleland and Toussant (1962)	Intermediate	172	Gates Reading Survey	American School Arithmetic	.49	.60
Erickson (1958)	6	269	Iowa Silent Reading Test / Reading Comprehension	I.T.B.S. Arithmetic Section	.62	.75
Muscio (1962)	6	206	Stanford Reading Tests Paragraph Meaning	Functional Evaluation in Mathematics Quantitative Understanding	.78	.89
			Word Meaning	Quantitative Understanding	.78	.89
Neale et al. (1970)	6–7	155	Gates Basic Reading Tests (Test C)	Quantitative Understanding	.68	.78
			Gates Basic Reading Tests (Test D)	Quantitative Understanding	.55	.63
			SRA Reading	SRA Mathematics	.78	.89

APPENDIX TABLE 3-E (continued)

STUDY	SAMPLE CHARACTERISTICS		READING COMPREHENSION MEASURE	ACHIEVEMENT MEASURE	OBSERVED r	CORRECTED r
	GRADE LEVEL	SIZE				
Coleman (1966b)	6	1,956,563	Reading Achievement	Mathematics	.68	.74
	9	2,265,319	Reading Achievement	Mathematics	.57	.62
	12	1,776,996	Reading Achievement	Mathematics	.51	.56
Shaw (1956)	9.1–9.9	275	Iowa Silent Reading Test	Lankton Algebra	.45	
SRA High School Placement Test Manual (1968)	9	275	SRA Reading Comprehension	SRA Arithmetic	.51	.58
Ivanoff, DeWane, and Praem (1965)	9	286	High School Placement Test (Reading)	High School Placement Arithmetic Test	.52	.59
				8th Grade Math Mark	.50	.60
Flanagan (1964)	9	3,915 M	Reading Comprehension	Mathematics Achievement	.64	.73
		3,864 F			.59	.67
	10	3,846 M	Reading Comprehension	Mathematics Achievement	.66	.76
		3,727 F			.59	.67
	11	3,619 M	Reading Comprehension	Mathematics Achievement	.66	.76
		3,557 F			.58	.66
	12	3,027 M	Reading Comprehension	Mathematics Achievement	.63	.72
		3,061 F			.56	.64
Pitts (1952)	11	210	Iowa Silent Reading	Davis Test of Functional Competence in Mathematics	.53	
SCIENCE						
Neale et al. (1970)	6–7	155	SRA Reading	SRA Science	.75	.84
SRA High School Placement Test Manual (1968)	9	275	SRA Reading	SRA Science	.55	.61
Flanagan (1964)	9	3,915 M	Reading Comprehension	Biological Science	.62 M	.83
		3,864 F			.58 F	.78
				Physical Science	.66 M	.80
					.62 F	.73
	10	3,846 M	Reading Comprehension	Biological Science	.59 M	.79
		3,727 F			.56 F	.75
				Physical Science	.64 M	.76
					.61 F	.72
	11	3,619 M	Reading Comprehension	Biological Science	.59 M	.79
		3,557 F			.56 F	.75
				Physical Science	.68 M	.80
					.61 F	.72

Source	Grade	Sample	Reading Test	Criterion Measure		
Thorndike (1973)	12	3,027 M 3,061 F	Reading Comprehension	Biological Science	.52 M	.70
					.58 F	.78
				Physical Science	.65 M	.77
					.61 F	.72
Thorndike (1973)	8 (approx.)	(National samples)	IEA Reading Achievement Tests	IEA Science Achievement Tests		
				Belgium (Flemish)	.53	.67
				Belgium (French)	.40	.49
				England	.73	.84
				Finland	.60	.73
				Hungary	.63	.74
				Italy	.51	.61
				Netherlands	.60	.71
				New Zealand	.70	.82
				Scotland	.73	.84
				Sweden	.65	.77
Thorndike (1973)	12 (approx.)	(National samples)	IEA Reading Achievement Tests	IEA Science Achievement Tests		
				Belgium (Flemish)	.50	.65
				Belgium (French)	.44	.57
				England	.38	.46
				Finland	.44	.53
				Hungary	.53	.66
				Italy	.41	.49
				Netherlands	.28	.33
				New Zealand	.37	.44
				Scotland	.46	.55
				Sweden	.53	.64

APPENDIX TO CHAPTER 4

APPENDIX TABLE 4-A. RELATION BETWEEN AFFECT TOWARD SUBJECT AND STUDENT ACHIEVEMENT

	SAMPLE CHARACTERISTICS				OBSERVED r		CORRECTED r	
STUDY	GRADE LEVEL	SIZE	AFFECTIVE MEASURE	CRITERION	PRED‡	CON	PRED	CON
MATHEMATICS								
Crosswhite (1972)	4		Pro-Math Composite	SMSG Achievement Tests				
		1,655		Computation 3		.22		.31
		1,516		Computation 4	.25		.36	
		1,654		Structure 3		.18		.24
		1,484		Structure 4	.24		.32	
				Math Grades				
		1,379		Math Grade 3	.29	.26	.40	.36
		1,503		Math Grades 4	.22			
Anttonen (1969)	5–6	154 M, 140 F	Elementary Attitude Scale toward Math	Iowa Arithmetic Total	.37			
Hungerman (1967)	6	200	Math Attitude Scale	California Arithmetic Test		.34		
						.37		
		305		California Math Test		.24		
						.32		
Crosswhite (1972)	6		Pro-Math Composite	SMSG Achievement Tests				
		1,519		Computation 5		.26		.35
		1,591		Computation 6	.26		.35	
		1,564		Structure 5		.23		.33
		1,603		Structure 6	.22		.32	
		1,504		Math Grades 5		.28		.39
		1,518		Math Grades 6	.30		.44	
Crosswhite (1972)	7		Pro-Math Composite	SMSG Achievement Tests				
		2,009		Computation 6	.26		.35	
		2,009		Structure 6	.26		.39	
		1,907		Computation 7		.29		.43
		1,903		Structure 7		.29		.45

Author (year)	Grade	Affect measure	Achievement measure	Sample				
Crosswhite (1972)	8	Pro-Math Composite	Math Grades 6	1,691	.27	.28		.39
			Math Grades 7	1,926	.28	.29		.39
		SMSG Achievement Tests						
			Computation 7	1,427	.31	.30		.45
			Computation 8	1,514	.30	.26		
			Structure 7	1,543			.37	.39
			Structure 8	1,524			.38	.39
			Math Grades 7	1,566			.42	.45
			Math Grades 8	1,562			.41	.36
Husén (1967)	8 (approx.)	Student wants to take more math	IEA Math Achievement Tests	National Samples		.41		
			Australia		.25			
			Belgium		.22			
			England		.39			
			Finland		.25			
			West Germany		.25			
			Japan		.25			
			Netherlands		.21			
			Scotland		.38			
			Sweden		.26			
			USA		.17			
Ryan (1967)	9	Dutton Attitude toward Math Scale	GPA in Math	37	.25	.42	.34	.57
		Aiken Attitude toward Math Scale	GPA in Math		.28	.48	.34	.58
Ryan (1969)	9	Dutton Attitude toward Math Scale	STEP Math Test	1,100	.32	.22	.44	.30
		Aiken Attitude toward Math Scale	STEP Math Test		.34	.23	.41	.28

‡PRED refers to correlations based on *predictive* measures of affect which were assessed prior to the achievement measures. CON refers to correlations based on *concurrent* measures of affect which were assessed at the same time as the achievement measures.

APPENDIX TABLE 4-A (continued)

STUDY	GRADE LEVEL	SIZE	AFFECTIVE MEASURE	CRITERION	OBSERVED r PRED‡	CON	CORRECTED r PRED	CON
MATHEMATICS (continued)								
Crosswhite (1972)	9		Pro-Math Composite	SMSG Achievement Tests				
		1,907		Computation		.24		.33
		1,818		Numbers Combined		.29		.40
		1,847		Algebra		.24		.34
		1,818		Geometry		.28		.42
		1,523		Geometry and Graph		.27		.42
		375		Number Composite		.15		.21
		1,920		Algebra (Combined)		.28		.40
		1,926		Math Grades 8		.27		.38
		1,939		Math Grades 9	.29		.41	
Crosswhite (1972)	10		Pro-Math Composite	SMSG Achievement Tests				
		1,289		Numbers		.26		.34
		1,289		Algebra		.29		.37
		1,289		Geometry		.19		.35
		1,170		Numeration		.21		.36
		1,170		Algebra 2		.27		.39
		1,170		Geometry 3	.26		.37	
		1,226		Math Grades 9		.29		.38
		1,209		Math Grades 10	.26		.34	
Anttonen (1969)	11	149 M	Secondary Math Attitude Scale	ITED Quantitative Score	.33			
		142 F			.36			
		156 M		GPA In Math	.40		.44	
		143 F			.47		.52	
Crosswhite (1972)	11		Pro-Math Composite	SMSG Achievement Tests				
		1,214		Geometric Inference		.24		.32
		1,170		Geometric Application		.32		.42

Study	Grade	N	Variable			
		607	Geometric Composite	.16		.23
		1,645	Non-Insightful			
			Geometry	.36		.49
		915	Algebra Composite	.26		.36
		784	Algebra Combined	.17		.22
		1,754	Math Grades 10	.35		
		1,333	Math Grades 11			.46
Anttonen (1969)	12	140 M / 155 F	Secondary Math Attitude Scale			
			ITED Quantitative Score	.16 M / .38 F	.29	.38
			GPA in Math	−.30 M / .36 F	.33	.40
Crosswhite (1972)	12	1,147	Pro-Math Composite			
			SMSG Achievement Tests			
			Non-Insightful			
			Geometry	.32		.46
		1,128	Algebra Equations	.33		.48
		818	Functions and Relations	.41		.51
		323	Numbers	.28		.39
		1,118	Geometry	.34		.52
		905	Math Grades 11	.28		.36
		649	Math Grades 12		.25	.32
Husén (1967)	12 (approx.)	National Samples	Student wants to take more math			
			IEA Math Achievement Tests			
			Australia	.32		
			Belgium	.17		
			England	.24		
			Finland	.38		
			West Germany	.25		
			Japan	.36		
			Netherlands	.29		
			Scotland	.29		
			Sweden	.37		
			USA	.33		

APPENDIX TABLE 4-A (continued)

STUDY	SAMPLE CHARACTERISTICS GRADE LEVEL	SIZE	AFFECTIVE MEASURE	CRITERION	OBSERVED r PRED‡	CON	CORRECTED r PRED	CON
OTHER SUBJECTS								
Groff (1962)	Reading 5, 6	142 M 136 F	Remmers Scale: Attitude toward particular school subjects	Critical reading score	.43			
					.39			
Jordon (1941)	Various subject areas 6–9	231 M	Attitudes toward particular subjects	Grades				
				French		.26		
				Math		.33		
				English		.25		
				History		.21		
				Geography		.21		
Wethington (1965)	English 8–12	708	Attitude toward English Scale	GPA in English		.46		
Shepler (1956)	Science 12	250	Scholastic preference interview in science	Harry-Durost Essential High School Content Battery (Science)		.37		
Thorndike (1973)	5		Hours reading for pleasure	Reading Comprehension				
				Belgium (Flemish)		−.09		
				Belgium (French)		.27		
				England		.38		
				Finland		.26		
				Hungary		.29		
				Israel		.31		
				Italy		.20		
				Netherlands		.30		
				Scotland		.39		
				Sweden		.21		
				United States		.28		

APPENDIX TABLE 4-B. RELATION BETWEEN AFFECT TOWARD SCHOOL AND STUDENT ACHIEVEMENT

STUDY	SAMPLE CHARACTERISTICS		AFFECTIVE MEASURE	CRITERION	OBSERVED r		CORRECTED r	
	GRADE LEVEL	SIZE			PRED ‡	CON	PRED	CON
Lunn (1969)	4–6	2,087	Lunn's Scale of Attitude toward School	English Grade		.20		
				Arithmetic Rank in Class		.21		
				Overall Rank in Class		.13		
			Interest in schoolwork	English Grade		.19		
				Arithmetic Rank in Class		.17		
				Overall Rank in Class		.12		
Glick (1969)	6	159 M 199 F	Pupil Opinion Question on schoolwork	Stanford Achievement	.39 M .44 F		.50 .57	
			Pupil Opinion Question on attitude toward school in general	Total	.21 M .44 F		.32 .35	
Shepps and Shepps (1971)	6	26	Attitude Scale from Survey of Study Habits and Attitudes (SSHA)	Iowa Test of Basic Skills, Arithmetic		.29		.34
Knight and Chansky (1964)	7	66	Attitude Scale from SSHA	Metropolitan Reading Achievement		.37		.43
				Reading Achievement		.35 M .52 F		.41 .60
				Language Achievement		.28 M .47 F		.33 .55
				Arithmetic Achievement		.62 M .51 F		.72 .59
Malpass (1953)	8	92	Sentence Completion Test	GPA		.57		.68
			School Picture Test			.45		.56
			Personal Document Test (attitudes toward different aspects of schooling)			.31		.37
Cullen and Katzenmeyer (1970)	8	372	Student Opinion Poll: (a) Satisfaction with teacher behavior	Ohio Survey Tests				
				Factual Reading		.14		
				Mathematics		.21		
				Grades				
				Language Arts		.35		
				Mathematics		.38		

APPENDIX TABLE 4-B (continued)

| STUDY | SAMPLE CHARACTERISTICS | | AFFECTIVE MEASURE | CRITERION | OBSERVED r | | CORRECTED r | |
	GRADE LEVEL	SIZE			PRED ‡	CON	PRED	CON
			(b) General subject matter interest	Ohio Survey Tests				
				Factual Reading		.08		
				Mathematics		.08		
				Grades				
				Language Arts		.28		
				Mathematics		.23		
Khan and Roberts (1969)	8	240	Subscales of SSHA: (a) Attitude toward teacher	Dominion Group ACT Tests				
				Verbal		.27		
				Arithmetic				
				Comprehension		.20		
				GPA		.33		.40
			(b) Attitude toward education	Dominion Group ACT Tests				
				Verbal		.08		
				Arithmetic				
				Comprehension		.03		
				GPA		.03		.03
Entwistle and Welsh (1969)	6–9	2,538	Entwistle Academic Motivation Scale	GPA		.48 M .43 F		
Khan (1969)	9	509 M	Subscales of SSHA: (a) Attitude toward teacher	Metropolitan Ach Tests				
				Reading		.34		.40
				Arithmetic		.17		.20
			(b) Academic interest	Reading		.24		.28
				Arithmetic		.18		.21
Farquhar (1963)	9–10	254 M 261 F	Generalized Situational Choice Inventory (attitude toward school)	GPA		.50 M .32 F		.62 M .39 F

Coleman (1966b)	(White Total)	Attitude toward school and reading	Metropolitan Achievement Tests	
3	2,071,035		Reading	.21
			Mathematics	.13
6	1,956,563		Reading	.30
			Mathematics	.23
9	2,205,319		Reading	.34
			Mathematics	.29
12	1,776,996		Reading	.35
			Mathematics	.24
Mayeske (1974)		Educational plans and desires	Composite Achievement Total	
6	650,000			.48
9	(for all three levels)			.49
12				.49

APPENDIX TABLE 4-C. RELATION BETWEEN ACADEMIC SELF-CONCEPT AND STUDENT ACHIEVEMENT

| | SAMPLE CHARACTERISTICS | | | | OBSERVED r | | CORRECTED r | |
STUDY	LEVEL	SIZE	AFFECTIVE MEASURE	CRITERION	PRED‡	CON	PRED	CON
Crosswhite (1972)	4	1,730	Math Self-concept	Computation 0		.29		.40
				Computation 1	.28		.36	
				Structure 0		.19		.26
				Structure 1	.26		.35	
	6	1,321	Math Self-concept	Computation 3	.35		.44	
				Computation 5	.35		.44	
				Structure 3	.33		.42	
				Structure 5	.33		.42	
	7	1,909	Math Self-concept	Level A		.34		.45
				Level B		.32		.44
				Computation with Rationals	.29		.35	
				Structure Combined	.33		.45	
	8	1,089	Math Self-concept	Computation 7	.37		.46	
				Computation 9	.34		.43	
				Structure 7	.36		.45	
				Structure 9	.35		.44	
	9	1,435	Math Self-concept	Numbers Combined	.33		.41	
				Computation with Rationals	.29		.36	
				Algebra Combined 1	.28		.35	
				Geometry Combined	.27		.36	
				Geometry and Graph	.29		.40	
				Number Composite	.25		.31	
				Algebra Combined 2	.30		.43	
	10	1,025	Math Self-concept	Numbers 1		.27		.34
				Algebra 1		.27		.32
				Geometry 2		.20		.35

				Numeration 2	.23		.37	
				Algebra 2	.27		.37	
				Geometry 3	.28		.37	
	11	703	Math Self-concept	Geometric Influence	.23		.29	
				Geometric Application	.28		.35	
				Geometric Composite	.19		.25	
				Non-insightful Geometry	.31		.45	
				Algebra Composite	.27		.35	
				Algebra Combined	.21		.26	
	12	466	Math Self-concept	Non-Insightful Geometry	.20		.30	
				Combined Algebraic Equations	.25		.36	
				Functions and Relations	.30		.36	
				Numbers 3	.07		.09	
				Geometry 6	.22		.33	
Crosswhite (1972)	3	1,730	Math Self-concept	Math Grades 3		.30		.41
				Math Grades 4	.33		.45	
	5	1,321		Math Grades 5		.42		.53
				Math Grades 6	.46		.58	
	6	1,909		Math Grades 6		.30		.38
				Math Grades 7	.44		.55	
	7	1,089		Math Grades 7		.39		.49
				Math Grades 8	.41		.51	
	8	1,435		Math Grades 8		.31		.39
				Math Grades 9	.45		.57	
	9	1,025		Math Grades 9		.34		.43
				Math Grades 10	.46		.58	
	10	703		Math Grades 10		.39		.48
				Math Grades 11	.42		.52	
	11	466		Math Grades 11		.39		.48
				Math Grades 12	.43		.53	

APPENDIX TABLE 4-C (continued)

STUDY	SAMPLE CHARACTERISTICS LEVEL	SIZE	AFFECTIVE MEASURE	CRITERION	OBSERVED r PRED‡	CON	CORRECTED r PRED	CON
Crandall and McGhee (1968)	12	68 M 84 F	Expectation of success in subject	Math Grades	.51 M .51 F			
				English Grades	.41 M .54 F			
				Natural Science Grades	.59 M .61 F			
				Social Science Grades	.47 M .53 F			
Alberti (1971)	1	129 M 100 F	Self-perception in school	Stanford Achievement Arithmetic		.16 M .25 F		.19 .29
	2	106 M 98 F		Reading		.26 M .15 F		.32 .19
				Arithmetic		.45 M .15 F		.54 .18
	3	98 M		Iowa Test of Basic Skills Reading		.40 M .16 F		.47 .19
		94 F		Arithmetic		.24 M .26 F		.28 .30
Torshen (1969)	5	400	Sears Academic Self-concept	Stanford Achievement Total		.36		.39
Linton (1972)	6	172	Self-Concept of Ability (Brookover)	Iowa Test of Basic Skills Total		.51 M .43 F		.55 .47
				Reading (Grade)		.40 M .40 F		.46 .46
				Arithmetic (Grade)		.52 M .35 F		.60 .40

Study	Grade	N	Self-concept measure	Achievement measure	Correlation 1	Correlation 2
Russell (1953)	5	144	Pupil evaluation of what their performance will be	Progressive Achievement Tests Composite	.54 M / .50 F	.34
	8	155			.35 M / .46 F	.33
Sears (1963)	Upper elementary	95 M / 100 F	Sears Academic Self-Concept	SRA Composite		.30 M / .29 F
Caplin (1969)	Intermediate	180	Miriam Goldberg Self-Concept Inventory (school related)	Iowa Test of Basic Skills Total	.31 M	.35 / .58
Farquhar and Christensen (1967)	11	344 M / 399 F	Word Rating List (based on Brookover's Self Concept of Ability)	Stanford Achievement Total	.30 M / .23 F	.34 / .26
Coleman (1966b)	3	2,071,035	Academic Self-concept	Metropolitan Reading Tests		.21
	6	1,956,563				.33
	9	2,205,319				.37
	12	1,776,996				.39
Torshen (1969)	5	400	Sears Academic Self Concept	GPA	.46	.53
Kifer (1973)	5	50 M / 47 F	Self Concept of Ability (Brookover)	GPA	.20 M / .23 F	.23 / .26
	7	51 M / 58 F			.51 M / .42 F	.59 / .48
Brookover, Shailer, and Paterson (1964)	7	1,050	Self Concept of Ability (Brookover)	GPA	.51 M / .67 F	.59 / .77
Bowen (1968)	9	389	Self-estimate of ability to do schoolwork	GPA	.64	
Farquhar (1963)	9–10	254 M / 261 F	Word Rating List (based on Brookover's Self Concept of Ability)	GPA	.51 M / .42 F	.59 / .49
Ponzo (1967)	9	176 M / 175 F	Self Concept of Ability (Brookover)	GPA	.64 M / .62 F	.74 / .71
	12	141 M / 150 F			.58 M / .63 F	.67 / .72

APPENDIX TABLE 4-C (continued)

| | SAMPLE CHARACTERISTICS | | | | OBSERVED r | | CORRECTED r | |
STUDY	LEVEL	SIZE	AFFECTIVE MEASURE	CRITERION	PRED‡	CON	PRED	CON
Rosenberg (1967)	10–12	1,198	Estimate of oneself as a good student	GPA		.52		
Payne (1962)	11	238 M 243 F	Word Rating List (based on Brookover's Self Concept of Ability)	GPA	.51 M .41 F	.48 M .42 F	.59 .48	.56 .49
Farquhar and Christensen (1967)	11	344 M 399 F	Word Rating List (based on Brookover's Self Concept of Ability)	GPA		.38 M .37 F		.44 .43
Green and Farquhar (1965)	11	750	Word Rating List (based on Brookover's Self Concept of Ability)	GPA		.51 M .34 F		.59 .40
Jones and Strowig (1968)	12	167 M 150 F	Self Concept of Ability (Brookover)	GPA		.51 M .67 F		.59 .77
Binder, Jones and Strowig (1970)	12	346	Self Concept of Ability (Brookover)	GPA		.56 M .71 F		.64 .82

APPENDIX TO CHAPTER 5

APPENDIX TABLE 5-A. RELATION BETWEEN USE OF CUES AND STUDENT ACHIEVEMENT (GROUP MEASURES)

| | SAMPLE CHARACTERISTICS | | | | | CORRELATION WITH | |
STUDY	GRADE LEVEL	NO. OF CLASSES	OBSERVATION	DESCRIPTOR	ACHIEVEMENT MEASURE	FINAL ACHIEVEMENT	ACHIEVEMENT GAIN
Chall and Feldmann (1966)	1 (disadvantaged)	12	Observer rating	"Does lesson appear to be too easy, just right, or too hard for the children?"	Stanford Achievement Test		
					Word Reading	.60	
					Paragraph Meaning	.59	
					Gates Word Recognition Test	.42	
				Rating on "whether or not the children seemed to be benefiting from her (teacher's) presentation."	Stanford Achievement Test		
					Word Reading	.26	
					Paragraph Meaning	.23	
					Vocabulary	.19	
					Gates Word Recognition Test	.27	
					Gilmore Oral Reading Test	.56	
Siegel and Rosenshine (1973)	1 (DISTAR)	24	Observer rating	"Teacher moves quickly after getting the children's attention, chains the parts of a complex task together, changes inflections, and talks at different levels of loudness."	Verbally administered criterion-referenced test on unit		.26
Wallen (1966)	1	36	Observer rating	Teacher is "able to explain concepts clearly . . . such that pupils seemed to be gaining understanding."	California Achievement Test		
					Arithmetic	.38	
					Reading Vocabulary	.33	
					Reading Comprehension	.37	
	3	40	Observer rating		California Achievement Test		
					Arithmetic	.50	
					Reading Vocabulary	.57	
					Reading Comprehension	.58	
	1	36	Observer rating	Teacher's teaching is "stimulating," "dynamic."	California Achievement Test		
					Arithmetic	.50	
					Reading Vocabulary	.28	
					Reading Comprehension	.32	
	3	40			California Achievement Test		
					Arithmetic	.45	
					Reading Vocabulary	.39	
					Reading Comprehension	.38	

Study	Setting/Grade	N	Method	Description	Criterion	r
Torrance (1966)	7–12	81	Student rating	"This teacher tries to make sure we all understand our work." "The test we use helps us get a good understanding of mathematics." "This teacher makes the lessons interesting." Materials teacher uses are "interesting," "easy to understand," have "diagrams and illustrations that helped."	Sequential Tests of Educational Progress, Total Math	.04 .24 .35
Belgard et al. (1968)	12	43	Student rating	"The content of the lesson is presented so that it is understandable to the pupils." "The purposes of the lesson are clear."	Social Studies Achievement Test (local)	.07 .44
Hiller, Fisher, and Kaess (1969)	12	32	Observer counting	Number of times teacher used vague terms and phrases divided by total number of words in lecture (15 min. duration).	Specially developed achievement test on *Yugoslavia*	.56 −.59
	12	23	Observer counting		Specially developed achievement test on *Thailand*	
Solomon, Rosenberg, and Bezdek (1964)	Credit evening course (median age was 20)	24	Observer rating Student questionnaire	*Clarity vs. Vagueness* Items that loaded high on this factor were: (w/factor loadings) coherence of lesson (observer) .82 well-organized (student) .75 clear and understandable (student) .84 monotonous and dull (student) −.76	Test measuring factual knowledge of course content (American government)	−.48 .58

APPENDIX TABLE 5-B. RELATION BETWEEN USE OF REINFORCEMENT AND STUDENT ACHIEVEMENT (GROUP MEASURES)

STUDY	SAMPLE CHARACTERISTICS		METHOD OF OBSERVATION	DESCRIPTOR	ACHIEVEMENT MEASURE	CORRELATIONS WITH	
	GRADE LEVEL	NO. OF CLASSES				FINAL ACHIEVEMENT	ACHIEVEMENT GAIN
Harris and Serwer (1966)	1 (disadvantaged)	48	Observer counting	Number of "statements intended to increase a pupil's motivation to learn, to reduce tension, or . . . to make him or her feel better."	Stanford Achievement Test		
					Word Reading		.10
					Paragraph Meaning		.16
					Vocabulary		.06
					Gates Word Recognition Test		.24
					Gilmore Oral Reading Test		.16
Wallen (1966)	1	36	Observer counting	"Frequency of minimum reinforcement." Reinforcement which confirms student correctness but does not give praise.	California Achievement Test		
					Arithmetic	.43	
					Reading Vocabulary	.29	
					Reading Comprehension	.38	
	3	40			California Achievement Test		
					Arithmetic	.18	
					Reading Vocabulary	.19	
					Reading Comprehension	.18	
Siegel and Rosenshine (1973)	1 (DISTAR)	24	Observer rating	"Praises the children for appropriate responding and attending behaviors; often repeats the correct response."	Verbally administered criterion-referenced test on unit		.42
Hurlock (1925)	4 and 6	Two groups Control (n=27) Experimental (n=26)	Experimental situation	Control group received no praise; experimental group received praise. "Each day, before the test papers were given out, praised group was asked to rise, come to front of room, face the class, and were praised."	Modified form of Courtis Research Tests in arithmetic, addition form	.57	
Flanders (1970)	2	15	Observer ratings	Interaction Analysis Praise: "Praises or encourages pupil action or behavior."	Portions of standardized achievement test covering language and number skills		.25
	6	30					.36
	4	16			Criterion-referenced test on two-week unit		-.13
	7	15					-.22
	8	16					.30

Study	Grade	N	Method	Treatment	Test	Effect
Anthony (1967)	5	21	Observer counting	"Extent of achievement rewards," including academic praise, gold stars, displays of pupil good work.	Stanford Achievement Test Word Meaning Paragraph Meaning Language Arithmetic Comprehension Arithmetic Application Total	.12 .25 .36 .36 .23 .28
Tuinman et al. (1971)	7 and 8	1 experimental and 1 control group (80 S's each)	Experimental situation	Experimental group offered material incentives for improvement, control group offered no special incentives.	Nelson Reading Test Vocabulary Comprehension Total Reading	.66 .51 .70
Torrance (1966)	7–12	81	Student rating	"This teacher praises the class for good work."	Sequential Tests of Educational Progress, Math	.49
Jayne (1945)	7–8	28	Observer counting	Number of times pupils were praised	Unit test in civics (two-week unit)	.48
Wright and Nuthall (1970)	3	17	Observer rating	Teacher's use of thanks and praise	Test (criterion-referenced) on three lessons	.49
Clark and Walberg (1968)	5–7 (aged 10–13) (remedial reading)	9 (5 exp.) (4 con.)	Experimental situation	The five teachers of the experimental groups were confidentially asked to double or triple number of rewards. Experimental groups were praised much more than control groups.	SRA reading test	.24

APPENDIX TABLE 5-C. RELATION BETWEEN USE OF PARTICIPATION AND STUDENT ACHIEVEMENT (GROUP MEASURES)

| | SAMPLE CHARACTERISTICS | | METHOD OF | | | CORRELATION WITH | |
| | GRADE | NO. OF | | | | FINAL | ACHIEVEMENT |
STUDY	LEVEL	CLASSES	OBSERVATION	DESCRIPTOR	ACHIEVEMENT MEASURE	ACHIEVEMENT	GAIN
Harris and Serwer (1966)	1 (disadvantaged)	48	Observer counting	"Episode which normally begins with a teacher question, continues with a pupil response, and ends with a reply from the teacher. . . ." Number of such episodes.	Stanford Achievement Test		(Adjusted for readiness)
					Word Reading		.35
					Paragraph Meaning		.17
					Vocabulary		.01
					Gates Word Recognition Test		.24
					Gilmore Oral Reading Test		.16
Conners and Eisenberg (1966)	Pre-school Headstart	38	Observer counting	Number of teacher-pupil interchanges focusing on intellectual growth	Peabody Picture Vocabulary Test		.12
Chall and Feldmann (1966)	1 (disadvantaged)	12	Observer rating	". . . extent to which the class, as a whole, generally appears to be participating in the class lesson."	Stanford Achievement Test		
					Word Reading	.25	
					Paragraph Meaning	.22	
					Vocabulary	.19	
					Gates Word Recognition Test	.26	
					Gilmore Oral Reading Test	.51	
Soar (1966)	3–6	55	Observer rating	Factor 6—Pupil Initiative High loading on pupil interest and attention	Iowa Test of Basic Skills		
					Vocabulary	.30	
					Reading	.06	
					Arithmetic Concepts	.29	
					Arithmetic Problems	.28	
					Total	.29	
Belgard et al. (1968)	12	43	Pupil rating of class	"Pupils come quickly to attention. They direct themselves to the task to be accomplished."	Local Social Studies Achievement Test (closely geared to lesson content)	.41	
				"The class is attentive. When appropriate, the pupils actively participate. . . ,"		.41	

						CORRELATION WITH
						ACHIEVEMENT GAIN
Morsh (1956)	Aircraft mechanics	120	Observer rating of behavior	Amount of inattentive behavior (e.g., looks around, ignores instructor, yawns, etc.)	Residual achievement gain on test based on course content	−.58

APPENDIX TABLE 5-D. RELATION BETWEEN USE OF PARTICIPATION AND STUDENT ACHIEVEMENT (INDIVIDUAL MEASURES)

	SAMPLE CHARACTERISTICS		METHOD OF OBSERVATION	DESCRIPTOR	ACHIEVEMENT MEASURE	CORRELATION WITH	
STUDY	GRADE LEVEL	SIZE				FINAL ACHIEVEMENT	ACHIEVEMENT GAIN
Turnure and Samuels (1972)	1	88	Observer coding of task-oriented behaviors	Pupil attention	Forty-five words, randomly selected from the Dolch list of basic sight-words		.44
Cobb (1970)	1	150 135	Observer coding of child behavior	Survival Skills, e.g., attention, talk-to-teacher about academic material, volunteer, talk-to-peer about academic material, etc. (multiple correlation of two best predictors)	Stanford Achievement Test Arithmetic Reading	.42 .59	
Cobb (1972)	4	School A, 60 School B, 43 (Arithmetic)¶	Observer coding of child behavior	Survival Skills (see above) (multiple correlation of three best predictors)	Stanford Achievement Test Arithmetic (School A) (School B) Reading (School A) (School B)	.63 .61 .56 .41	
Attwell et al. (1967)	K§ and 5	57	Observer behavior ratings during testing process in kindergarten	Attention—"The ability of the subjects to put forth a mental effort and to concentrate on the task. . . ."	California Achievement Test—Grade 5 Reading Vocabulary Reading Comprehension Arithmetic Reasoning Arithmetic Fundamentals	.40 .43 .38 .26	

¶Pupil's behavior in arithmetic class related to achievement in arithmetic and reading.

§Ratings of attention observed in kindergarten related to achievement in grade 5.

| SAMPLE CHARACTERISTICS | | | | | | CORRELATION WITH | |
STUDY	GRADE LEVEL	SIZE	METHOD OF OBSERVATION	DESCRIPTOR	ACHIEVEMENT MEASURE	FINAL ACHIEVEMENT	ACHIEVEMENT GAIN
Lahaderne (1967)	6	61 boys	Observer counting of frequency of student's attentiveness or participation	Pupil Attention	Mechanics of English Composite		.30
		63 girls					.40
					Scott Foresman Reading Test	.51	
						.49	
		56 boys			Standard Achievement Test—Intermediate II		
					Reading	.46	
					Arithmetic	.53	
					Language	.48	
		55 girls			Reading	.39	
					Arithmetic	.39	
					Language	.37	
Lahaderne (1967)	6	61 boys	Observer counting	"Frequency of Instructional Interactions." Number of messages between a given student and teacher which are instructional in nature.	Scott Foresman Reading Test	.28	
		63 girls				.45	
		56 boys			Stanford Achievement Test—Intermediate II		
					Reading	.38	
					Arithmetic	.35	
					Language	.41	
		55 girls			Reading	.50	
					Arithmetic	.44	
					Language	.49	
Lahaderne (1967)	6	61 boys	Observer counting	"% of Instructional Interactions" (percent of messages between a given student and teacher which were instructional rather than prohibitory or managerial)	Scott Foresman Reading Test	.52	
		63 girls				.29	
		56 boys			Stanford Achievement Test—Intermediate II		
					Reading	.28	
					Arithmetic	.46	
					Language	.46	
		55 girls			Reading	.22	
					Arithmetic	.31	
					Language	.21	

Study	Grade/Age	N	Method	Measure	Criterion	r	r
Anderson (1973)	7 8 9	27 82 28	Observer coding of overt on-task behaviors plus observer counting of student recall of thoughts (covert)	Time-on-task	Examination based on the content and objectives of the units studied		.59 .58 .62
Edminston and Rhoades (1959)	12	94	Observer ratings during study and testing periods	Pupil attention	High school GPA California Achievement Test Composite	.51 .58	
Olson (1931)	High school	24	Observer coding of student behavior	Amout of whispering	Grade-point average	−.31	
Bloom (1954)	College freshman	45	Observer counting based on student's recall of thoughts	Proportion of relevant thoughts during class discussion (covert)	Average comprehensive examination score, science, mathematics, social science, humanities		.61
			Teacher rating of pupil	Extent of class participation (overt)			.57
			Observer counting based on student recall plus teacher rating	Proportion of relevant thoughts and extent of class participation (covert and overt)			.87
Krauskopf (1963)	13	54	Observer rating based on student's recall of thoughts	Rating of relevant thoughts during class lecture	Exam based on material covered in lecture		.56
Siegel et al. (1963)	13–14	47	Observer rating based on student's recall of thoughts	Rating of relevant thoughts during class lecture	Exam containing items based on lecture		.59
Sjogren (1967)	Adult	200	Experimental situation providing varying amounts of time for learning task	Individual's time-on-task (in relation to amount of time he or she required to complete a parallel task)	Local Math, Astronomy, and Social Studies test, combined scores		.46

APPENDIX REFERENCES

Aaron, S. *The Predictive Value of Cumulative Test Results.* Unpublished doctoral dissertation, Stanford University, 1946.

Adam, H. Reading Interests of Boys in a Vocational High School. *High Points,* 1940, *22,* 34–38.

Alberti, J. M. *Correlates of Self-perception in School.* Paper presented at American Educational Research Association Annual Meeting, New York, Feb. 5, 1971.

Alexander, M. *Relation of Environment to Intelligence and Achievement: A Longitudinal Study.* Unpublished master's study, University of Chicago, 1961.

Anderson, L. W. *Time and School Learning.* Unpublished doctoral dissertation, University of Chicago, 1973.

Anthony, B. *The Identification and Measurement of Classroom Environmental Variables Related to Academic Achievement.* Unpublished doctoral dissertation, University of Chicago, 1967.

Anttonen, R. G. Longitudinal Study in Mathematics Attitude. *Journal of Educational Research,* 1969, *62.*

Attwell, A. A., Orpet, R. E., & Meyers, C. E. Kindergarten Behavior Ratings as a Predictor of Academic Achievement. *Journal of School Psychology,* 1967, *6,* 43–46.

Balow, I. H. Reading Computation Ability as Determinants of Problem Solving. *Arithmetic Teacher,* 1964, *11,* 18–22.

Belgard, M., Rosenshine, B., & Gage, N. L. The Teacher's Effectiveness in Explaining: Evidence on Its Generality and Correlation with Pupils' Ratings and Attention Scores. In Gage et al., *Technical Report No. 4.* Stanford: Stanford Center for Research and Development in Teaching, 1968.

Binder, D. M., Jones, J. G., & Strowig, R. W. Non-Intellective Self-report Variables as Predictors of Scholastic Achievement. *Journal of Educational Research,* 1969–1970, *63.*

Bloom, B. S. Thought Processes of Students in Discussion Classes. In S. J. French (Ed.), *Accent on Teaching.* New York: Harper and Brothers, 1954.

Bowen, C. W. *The Use of Self-estimates of Ability and Measures of Ability in the Prediction of Academic Performance.* Unpublished doctoral dissertation, Oklahoma State University, 1968.

Brookover, W. B., Shailer, T., & Paterson, A. Self-concept of Ability and School Achievement. *Sociology of Education,* 1964, *37.*

Calfee, R. C., & Venezky, R. L. Component Skills in Beginning Reading. *Technical Report No. 60.* Madison, Wis.: Wisconsin Research and Development Center for Cognitive Learning, University of Wisconsin, 1968.

California Achievement Tests Manual, Grades 1–2. Monterey, Calif.: California Testing Bureau, 1957–63.

267

Caplin, M. D. The Relationship between Self-concept and Academic Achievement. *Journal of Experimental Education,* 1969, 37.

Carroll, J. B. Use of the Modern Language Aptitude Test in Secondary Schools. *Yearbook of the National Council of Measurement in Education,* 1959, *16,* 155–159.

Chall, J. S., & Feldmann, S. C. *A Study in Depth of First Grade Reading.* New York: The City College of the City University of New York, 1966. (U.S.O.E. Co-op Research Project No. 2728.)

Chase, C. I. The Position of Certain Variables in the Prediction of Problem Solving in Arithmetic. *Journal of Educational Research,* 1960, *54,* 9–14.

Clark, C. A., & Walberg, H. J. The Influence of Massive Rewards on Reading Achievement in Potential Urban School Dropouts. *American Educational Research Journal,* 1968, *5,* 305–311.

Cleland, D. L., & Toussant, I. H. The Interrelationships of Reading, Listening, Arithmetic Comprehension and Intelligence. *Reading Teacher,* 1962, *15,* 228–331.

Cobb, J. A. *Survival Skills and First-grade Academic Achievement.* Center at Oregon for Research in the Behavioral Education of the Handicapped, Department of Special Education, University of Oregon, 1970.

Cobb, J. A. Relationship of Discrete Classroom Behaviors to Fourth-grade Academic Achievement. *Journal of Educational Psychology,* 1972, *63,* 74–80.

Coleman, J. S., et al. *Equality of Educational Opportunity.* Washington, D.C.: U.S. Government Printing Office, 1966a.

Coleman, J. S., et al. *Equality of Educational Opportunity—Supplemental Appendix.* Washington, D.C.: U.S. Government Printing Office, 1966b.

Conners, C. K. & Eisenberg, L. *The Effect of Teacher Behavior on Verbal Intelligence in Operation Headstart Children.* Baltimore: Johns Hopkins University School of Medicine, 1966. (U.S.E.O. Headstart Contract No. 510.)

Cottrell, R. S. *A Study of Selected Language Factors Associated with Arithmetic Achievement of Third Grade Students.* Unpublished doctoral dissertation, Syracuse University, 1968.

Craig, G. S. Science and Elementary Education. *Teachers College Record,* 1937, *38,* 660–677.

Crandall, V. S., & McGhee, P. E. Expectancy of Reinforcement and Academic Competence. *Journal of Personality,* 1968, *36,* 635–648.

Crosswhite, F. J. Correlates of Attitudes toward Mathematics. In J. W. Wilson & E. G. Begle (Eds.), *National Longitudinal Study in Mathamatics Achievement,* Report 5, No. 20. Palo Alto, Calif.: School Mathematics Study Group, 1972.

Cullen, R. J., & Katzenmeyer, C. G. *Achievement and Ability Correlates of Components of School Attitude among Eighth Grade Students.* Paper presented at American Educational Research Association Annual Meeting, Minneapolis, Minn., March 1970.

Davis Reading Test: Manual. New York: Psychological Corp., 1958.

Dean, C. D. Predicting First Grade Reading Achievement. *Elementary School Journal,* 1939, *39,* 609–616.

Deputy, E. C. Predicting First-grade Reading Achievement: A Study in Reading Readiness. *Contributions to Education.* Teachers College, 1930, No. 426.

Dicter, M. R. Predicting Algebraic Ability. *School Review,* 1933, *41,* 604–606.

Edminston, R. W., & Hollahan, C. E. Measurement Prediction of First Grade Achievement. *School and Society,* 1946, *63,* 268–269.

Edminston, R. W., & Rhoades, B. J. Predicting Achievement. *Journal of Educational Research,* 1959, *52,* 177–180.

Entwistle, N. J., & Welsh, J. Correlates of School Attainment at Different Ability Levels. *British Journal of Educational Psychology,* 1969, *39.*

Erickson, L. H. Certain Ability Factors and Their Effect on Arithmetic Achievement. *Arithmetic Teacher,* 1958, *5,* 287–293.

Farquhar, W. W. *Motivational Factors Related to Academic Achievement.* Cooperative Research Project No. 846. East Lansing, Mich.: Office of Research and Publications, College of Education, Michigan State University, 1963.

Farquhar, W. W., & Christensen, E. W. *Academic Achievements of Eleventh Grade Puerto Rican High School Students.* East Lansing, Mich.: Educational Publication Series No. 43, College of Education, Michigan State University, 1967.

Flanagan, J. C. *Project Talent: The American High School Student.* Pittsburgh, Pa.: University of Pittsburgh, 1964.

Flanders, N. A. *Analyzing Teaching Behavior.* Reading, Mass.: Addison-Wesley, 1970.

Gardner, R. C., & Lambert, W. E. Language Aptitude, Intelligence and Second Language Achievement. *Journal of Educational Psychology,* 1965, *56,* 191–199.

Gates, A. I. An Experimental Evaluation of Reading-Readiness Tests. *Elementary School Journal,* 1939, *39,* 497–508.

Gates, A. I. A Further Evaluation of Reading Readiness Tests. *Elementary School Journal,* 1940, *40,* 577–591.

Gates, A. I., et al. Methods of Determining Reading Readiness. *Elementary School Journal,* 1939, *40,* 165–167.

Glick, O. *The Interdependence of Sixth Graders' School Attitudes and Academic Performance.* Paper presented at the Western Psychological Association Convention, Vancouver, British Columbia, June 1969.

Gnauck, J., & Kaczkowski, H. Prediction of Junior High School Performance. *Educational and Psychological Measurement,* 1961, *21,* 485–488.

Green, R. L., & Farquhar, W. W. Negro Academic Motivation and Scholastic Achievement. *Journal of Educational Psychology,* 1965, *56.*

Groff, P. J. Children's Attitude Towards Reading and Their Critical Reading Abilities in Four Content-Type Materials. *Journal of Educational Research,* 1962, *55.*

Hanna, G. S., Bligh, H. F., Lenke, J. M., & Orleans, J. B. Predicting Algebra Achievement with an Algebra Prognosis Test, IQs, Teacher Predictions, and Mathematics Grades. *Educational and Psychological Measurement,* 1969, *29,* 903–907.

Harris, A. J., & Serwer, B. *A Comparison of Reading Approaches in First-Grade Teaching with Disadvantaged Children* (The CRAFT Project). New York: City University of New York, 1966. (U.S.O.E. Cooperative Research Project No. 2677.)

Harrison, M. L. Principles for Increasing the Readiness to Read. *National Elementary Principal,* 1938, *17,* 264–272.

Hicklin, W. J. *A Study of Long Range Techniques for Predicting Patterns of Scholastic Behavior.* Unpublished doctoral dissertation, University of Chicago, 1962.

Hiller, J. H., Fisher, G. A., & Kaess, W. A Computer Investigation of Verbal Characteristics of Effective Classroom Lecturing. *American Educational Research Journal,* 1969, *6,* 661–675.

Hopkins, K. D., & Sitkei, E. G. Predicting Grade One Reading Performance: Intelligence vs. Reading Readiness Tests. *Journal of Experimental Education,* 1969, *37,* 31–33.

Huggett, A. J. An Experiment in Reading Readiness. *Journal of Educational Research,* 1938, *32,* 263–270.

Hungerman, A. D. Achievement and Attitude of Sixth-Grade Pupils in Conventional and Contemporary Math Programs. *Arithmetic Teacher,* 1967, *14.*

Hurlock, E. B. An Evaluation of Certain Incentives Used in School Work. *Journal of Educational Psychology,* 1925, *16,* 145–159.

Husén, T. (Ed.). *International Study of Achievement in Mathematics: A Comparison of Twelve Countries* (Vols. I and II). New York: John Wiley & Sons, 1967.

Iowa Test of Basic Skills: Technical Manual. Boston: Houghton Mifflin Co., 1955–56.

Ivanoff, J. M., DeWane, E. T., & Praem, O. Use of Discriminant Analysis for Selecting Students for Ninth Grade Algebra or General Mathematics. *Mathematics Teacher,* 1965, *58,* 412–416.

Jacobs, R., & Spaulding, G. An Evaluation of the 1953 Revision of the Stanford Achievement Test Battery. *Educational Research Bureau,* 1954, 48–66, No. 62.

Jayne, C. D. A Study of the Relationship between Teaching Procedures and Educational Outcomes. *Journal of Experimental Education.* 1945, *14,* 101–134.

Jones, J. G., & Strowig, R. W. Adolescent Identity and Self-perception as Predictors of School Achievement. *Journal of Educational Psychology,* 1968, *62,* 78–82.

Jordon, D. The Attitude of Central School Pupils to Certain School Subjects and Correlation Between Attitudes and Attainment. *British Journal of Educational Psychology,* 1941, *11.*

Khan, S. B. Affective Correlates of Academic Achievement. *Journal of Educational Psychology,* 1969, *60.*

Khan, S. B., & Roberts, P. M. Relationships among Study Habits and Attitudes, Aptitudes, and Eighth Grade Achievement. *Educational and Psychological Measurement,* 1969, *29.*

Kifer, E. *The Effects of School Achievement on the Affective Traits of the Learner.* Unpublished doctoral dissertation, University of Chicago, 1973.

Knight, J., & Chansky, N. M. Anxiety, Study Problems, and Achievement. *Personnel and Guidance Journal,* 1964, *43,* 45–46.

Kottmeyer, W. Readiness for Reading. *Elementary English,* 1947, *24,* 355–366, 528–535.

Kraus, P. E. *Yesterday's Children.* New York: John Wiley & Sons, 1973.

Krauskopf, C. J. Use of Written Responses in the Stimulated Recall Method. *Journal of Educational Psychology,* 1963, *54,* 172–176.

Kvaraceus, W. C., & Lanigan, M. A. Pupil Performance on the Iowa Every-Pupil Tests of Basic Skills Administered at Half-year Intervals in the Junior High School. *Educational and Psychological Measurement,* 1948, *8,* 93–100.

Lahaderne, H. M. *Adaptation to School Settings: A Study of Children's Attitudes and Classroom Behavior.* Unpublished doctoral dissertation, University of Chicago, 1967.

Layton, R. B. A Study of Prognosis in High School Algebra. *Journal of Educational Research,* 1941, *34,* 601–605.

Lee, J., & Hughes, W. Predicting Success in Algebra and Geometry. *School Review,* 1934, *42,* 188–196.

Lee, J. M., Clark, W. W., & Lee, D. M. Measuring Reading Readiness. *Elementary School Journal,* 1934, *34,* 655–666.

Lenke, J. M., Bligh, H. F., & Kane, B. H. Cross-validation of the Orleans-Hanna Algebra

Prognosis Test and the Orleans-Hanna Geometry Prognosis Test. *Educational and Psychological Measurement,* 1971, *31,* 521–523.

Linton, T. *A Study of the Relationship of Global Self-concept, Academic Self-concept, and Academic Achievement among Anglo and Mexican American Sixth Grade Students.* Paper presented at American Educational Research Association Annual Meeting, Chicago, April 1972.

Lunn, J. C. B. The Development of Scales to Measure Junior School Children's Attitudes. *British Journal of Educational Psychology,* 1969, *39.*

Malpass, L. F. Some Relationships Between Students' Perceptions of School and Their Achievement. *Journal of Educational Psychology,* 1953, *44.*

Mayeske, G. W. *A Study of the Achievement of Our Nation's Students.* Washington, D.C.: U.S. Government Printing Office, 1974.

Metropolitan Achievement Tests: Manual. New York: Harcourt Brace Jovanovich, Inc., 1965.

Mitchell, B. C. Metropolitan Readiness Tests as Predictors of First Grade Achievement. *Educational and Psychological Measurement,* 1962, *22,* 765–772.

Morsh, J. E. *Systematic Observations of Instructor Behavior.* Developmental Report, AFPTRC—TN-56-32. San Antonio, Tex.: Air Force Personnel and Training Research Center, Lackland AFB, 1956.

Muscio, R. D. Factors Related to Quantitative Understanding in the Sixth Grade. *Arithmetic Teacher,* 1962, *9,* 258–262.

Neale, D. C., Gill, N., & Tismer, N. The Relation Between Attitude Toward School Subjects and School Achievement. *Journal of Educational Research,* 1970, *63,* 232–237.

Olson, W. C. A Study of Classroom Behavior. *Journal of Educational Psychology,* 1931, *22,* 449–454.

Osburn, H. G., & Melton, R. S. Prediction of Proficiency in a Modern and Traditional Course in Beginning Algebra. *Educational and Psychological Measurement,* 1963, *23,* 277–287.

Payne, D. A. Concurrent and Predictive Validity of an Objective Measure of Academic Self-concept. *Educational and Psychological Measurement,* 1962, *22.*

Payne, M. A. *The Use of Data in Curriculum Decisions.* Unpublished doctoral dissertation, University of Chicago, 1963.

Pitts, R. J. Relationship Between Functional Competence in Mathematics and Reading Grade Levels, Mental Ability, and Age. *Journal of Educational Psychology,* 1952, *43,* 486–492.

Ponzo, Z. *A Study to Determine Relations in Role Identity, Scholastic Aptitude, Achievement, and Non-academic Factors Among Male and Female Students.* Final Report, 1967. (DHEW Project #7-E-085, Contract #OE6-1-7-020065-3497.)

Powell, M., & Parsley, K. M. The Relations between First Grade Reading Readiness and Second Grade Reading Achievement. *Journal of Educational Research* 1961, *54,* 229–233.

Rosenberg, M. Psychological Selectivity in Self-esteem Formation. In Sherif & Sherif (Eds.), *Attitude, Ego-involvement and Change.* New York: Wiley & Sons, 1967.

Russell, D. H. What Does Research Say About Self-evaluation? *Journal of Educational Research,* 1953, *46.*

Ryan, J. J. *Effects of Experimental Programs in Mathematics on Relevant Attitudes and*

Interests of Ninth Grade Pupils as Measured by Questionnaire Indices. St. Paul, Minn.: Minnesota State Department of Education, 1967. (Interim Report Project No. 5-1028, Contract No. OE-5-10-051.)

Ryan, J. J. *Effects of Modern and Conventional Math Curricula on Pupil Attitudes, Interests, and Perception of Proficiency.* Final Report, OE-5-10-051. Washington, D.C.: U.S.O.E. Bureau of Research, 1969.

Sabers, D. L., & Feldt, L. S. Predictive Validity of Iowa Algebra Aptitude Test for Achievement in Modern Math and Algebra. *Educational and Psychological Measurement,* 1968, *28,* 901–907.

Science Research Associates. *High School Placement Test, Manual.* Chicago, Ill.: Science Research Associates, 1968.

Sears, P. S. *The Effect of Classroom Conditions on the Strength of Achievement Motive and Work Output of Elementary School Children.* Final Report, U.S. Cooperative Research Project, 1963, No. 873.

Shaw, G. S. Prediction of Success in Elementary Algebra. *The Mathematics Teacher,* 1956, *49,* 173–178.

Shepler, W. D. *A Study of Scholastic Achievement in Secondary School Science in Relation to Pupils' Relative Preference for This Subject.* Unpublished doctoral dissertation, University of Pittsburgh, 1956.

Shepps, F. P., & Shepps, R. R. Relationships of Study Habits and School Attitudes to Achievement in Mathematics and Reading. *Journal of Educational Research,* 1971, 65.

Siegel, L., et al. Students' Thoughts during Class: A Criterion of Educational Research. *Journal of Educational Psychology,* 1963, 54, 45–61.

Siegel, M. A., & Rosenshine, B. *Teacher Behavior and Student Achievement in the Bereiter-Engelman Follow-through Program.* Paper presented at AERA meeting, New Orleans, February 1973. (ERIC:ED:076 564.)

Sjogren, D. D. Achievement as a Function of Study Time. *American Educational Research Journal,* 1967, *4,* 337–343.

Soar, R. S. *An Integrative Approach to Classroom Learning.* Philadelphia, Pa. Temple University. Final Report, 1966. (Public Health Service Grant No. 5-R11-MH 02045.)

Solomon, D., Rosenberg, L., & Bezdek, W. E. Teacher Behavior and Student Learning. *Journal of Educational Psychology,* 1964, 55, 23–30.

Spaulding, G. The Relation between Performance of Independent School Pupils on the Harrison-Stroud Reading Readiness Tests and Reading Achievement a Year Later. *Educational Records Bulletin,* 1956, *67,* 73–76.

Thorndike, R. L. *Reading Comprehension Education in Fifteen Countries: International Studies in Evaluation* (Vol. III). New York: John Wiley and Sons, 1973.

Torrance, E. P. *Characteristics of Mathematics Teachers that Affect Students' Learning.* Final Report, U.S.O.E., Bureau of Research (Coop. Res. Proj. No. 1020. Contract No. SAE-8993), 1966. (ERIC No. ED 010 378.)

Torshen, K. *The Relation of Classroom Evaluation to Students' Self-Concepts.* Unpublished doctoral dissertation, University of Chicago, 1969.

Townsend, A. The Use of Form R of Metropolitan Achievement Tests in the Spring, 1948, Testing Program. *Educational Records Bulletin,* 1948, *50,* 62–73.

Townsend, A. Growth of Independent-School Pupils in Achievement on Stanford Achievement Test. *Educational Records Bulletin,* 1950, *56,* 61–72.

Traxler, A. E. Reliability and Predictive Value of the Metropolitan Readiness Tests. *Educational Records Bulletin*, 1947, 47, 49–58.

Traxler, A. E. Correlations Between Scores on Various Reading Tests Administered Several Months Apart. *Educational Records Bureau*, 1949a, 52, 78–82.

Traxler, A. E. Reading Growth of Secondary-School Pupils during a Five-year Period. *Educational Records Bureau*, 1949b, 54, 96–107.

Tuinman, J. J., et al. *Increases on Test Scores as a Function of Material Rewards*. Bloomington, Ind.: Indiana University, Institute of Child Study, 1971.

Turnure, J. E., & Samuels, S. J. *Attention and Reading Achievement in First Grade Boys and Girls*. Research Report No. 43, University of Minnesota Research Development and Demonstration Center in Education of Handicapped Children, 1972.

University City School District, Missouri, ED 043-683 Spons. Agency: Office of Education (DHEW). *Primary Mental Abilities and the Metropolitan Readiness Tests as Predictors of Achievement in the First Primary Year*. Washington, D.C.: Bureau of Research, June 1970. (Contract OEC 3-7061328-0322.)

Wallen, N. E. *Relationships between Teacher Characteristics and Student Behavior* (Part III). Salt Lake City: University of Utah, 1966. (U.S.O.E. Coop Res. Proj. No. SAE OE 5-10-181.)

Weiner, M., & Feldmann, S. Validation Studies of a Reading Prognosis Test for Children of Lower and Middle Socio-economic Status. *Educational and Psychological Measurement*, 1963, 23, 807–814.

Wethington, C. T. *A Study of the Relationship between Attitude toward English and Several Selected Variables*. Unpublished doctoral dissertation, University of Kentucky, 1965.

Wilmore, W. W. *Relative Validity of Three Group Readiness Tests in Predicting Reading Achievement*. Master's thesis, University of Kansas, Lawrence, 1939.

Wilson, F. T., & Burke, A. Reading Readiness in a Progressive School. *Teachers College Record*, 1937, 38, 565–580.

Wilson, J. W., & Begle, E. G. (Eds.). *National Longitudinal Studies in Math. Achievement, No. 33, Intercorrelations of Mathematical and Psychological Variables*. Palo Alto, Calif.: School Mathematics Study Group, 1972.

Wright, C. J., and Nuthall, G. Relationships between Teacher Behaviors and Pupil Achievement in Three Experimental Elementary Science Lessons. *American Educational Research Journal*, 1970, 7, 477–493.

NAME INDEX

A

Aaron, S., 230
Adam, H., 230
Airasian, P. W., 22, 23, 36
Alberti, J. M., 254
Alexander, M., 230
Anderson, L. W., 56, 57, 62, 99, 102, 128, 130, 133, 134, 182, 186–192, 265
Anthony, B., 126–127, 261
Anttonen, R. G., 244, 246–247
Arlin, M. N., 56, 57, 60, 99, 101, 128, 130, 133, 134, 183, 188–190, 192
Atkinson, J. W., 146
Atkinson, R. C., 122, 188
Attwell, A. A., 263

B

Baker, D., 150
Balow, I. H., 239
Barr, A. S., 110
Bart, W. M., 36
Begle, E. G., 236
Belgard, M., 259, 262
Bellack, A. A., 21
Bezdek, W. E., 259
Biddle, B. J., 111
Binder, D. M., 256
Binor, S., 59, 128, 131, 134, 184, 192, 193
Bligh, H. F., 233
Block, J. H., 5, 22, 57, 61, 65, 99, 101, 125–126, 128, 131, 133, 134, 139n., 182, 187–190, 192, 196, 199, 206
Bloom, B. S., 2, 9, 22, 32, 36, 40, 54, 121, 122, 143, 150, 206, 216, 265
Bloom, S., 112, 124

Bostow, D. E., 200
Boswell, J., 1
Bowen, C. W., 255
Bower, E. M., 159
Bower, G. H., 112, 116, 119, 172
Bracht, G. H., 9, 32, 39, 40, 143
Brookover, W. B., 93, 255
Brookover Test of Self-Concept of Ability, 93, 95, 154
Brophy, J. E., 121
Burke, A., 233
Burns, R. B., 199

C

Calfee, R. C., 233, 235
California Achievement Tests: Manual, 238
Caplin, M. D., 255
Carroll, J. B., 4, 75, 81n., 108n., 111–112, 188, 234, 236
Carroll Model of School Learning, 4, 7, 22, 172
Chall, J. S., 258, 262
Chansky, N. M., 249
Chase, C. I., 239
Christensen, E. W., 93, 255–256
Clark, C. A., 261
Clark, W. W., 232–233
Cleland, D. L., 239
Cobb, J. A., 263
Coleman, J. S., 2, 8, 108, 110, 111, 151, 213, 240, 251, 255
Comber, L. C., 2, 8, 20, 81n., 90n., 108n., 213
Comenius, J., 4

Condo, P., 200
Conners, C. K., 262
Cottrell, R. S., 238
Craig, G. S., 232
Crandall, V. S., 254
Crawford, J., 3
Cronbach, L. J., 116
Crosswhite, F. J., 80, 97, 147, 244–247, 252–253
Cullen, R. J., 249

D

Dahlöff, U., 121
Dave, R. H., 2, 108
Davis Reading Test: Manual, 237–238
Dean, C. D., 232–233
Deputy, E. C., 233
DeWane, E. T., 240
Dickter, M. R., 233
Distar reading program, 201
Dolan, L., 97
Dollard, J., 112, 119, 172
Domas, S. J., 110
Dreeben, R., 142
Duker, J., 3
Dunkin, M. J., 111

E

Edminston, R. W., 232, 265
Eisenberg, L., 262
Entwistle, N. J., 250
Erickson, L. H., 239
Erikson, E. H., 159

F

Farquhar, W. W., 93, 250, 255–256
Faure, E., 152
Feather, N. T., 93, 146
Feldmann, S. C., 232, 235, 258, 262
Feldt, L. S., 234
Fisher, G. A., 259
Flanagan, J. C., 230–231, 237, 240
Flanders, N. A., 21, 260
Flemming, C. W., 150

G

Gagné, R. M., 25, 37, 51
Gardner, R. C., 236
Gates, A. I., 232–233
Glaser, R., 32, 122, 167, 188
Glick, O., 249
Glidewell, J. C., 157
Gnauck, J., 228–229
Good, T. L., 121
Green, R. L., 256
Groff, P. J., 248

H

Haggerty, L. H., 40
Hanna, G. S., 233
Hanson, R. A., 2
Harris, A. J., 260, 262
Harrison, M. L., 233
Hastings, J. T., 22, 36
Havighurst, R. J., 120
Herbart, J., 4
Hess, R. L., 86
Hicklin, W. J., 32, 143, 230
Hilgard, E. R., 112, 116, 119, 172
Hiller, J. H., 259
Hollahan, C. E., 232
Hopkins, K. D., 9, 32, 39, 40, 143, 232
Huggett, A. J., 232
Hughes, W., 234
Hungerman, A. D., 244
Hurlock, E. B., 260
Husén, T., 2, 8, 20, 79, 81n., 90n., 108n., 149, 213, 245, 247

I

International Study of Educational Achievement (IEA), 49–50, 76, 79–84, 88–89, 108, 110, 111
International Study of Educational Achievement in Mathematics (IEA), 79–80, 88–91
Iowa Tests of Basic Skills (ITBS): Technical Manual, 237, 239
Ivanoff, J. M., 240

J

Jackson, P. W., 111, 142
Jacobs, R., 228–229
Jamison, D., 111
Jayne, C. D., 261
Jesuit schools, 4
Jones, E. L., 57, 58, 197, 198
Jones, J. G., 256
Jones, R. A., 150
Jordon, D., 248

K

Kaczkowski, H., 228–229
Kaess, W. A., 259
Kane, B. H., 233
Kaplan, J. D., 25
Katzenmeyer, C. G., 249
Keeves, J. P., 2, 8, 20, 81n., 90n., 108n., 213
Keller Personalized System of
    Instruction, 198–200
Kersh, M. E., 197
Khan, S. B., 150, 250
Kifer, E., 94–96, 153–156, 255
Kim, H., 116
Knight, J., 249
Kottmeyer, W., 232
Kraus, P. E., 230, 239
Krauskopf, C. J., 265
Kurtz, J. J., 150
Kvaraceus, W. C., 230

L

Lahaderne, H. M., 263–264
Lambert, W. E., 236
Lanigan, M. A., 230
Lavin, D. E., 52
Layton, R. B., 233
Lee, D. M., 232–233
Lee, J., 234
Lee, J. M., 232–233
Lee, Y. D., 197, 198
Lenke, J. M., 233
Levin, T., 57, 63, 99, 103, 128, 132, 134,
    183, 192, 195
Lewis, E. G., 81n., 108n.

Linton, T., 254
Longo, A. A., 197
Lunn, J. C. B., 249

M

McClelland, D., 120
MacDermot, H. G., 200
McGhee, P. E., 254
Madaus, G., 22, 36
Malpass, L. F., 97, 249
Marjoribanks, K., 2, 111
Massad, C. F., 81n., 108n.
Mayeske, G. W., 251
Mayo, G. D., 197
Melton, R. S., 234
Metropolitan Achievement Tests:
    Manual, 235
Meux, M. O., 21
Michael, W. B., 150
Miller, N. E., 112, 119, 172
Mitchell, B. C., 233
Moore, J. W., 200
Morrison, H. C., 4
Morsh, J. E., 110, 262
Muscio, R. D., 239

N

National Longitudinal Study of
    Mathematics Achievement, 80, 85
Neale, D. C., 239–240
Nuthall, G., 261

O

O'Connor, R. J., 200
Olson, W. C., 265
Orleans, J. B., 233
Osburn, H. G., 234
Overly, N. V., 142
Özcelik, D. A., 57, 58, 99, 100, 102, 128,
    133, 134, 187

P

Paradise, N. E., 25, 37, 51
Parsley, K. M., 233

Paterson, A., 93, 255
Payne, M. A., 9, 32, 41, 52, 53, 143, 228–231, 239, 256
Pearson, W., 67, 116
Pestalozzi, J., 4
Peterson, P., 5
Pillet, E. E., 57, 58, 128, 132, 134, 197
Pitts, R. J., 240
Plowden Report, 2, 8, 108, 110, 111, 213
Ponzo, Z., 255
Powell, M., 233
Praem, O., 240
Pringle, M. K., 139n.
Purves, A. C., 2, 8, 81n., 90n., 108n., 213

R

Resnick, L. B., 25, 37
Rhoades, B. J., 265
Roberts, P. M., 250
Rosenberg, L., 259
Rosenberg, M., 256
Rosenshine, B., 111, 258, 260
Russell, D. H., 255
Russell, I. L., 150
Ryan, J. J., 245

S

Sabers, D. L., 234
Samuels, S. J., 263
Scannell, D. P., 40
Science Research Associates (SRA) High School Placement Test: Manual, 237, 240
Sears, P. S., 93, 156, 255
Serwer, B., 260, 262
Shailer, T., 93, 255
Shaw, G. S., 233, 240
Shepler, W. D., 248
Sheppard, W. C., 200
Shepps, F. P., 249
Shepps, R. R., 249
Shipman, V., 86
Siegel, L., 265
Siegel, M. A., 258, 260
Sitkei, E. G., 232

Sjogren, D. D., 265
Smith, B. O., 21
Smith, M. I., 200
Snow, R. E., 116
Soar, R. S., 262
Solomon, D., 259
Spaulding, G., 228–229, 232
Stephens, J. M., 1, 111
Stringer, L. A., 157
Strowig, R. W., 256
Suppes, P., 111
Swenson, E. J., 150

T

Thorndike, R. L., 2, 8, 49–50, 81n., 90n., 108n., 213, 216, 237–238, 241, 248
Tiedeman, D., 110
Torrance, E. P., 259, 261
Torshen, K., 94, 155–157, 254–255
Toussant, I. H., 239
Townsend, A., 228–229
Traxler, A. E., 228, 230, 232, 235
Tuinman, J. J., 261
Turnure, J. E., 263
Tyler, R. W., 21

U

UNESCO, 152
University of Chicago, 55, 56, 98, 127
University of Chicago Laboratory School, 4
University City School District (Missouri), 232, 235

V

Varma, V. P., 139n.
Venezky, R. L., 233, 235

W

Walberg, H. J., 126, 261
Wallen, N. E., 258, 260
Wang, M. C., 25

Washburne, C. W., 4
Weiner, M., 232, 235
Weiss, J., 150
Wells, S., 111
Welsh, J., 250
Wethington, C. T., 248
White, M. A., 3
White, R. W., 120, 146, 159

Wilder, E. W., 110
Williams, T. H., 2
Wilmore, W. W., 232
Wilson, F. T., 233
Wilson, J. W., 236
Winnetka Plan, 4
Wolf, R., 2, 108
Wright, C. J., 261

SUBJECT INDEX

A

Academic self-concept, 92–98, 152–157, 252–256; *illus.*, 91, 96, 154
Achievement:
  and academic self-concept, 93–95, 156–157, 252–256; *illus.*, 91
  and affective entry characteristics, 76, 81–85, 88–92, 168–171
  and classroom characteristics, 110–112
  and cognitive entry behaviors, 167–168
  and cues, 117–118
  cumulative effect of, 94–95; *illus.*, 96
  development in the home, 1, 2
  distribution of, 35–36, 47–48; *illus.*, 48
  and feedback/correctives, 126
  and learning tasks, 56–64; *illus.*, 57, 59–64
  and learning time, 185–191
  and mental health of students, 157–159
  and participation, 123, 262–265
  predicting levels of, 32, 38–44, 97, 104, 203, 204; *illus.*, 40
  prior and later studies, 39–48
  and quality of instruction, 108, 129, 173–174; *illus.*, 118, 128, 130–132
  and reinforcement, 120–121, 260–261
  and school characteristics, 110–112
  and school-related affect, 88–92, 149–152, 249–251; *illus.*, 89, 91
  and subject-related affect, 81–85, 98–103, 146–148, 244–248; *illus.*, 82–83, 99
  and teachers' characteristics, 110–112
  and variation in school setting, 162–167; *illus.*, 163, 165, 169

AEC (*see* Affective entry characteristics)
Affective entry characteristics (AEC), 73–107, 161–196
  alterability of, 105–106
  basic assumptions, 75–76
  as causal variables, 104
  defined, 75
  implications, 104–107
  macro-level studies, 77–98
  and mathematics achievement, 79–80
  micro-level studies, 98–103
Affective outcomes, 11, 139–160
  and academic self-concept, 152–157
  curriculum for, 141–144
  and mental health of students, 157–159
  and school-related affect, 149–152
  and subject-related affect, 144–149
Alterability:
  of affective entry characteristics, 105–106
  of cognitive entry behaviors, 70–71
  of quality of instruction, 136–137
Aptitude:
  and achievement, 38, 43–46, 52, 232–236; *illus.*, 42
  defined, 44
  and instruction, 4, 19

C

Causal variables:
  affective entry characteristics, 104
  cognitive entry behaviors, 68–69
  quality of instruction, 135–136
CEB (*see* Cognitive entry behaviors)
Class size, 9–10, 20, 28, 111, 124, 171, 173, 212, 213
  (*See also* Group instruction)

Cognitive entry behaviors (CEB), 30–72, 161–196
  alterability of, 70–71
  alternatives when CEB not available, 65–68
  as causal variables, 68–69
  defined, 32–33
  effect on achievement distributions, 47–48
  and general intelligence measures, 51–55
  and generalized entry measures, 48–55
  identification of, 36–38
  implications, 68–71
  and the learning process, 47
  macro-level studies, 39–48
  micro-level studies, 55–65
Competition in schools, 143, 158
  (*See also* Peer interaction)
Correctives, 5, 10, 56–57, 64, 114, 124–127, 129, 133, 173, 176, 179, 191, 194, 198, 212; *illus.*, 118, 130–132, 177
Cues, 113, 115–117, 119, 172, 173, 176, 179; *illus.*, 118
Curriculum, 1, 3, 7, 34, 37, 65, 68, 79, 97–98, 105, 117, 141–144, 168, 201, 204, 206, 208, 214–217

F

Feedback, 5, 28, 56–57, 64, 104, 114, 120, 124–127, 129, 133, 171, 173, 176, 178–180, 185, 191, 194, 198, 212; *illus.*, 118, 130–132
Formative tests, 23, 56, 64, 125, 127, 129, 175, 196, 198

G

General intelligence, 51–55
Grades (marks), 92–95, 105, 143–149, 155–157, 171, 233–238, 244–256
Group instruction, 9–10, 20, 26, 111, 114–115, 117, 121, 122, 124, 127, 143, 161
  and errors in learning, 10, 28–29, 124, 134–136, 173–174, 179, 211–214

H

History of the learner, 13–14, 18–19, 30–31, 69–70, 74–75, 94, 104–105, 136, 202
Homes, 1–2, 9, 16, 18, 45, 108, 159, 164, 209, 211–213
  (*See also* Parents)
Human nature, 206–211

I

Individual differences in learning, 1–17, 206–207, 208–209, 214–217
Instructional material, 5, 7, 20–23, 48–49, 66, 117, 125, 127, 173, 175, 215, 216
  (*See also* Textbooks)
Intelligence, general, 51–55

L

Latent curriculum, 141–144
Learning tasks:
  and academic self-concept, 153
  and achievement, 56–64; *illus.*, 57, 59–63
  and affective entry characteristics, 73–107
  altering, 65–68
  characteristics of, 22–26
  and cognitive entry behaviors, 30–72
  and curriculum, 142–144
  defined, 11, 20–22
  developmental sequences in, 32–38; *illus.*, 35, 36
  and learning time, 185–191; *illus.*, 189, 190
  and mastery learning, 174–180; *illus.*, 177
  and process changes, 180–191; *illus.*, 182–184, 189, 190
  psychomotor, 15, 23, 69
  and quality of instruction, 109, 127–134
  relations among, 26–29
  and subjects, 144–149
  and tutors, 112–114
  types of, 23
  (*See also* Learning units)

Learning time, 4, 5, 31, 33, 122, 125, 133,
166, 175, 178, 185–191, 207, 213,
214; *illus.,* 189, 190
Learning units, 18–29
sequential, 25–28, 32–38, 164–166,
173, 175, 216; *illus.,* 24, 27, 28, 35,
36, 165
(*See also* Learning tasks)

M

Manifest curriculum, 141–144
Marks (*see* Grades)
Mastery learning (ML), 3–7, 22, 55–65,
98, 103, 127, 129, 133, 164–166, 202,
207; *illus.,* 57, 59–63, 130–132
and Keller system of instruction, 198–
199; *illus.,* 200
and learning tasks, 174–180; *illus.,* 177
and process changes, 180–191; *illus.,*
182–184, 189
and summative tests, 196; *illus.,* 197
Mental health, students', 157–159
ML (*see* Mastery learning)

P

Parents, 3, 73, 86–88, 93–95, 120, 142–
143, 145, 151, 158–159, 171, 209
(*See also* Homes)
Participation, 113–114, 121–123, 172,
173, 176, 179–180, 262–265; *illus.,*
118
Peer interaction, 73, 87–88, 94, 95, 120,
143, 148, 151, 171, 173
Practice (*see* Participation)
Prerequisite learning, 30–38, 43–47
(*See also* Cognitive entry behaviors)
Process changes, 180–191; *illus.,* 182–
184, 189
Psychomotor learning tasks, 15, 23, 69
Psychomotor skills, 33, 210

Q

Q of I (*see* Quality of instruction)
Quality of instruction (Q of I), 11, 108–
138, 161–201

Quality of instruction (Q of I) (*Cont.*):
and achievement, 117–127, 129–132
and affective entry characteristics,
109–110
alterability of, 136–137
as causal variable, 135–136
and cognitive entry behaviors, 109
components of (*see* Correctives;
Cues; Feedback; Participation;
Reinforcement)
implications, 134–138
and learning process, 133–134
macro-level studies, 115–127
micro-level studies, 127–134
and tutors, 112–115
(*See also* Teachers)

R

Reading comprehension, 48–52, 66, 68,
84, 150–151, 237–241; *illus.,* 49, 50, 53
Reinforcement, 113–114, 119–121, 158–
159, 172, 173, 176, 179, 260–261;
illus., 118

S

School-related affect, 85–92, 95, 97–98,
149–152; *illus.,* 89, 91, 151
School years, 2, 7, 17–19, 86, 141, 211–212
Schooling process, 7–10
Subject-related affect, 77–85, 95–103,
144–149, 244–248; *illus.,* 82–83, 99,
101–102, 147
Subjects:
as center of school learning, 20, 26
and learning tasks, 34, 144–149
students' attitudes toward (*see* Subject-
related affect)
use in grouping learning tasks, 34
Summative measures, 57–58, 64, 126,
165, 176, 180, 181, 193, 196–199

T

Talent, 209–211
Teachers:
and academic self-concept, 92–95

Teachers (*Cont.*):
  and alterability of affect, 105
  capability of, 110–112, 114, 171, 174,
      201
  characteristics of, 110–112
  and children's attitudes toward
      schooling, 86–88
  determining cognitive entry behaviors,
      34
  responsibilities of, 215
  role of, in school, 7, 21

Teachers (*Cont.*):
  standards set by, 143, 144, 158
  (*See also* Quality of instruction; Tutors)
Teachers' aides, 5, 21, 127, 173
Textbooks, 68, 117, 144
  (*See also* Instructional material)
Time-on-task (*see* Learning time)
Tutors, 10, 21, 22, 28, 65, 109, 112–115,
      122, 124–125, 127, 172–174, 176,
      178–180, 201, 212
  (*See also* Teachers)